AF412276

Originally published in 1856
by Arthur Hall, Virtue, and Co., London

Reprinted 1969 by
Negro Universities Press
A DIVISION OF GREENWOOD PUBLISHING CORP.
NEW YORK

SBN 8371-1134-X

PRINTED IN UNITED STATES OF AMERICA

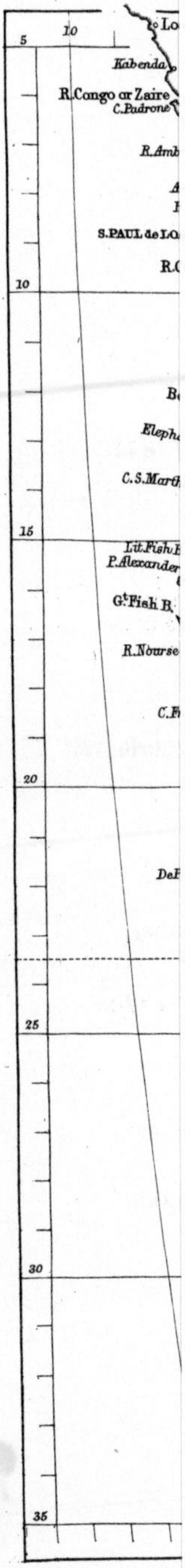

10
5
Lo
Kabenda
R.Congo or Zaire
C.Padrone
R.Amb
A
S.PAUL de LO
R.C
10
B
Eleph
C.S.Mart
15
Lit.Fish R
P.Alexander
Gt.Fish R.
R.Nourse
C.F
20
DeF
25
30
35

ERRATA.

Page.	line.				
16	19	*for*	republic	*read*	republics
40	13	—	Zunreberg	—	Zuureberg
65	7	—	Gebirgc	—	Gebirge
73	20	*after*	metallic	—	and
80	7	*for*	Bechaanas	—	Bechuana's
85	2	*after*	the	—	most
116	6	*for*	Hork	—	Hoek
148	23	—	$1\frac{75}{100}$	—	$1\frac{3}{4}$
190	8	—	Winter-vogee	—	Winter-vogel
209	6	—	eight	—	eighth
256	28	—	amapayati	—	amapakati
274	3	—	become	—	becoming
276	5	—	suffices	—	suffice
345	1	*dele*	of		
422	27	*for*	Loanda	—	Loando
423	7	—	Loanda	—	Loando
423	16	—	Loanda	—	Loando
426	10	—	Loanda	—	Loando
427	13	—	Loanda	—	Loando

CONTENTS.

CHAPTER X.

CHAPTER XI.

CHAPTER XII.

CHAPTER XIII.

ENGRAVINGS.

PREFACE.

THREE considerations have combined, in inducing the publication of the present Work.

First—The numerous and repeated solicitations of friends, and more especially of my clerical brethren, "that I would supply them with a book, descriptive of South Africa, and its various tribes; from which, without the expenditure of much time, they might be able to derive useful, as well as general, and authentic information." For those who are interested in the welfare of the African heathen, and the extension of our Mission Fields, amongst their numerous tribes, such a work seemed certainly wanted.

Secondly—Missionaries, Officers, Emigrants, Travellers, and others going to this country, necessarily, and urgently, require a "Guide Book;" in which notices may easily be found, bearing on *all* points of general interest and utility in connection with it.

And *Lastly*—The non-existence of such a work, as the one above described.

These combined, have induced me to try and turn my past experience and information (derived from a sojourn of nearly five years in the country) to some account, by attempting the compilation of the present volume.

The difficulty of obtaining the *exact* information required on any particular subject, connected with the Cape and its dependencies, was one often keenly felt by myself, whilst residing there. The various works of travellers, are so *voluminous;* whilst those of Officers, or other casual visitors, are so *locally confined* in the information given, that, either hours have to be spent in searching through several ponderous tomes in some library, or else, they are wholly thrown away, by the perusal of the *wrong* book, before the point requiring elucidation can be arrived at.

The favourable and flattering reception by the public of both editions of my former little work on "Kaffraria," together with the suggestions offered by some of the reviewers of it, has, also, further emboldened me to attempt the present more extended volume.

In forming this, I have sought to attain my object, as much by careful and judicious *compilation*, as by original *composition;* and, consequently, although much may appear in it "not very new," still, I dare to hope, that from the combination of the notices, "new and old," which it contains, it may be found a useful, if not an amusing, book.

The attainment of the latter qualification has not been wholly lost sight of, and I have, therefore, endeavoured to intersperse through the chapters and pages, a few remarks and anecdotes, calculated to render them amusing and pleasing to the more general reader.

The labour of my work has been in compiling from the many and large works of previous authors; for, whilst my opportunities in the colonies themselves, or at home, brought to my notice *any* book, bearing on the subject, I felt in duty bound to read, and to use it. For the rest, my own ample note-books have supplied my need.

Through the renewed kindness of J. Arrowsmith, Esq., F. R. G. S., I am enabled to add much to the value of the volume, by the admirable map prepared by him; deserving, and for which I here record, my warmest and most sincere thanks.

To Dr. Norton Shaw, M. D., F. R. G. S., Secretary to the Royal Geographical Society, the same is due, for his kindness and assistance lent to me, in addition to that of many other friends at home and abroad.

The Engravings and Vignettes have been executed from original drawings taken on the spot, and most of them selected from portfolios of the Author and his brother, (who, whilst with his regiment, was also many years resident in that country.) A few of them have been furnished by others.

In conclusion, I have but to add, that, whilst fully conscious of many unintentional imperfections, and faults otherwise arising, I still sanguinely trust, that the present publication may not totally fail in the object for which it is written, namely—" To afford, in a portable and readable form, a volume containing general information on all points connected with the country, colonies, and tribes of Southern Africa."

PARK SIDE, CAMBRIDGE,
July, 1856.

Ky Ga

E R

2 Modder

A

oom. Plaat

3 Philippo

tha's Dr.

erg

E R

3 Zuurberg 3D

Sek Poort R.

3 D O

Tarka R.

BonaB

E T

3

A

B.

idbur

gga

at

sh

El

Tur

abeth

G o a B

& L. Ho.

26

but was sometimes also used among them in the same extensive application as that of Africa was by the Romans. This word is supposed to be of Hebrew origin, denoting that the inhabitants (the *Lubim* of the Old Testament) were placed under a burning sky.

The appellation by which we now distinguish this very extensive, and, in many respects, most highly interesting portion of our globe, is one, which, although we can thus trace it to an antiquated origin, seems to have been formed wholly irrespective of that portion of this continent, alluded to in the following pages as "Southern Africa."

The true extent of geographical knowledge of the continent possessed by the ancients, is not now clearly to be ascertained. It is supposed to have extended on the Western shore to Cape Blanco, or Cape de Verd : and on the Eastern side, to the island of Pembo.

The valley of the Nile was certainly known, in early history, under the same name which it now bears; but the neighbouring countries to it were veiled in darkness, and were comprehended under the general title of *Nigritia* or Negroland. The Greeks, according to Herodotus, and, afterwards, the Romans, having acquired a better knowledge of the coasts of the Mediterranean, may perchance have sailed up the Joliba; but it is certain that they never penetrated further than to the limits of Numidia, and were at least totally unacquainted with "Southern Africa."

Whatever great and remarkable transactions, therefore, may have occurred on the Northern shore of this continent 3,500 years ago—rendering them known and famous amongst the ancients—they cannot now be claimed as bearing any relation to its Southern extremity, more than having given to it a name, the derivation of which, in its Greek form, is quite inapplicable to it—though bright and sunny it may be, or productive and abundant in corn and wine and oil—a land indeed of plenty.

Africa, viewed as a continent in respect to its physical features, is the most compact of any of the four great primitive divisions of the globe—it is, to use the expression of Ritter, "like a trunk without limbs." Hence its periphery is, in comparison with its superficial extent, much less than that of either Asia, America, or Europe. Bays, capes, and necks of land deeply indent and elongate the coast lines of these continents; whilst, in Africa, these are few in number. The islands likewise are scanty, and none of them (if we except Madagascar) seem to possess any relation to the main land in their physical structure.

It has been surmised* that the two continents of Africa and America were once united, since the projecting part of Africa exactly fits the gulf of Mexico; while the projecting part of South America, about Paraiba and Pernambuco, would, in size and shape, fill up the gulf of Guinea.

According to M. Cordier, the North coast of this continent is sinking, at the rate of one foot in a century. If this be the case, and the globe remain sufficiently long in its present organization, it may be readily conjectured that, ultimately, the Mediterranean Sea and Indian Ocean will become united, whilst the Red Sea will reach to the mountains under the 10th parallel of latitude.† Be this as it may, this continent, as now presented to us, is of an extent sufficient, without improbable conjectures, to employ our most extended research; for although the third largest division of the terrane surface of our planet, it is still the least known.

Its extent, according to most of our British geographers, is computed at 11,500,000 square miles, inclusive of the islands. With this calculation, most of the continental professors differ. Malte Brun rates it at 13,430,000 square miles.

* See Article under head of " Africa," in 7th Edition of Encyclopædia Britannica.

† See Bell's Geography, vol. iii, p. 263.

Ukert makes it to contain 11,961,675 square miles, or, without its islands, 11,724,885 miles, with which computation Gräberg pretty nearly corresponds.

According to the Abbé Guyot, its surface covers 8,720,000 square miles, while its coast extends over 14,000 geographical miles. Thus he makes it to possess 623 miles of surface to every one mile of coast. This is much more than in Europe, which possesses but one mile of coast to every 156 square miles of surface. Hence he shows that Europe is the continent most open to the sea for foreign connections; while Africa, (which is three times its extent in surface), by reason of being less individualized in local and independent districts, is incapacitated from even competing with her, in this respect; although possessing far more internal and indigenous capabilities and products, fitting her to extend commerce.

But of these stores of wealth, with which to increase and engender commerce, we yet know comparatively nothing. It remains for the enterprising, amidst this and succeeding generations, to open up the mines of ores and minerals, that still lie hidden beneath its surface. Nor need it be a matter of much wonder to us, that the ancients knew so little of this vast continent, and nothing respecting its extremity, or interior; when, for upwards of three centuries, our own ships have now sailed round its shores, and yet our *modern* acquaintance with its coast is still, at the best, very inaccurate and incomplete, and our ignorance of its vast interior, profound. Neither commerce, stimulated by the grasping avarice of man, nor yet religion, impelled by her warmest zeal, have done more than to send a few to traverse, for a few hundreds of miles, beyond our immediate colonies. Nor has science or curiosity, ambition or speculation, aided much towards exploring its unknown plains. And thus time has travelled on to this, the nineteenth century, and we are yet, comparatively speaking, resting in ignorance of the resources, and even the geography, of this vast continent.

A few noble pioneers, indeed, we do number—men who have laid down their lives in trying to increase the store of our African geographical knowledge. Mr. Park, and his enterprising son, a Houghton, a Roentzen, and a Cochelet, have each fallen victims in this noble cause; as well as a Laing, who penetrated to the centre of the land, there only to meet with a tragical death. Others too, more fortunate than they were, have lived and returned to tell their tales, and add, thereby, to our store of information. But beginning with the Portuguese discoveries, in 1402, of the Canary Islands; Cape Nun, by Prince Henry, in 1412; Cape of Good Hope, in 1486, by Bartholomew Diaz; and, including those to the present day, our last extended explorations but put us in possession of information respecting about 28,000 square leagues of the superficies of Africa as a continent (and this is a very liberal computation.)   And what is this extent when compared with the 1,400,000 square leagues which it contains?   Scarcely a *fifth* of the surface is yet visited or known.

Or even confine this remark to Southern Africa, and what can we say? A few of the Missionaries have penetrated to the 24th Southern parallel of latitude. Messrs. Oswell and Livingston to 18°.20'. South Latitude.   The general course of the Gareep or Orange River is determined; the River Zack on its left bank, and the feeders of the Elephant's River, more again to the South, have been carefully visited; the accurate positions of one or two great salt lakes in the interior, and one or two rivers running out of them have been recently determined: but how much yet has to be ascertained? The certain sources of both branches of the Kuman and Oup Rivers, that of the Fish River, as well also as the Limpopo; the connection of the various chains of mountains; the issue of the River Nokannan, also of those of Kuisip, and Kubakop more to the North; the extent and direction of the longitudinal chain of the Kamhanni mountains; the geography of the Lupata chain, and of the lake Maravi to the Eastward, together with Marapi on the North East, as well as the sources of the Sesheké and Zambesi Rivers. Enough, indeed, yet remains to stimulate the most apathetic towards a continued exertion in the great work of exploring this still unknown, but interesting, and we believe, rich and auriferous continent. Nor can we but sanguinely hope that a great national effort on the part of Britain, conducted through the direction of the Royal Geographical Society, may, ere long, not only be contemplated, but put in action, to accomplish part of these discoveries, and to extend further our knowledge in this direction.

Confining *our* sketches, however, to what we, with any degree of certainty, *do know* respecting the physical and political geography of "Southern Africa," (stretching this tract northwards from the Cape of Good Hope to about 8° or 10° South latitude,) we shall endeavour to condense, to a small compass, most of what is interesting, truthful, and instructive respecting this country; and those races, animals, and indigenous products which are found there.

In doing this, while the information afforded

by all intelligent and authentic travellers will
be used and compiled from, we shall also trust
to our own note-book for many of the details
connected with those immediate parts of these
districts, which we have personally visited. Together with these, such anecdotes and incidents
as may tend to render the account more interesting to the general reader, will be introduced;
thus hoping to present a volume containing,
in a small compass, both useful and interesting
matter.

OUTWARD BOUND.

CHAPTER II.

THE Geography, and the History of "South
Africa" may be said to commence at the period
when it first became known to Europeans, while
the little to be gathered from ancient sources,
relating to it, is as follows :—

Some Phœnicians who, in the reign of Pharoah
Necho, King of Egypt, about the year 610 A.C.
and at his command, set sail from the Red Sea,
(which lay to the East of his dominions,) for
the purpose of exploring this region, spent, we
are told, three years in the voyage. Disembarking on the coast, in the autumn, they sowed
their grain, waited for the return of harvest,
and then progressed. This they did for two
successive years, and in the third, to their great
joy and astonishment, they arrived at the Straits
of Gibraltar, and so, passing between the "Pillars of Hercules," they reached in safety the
shores of Egypt.

But when, in describing their voyage, these
Phœnicians recounted to the ancients that, while

passing round the Southern part of Africa, the sun was on their right hand, their account was disbelieved; although their mention of this very fact, viz., that they saw the sun describe its course from East to West in the Northern heavens, (although contrary to their former experience,) seems to us now the more clearly to demonstrate that they *did* circumnavigate this continent. It was not, however, then accredited, for Herodotus, speaking of this, says, "They brought back a strange account, perfectly incredible to me, another may believe it if he pleases; but when they sailed round Lybia, they had the sun on their right hand."

Referring to this voyage, Col. Wilkie, in a very ably written article, which appeared in the United Service Journal some years ago, remarks, that "a combination of natural causes would render the navigation of those early days not so difficult, as may at first appear, to such frail vessels that probably never lost sight of land. After leaving the Straits of Babel-mandel, and doubling Cape Guardafui, they would have, during their N. E. monsoon, a fair wind until they were well to the Southward and Westward of Madagascar, and keeping along shore, they would soon fall into the powerful current that runs along the L'Agullas bank, to the Westward."

The same writer alludes further to this voyage as not the most unlikely means or opportunity for peopling South Africa with its Hottentot tribes. He says, "amongst the possibilities that have peopled the Southern corner of Africa, with two such curious races, (referring to the Hottentots and Kaffirs) it may not be too bold a conjecture to attribute it to this ancient Egyptian voyage, in the reign of Pharoah Necho. The crews of the vessels would be composed of Egyptians, in their progress down the Red Sea, they would touch at the Ethiopian ports, and carry with them a few of the most adventurous of the people. Arrived at the Cape, a portion of these navigators, tired with the length of the voyage, on finding an unoccupied country, full of wild animals, might naturally wish to try their fortune at hunting, and be left behind. I have noticed the *striking* resemblance between the persons of the Hottentots and those of the ancient Egyptians delineated on ancient monuments, as well as the singularity of the female form—*to be found nowhere else than in Nubia, and South Africa.*"*

From these Phœnicians, however, we hear nothing of even the existence of so remarkable a promontory as "The Cape:" and hence it may reasonably be conjectured that these enter-

* United Service Journal, February, 1841.

prising navigators, like many others since them, doubled it without being aware of its exact locality. About 500 years B.C., the Carthaginians made the next attempt at Southern geographical discovery, beyond the Herculean Straits; leaving which, Hanno, in command of a fleet, proceeded towards the South, sailing along the coast. Some of the ships under his command steered round by Mount Atlas, "the pillar of heaven," and doubled "the African forehead," as its great Western promontory was called. Here they beheld the various species of monkeys, specially the Baboon and Ouran-Outang —and such was the birth of Satyrs!

We also receive from them a history of primæval commerce, in their account of their bartering with the natives here.

"Having made a signal with smoke, the savages placed the goods they had to dispose of, on the coast, and retired; while they, having deposited the equivalent, removed them. If that which they laid down did not satisfy the natives, it was not removed until a suitable addition had been made."

They further describe the country, "as hot and still by day, but resounding with the echoes of cymbals, gongs, and flutes, by night, when the mountains seemed clothed in fire, reaching even to the sea shore."

Hence ignorance and fear soon peopled the Lybian wastes or deserts of Africa, with the Gorgons, and other like monstrous creations of fancy. Nor can we, when viewing now the habits of the African tribes, but corroborate the statements of Hanno's Punic Sailors: when we see the people lying in listless indolence by day, and dancing, singing, and rejoicing in the cool of night. Or, when setting fire to the dry and parched grass of summer, they thus clothe the hills in fire by night and day; but which are soon again, after the falling of the tropical rains, covered with fresh and tender grass for their cattle to feed upon.

Although no mention is, however, made of Southern Africa by these either, yet Pliny tells us that this voyage was effected round the whole extent of the African continent.

We next read of Sataspes, a Persian nobleman, condemned to death by Xerxes, but whose sentence was commuted to the accomplishment of a voyage round Africa. He sailed from Egypt (B.C. 480) through the straits of Gibraltar, and then Southwards, but frightened and terror-stricken by the mighty waves of the Atlantic, dashing against the shores of the great unknown desert; he (after beating about for a few months) returned home, and suffered according to his original sentence.

Centuries then roll by, without the record of any attempt being made to resume this effort. About 150 years B.C. the accounts of Africa having ever been circumnavigated, appear indeed to have become apocryphal. And when, after the time of Ptolemy, all science and learning began to decay—rapidly declining, until finally extinguished in the dark night of ignorance which followed—the idea of geographical research died out also.

In the time of Epiphanius (born A.D. 430) we have him giving this exposition of the contemptable ignorance of the age, in the science of geography. "The Pison," he says, "is the same as the Indians and Ethiopians call Ganges, and the Greeks "Indus"; it flows through the whole of Ethiopia, and discharges itself at last into the Ocean at Gades." (Gibraltar!)

Such are the few faint traces of ancient knowledge respecting South Africa, nor do we again find mention of it, or any expedition likely to bring its exact locality into note, until the days immediately preceding those of "the great discoverer of it," Bartholomew Diaz.

The haughty Venetians, in first introducing the mariner's compass from Asia to Europe, little thought that they were bringing it into the hands of their jealous Portuguese neighbours, as the insignificant, though certain instrument of their own downfall; by enabling them thereby, to discover the Cape of Good Hope, and with it, the East Indian passage. Yet such was the unforeseen result.

In the early part of the fifteenth century, John I., King of Portugal, effected some very important conquests over the Moors, on the North of Africa; and, with the assistance of some English merchants, he took the City of Ceuta, in Barbary. While here, in company with his father, it is said that Prince Henry* received some important information respecting the coast of Guinea, which induced him to turn all his energies to the circumnavigation of Africa. In effecting this, he had in view the opening of a maritime route to the rich nations of the East; and so putting an end to the monopoly of their wealth, which hitherto had belonged to the republic of Venice and Genoa; and which had succeeded, in a short time, to raise these from comparative insignificance, to extraordinary opulence, and haughty arrogance.

At this period, the most Southerly point of Africa known was Cape Nun, in about 27° North latitude. The promontory had received this appellation from the supposition that it

* He was son of John the first of Portugal, surnamed the Avenger, and his mother was Phillippa of Lancaster, sister of Henry IV of England.

was utterly impossible to traverse beyond it, but the officers under Prince Henry having, at length doubled it, found Cape Bojador in the distance, whose formidable coast, clothed in foam and breakers, appalled and terrified them. A superstitious dread, respecting any who should dare to proceed beyond this was soon engendered, but this, together with an equally prevalent one which existed; namely, that the earth was girdled at the equator with a zone of intolerable heat, which separated the two hemispheres, was speedily dispelled with the aid of science, by their enterprising leader, Prince Henry.

Cape Bojador was not only doubled, but the Azores and Cape de Verd Islands were discovered, and the African coast explored beyond the tropics, so as to divest the torrid zone of all its fanciful horrors.

In 1471, the line was reached, and, in 1484, they had extended their explorations to fifteen hundred miles South of it. The death of the enterprising Prince Henry, which occurred in 1473, deprived him of the gratification of beholding the achievement of the purpose which his daring genius had so ably planned and commenced. Still the thirst for geographical research and discovery, which he had awakened, was not permitted to expire.

His grand-nephew, John II., had imbibed the passion for discovery, and his Portuguese subjects eagerly carried out his most impatient wishes, under Diego Cam.

At length the enterprising mariner, Bartholomew Diaz, put to sea with three ships. He passed Cape Cross or De Padrono, (in 22° South latitude) the furthest point to which Diego Cam had reached, and proceeded until he arrived at Sierra Parda, (in 24° South latitude.) Here he raised his first cross, calling it Padraô de Santiago. He then passed on as far as Cape das Voltas, (about 29° South latitude) where he was detained for five days. Upon leaving this point, he fell in with foul weather and was driven out to sea; and upon his next nearing the land, he made the Western point of Mossel Bay, which he named the Angra dos Vagneiros (Cape Vaches Vaccas, or Bay of Herdsmen.) He here found that the land stretched to the North.—Without knowing it, he had in reality, doubled the Cape.

Still continuing his voyage from this, he came to the small island in Algoa Bay; where, anchoring and landing on Thursday, the 14th of September, 1486, (being the Festival of Holy Cross,) he raised his second cross. And here, amid the roaring foam of the untamed flood; here on a rude islet in a remote and tempestuous ocean, that illustrious, but ill-requited discoverer —partaking of the Holy Sacrament, together with his gallant crews, beneath that rough and simple emblem, mingled their wild music with the holy anthem that then was rising to the Redeemer of men, under the magnificent roof of St. Mark's in Venice. Thus they, from whom that day "*the sceptre was departing*," and those, by whose instrumentality they were deprived of it, were yet employed alike, united by the bonds of religion. For this discovery by Diaz, it must be remembered, at once arrested the spring course of the Venetian wealth and pre-eminence, plucked the oriental diadem from her imperial brow, and transferred to Portugal, his ungrateful country, the sovereignty of commerce. Diaz' crews, however, becoming dissatisfied, and urging their objection to proceeding further, in firm, though respectful terms, he yielded to their wishes; but made his officers sign a paper, recording it as their desire that he should do so. And even after this had been done, Diaz prayed them, that they would, to indulge him, sail but two days further; pledging himself, should nothing of importance occur or be discovered, to accede then to their wishes, and return at once. This they agreed to, and during this interval they discovered the mouth of the great Fish River, which received its primitive name of Rio d'Infante, from Joas Infanté, Captain of the Santa Pantaleone, who was the first European who landed there. The Portuguese entered this river with their ships, and remained at anchor for three days. Failing, however, to obtain any information respecting India from the natives, whom they describe as "a savage sort of people," they finally weighed anchor, and returned to the little island to which they had given the name which it still retains, Santa Cruz, and on which are yet to be seen the remnants of their rude cross. Diaz (says the chronicler of this voyage) on leaving this scene of his labours was moved to tears, and parted with the cross that he had set up on this barren rock, "as if he had been leaving a son in perpetual banishment." On his voyage back he came in sight of the long sought promontory, which we now call "*The Cape*," or the Head of Africa; but which he named Cabo Tormentoso, or Cabo de los Tormentos, (Cape of Storms.) This appellation was, however, changed by his master, King John II., to Cabo de Buena Esperanza, *(The Cape of Good Hope;)* on account of the hopes he entertained, and which were shortly realised, of discovering a passage round it by sea to the East Indies.

This scene of tender emotions to Bartholomew Diaz, he was never destined to see again. While trying to round this very head-land, eleven years afterwards, in a fleet sailing under the command of Pedro Alvarez Cabral, he was drowned: and thus it became, as has been well said, "at once his trophy and his tomb." Shortly after these discoveries, the Portuguese Admiral, Joas d'Infante, Captain of the Santa Pantaleone, already mentioned, strongly urged his Government to establish a Colony at the great Fish River, and he himself again doubled the Cape. Several attempts also were subsequently made, by Portuguese navigators, to colonize this country; but all failed, owing, it is said, to the constant and harassing inroads of the natives.

On the evening of the 11th of November, 1497, the great expedition, commanded by the Conqueror Vasques de Gama, came in sight of the Cape of Good Hope; when, owing to contrary winds, they stood out to sea, but turning again towards the shore at night. They thus tacked until the 20th, when they doubled the Cape, and found themselves at large in the Indian Ocean. He landed at a place called Angra del Blas, (possibly near the great Kei River,) on the 24th, and here raised a pillar, with the King of Portugal's Arms upon it. This was immediately pulled down by the *negroes*, as they are styled; who, although they at first seemed friendly, finally meditated mischief. The Portuguese, returning to their ships, fired two pieces of ordnance, "which," says the old chronicler, "so much affrighted the savages, that they dropped their weapons and disappeared."

On the 11th of January, in the next year, but during the same voyage, Vasco de Gama, touched on this coast again, much further to the Eastward, near the Mozambique Channel; and then, standing away to the Northward and Eastward, he had his perseverance and skill ultimately rewarded by the discovery of the coast of Malabar and India.

After the discovery of the Cape, the Portuguese fleets continued for several years to resort to the various bays in the present Colony, for the purposes of refreshment. They do not, however, appear to have ever taken possession of any part of the territory for the purpose of a Settlement. At length, their ships and merchants were chased from the Eastern Seas and their Indian empire, by their zealous rivals, and indefatigable enemies, the Dutch.

On one occasion only, during this period of the Cape history, do we find it recorded as the scene of any eventful incidents. The one alluded to, is that, when Francisco d' Almeida, first Portuguese viceroy of India, was shot by the natives with a poisoned arrow, and, at the same time, two of his captains and seventy-two other persons were slain.*

In 1614, the English attempted to form a settlement at the Cape hoping, thereby, to facilitate their efforts for sharing the Eastern commerce with the Dutch.   For this purpose, they landed a few convicts on Robben Island, in Table Bay. These were, however, soon dispersed; some of them being killed in an affray with the natives on the mainland, while the remainder returned to England.

In 1620, a fleet from Holland entered Table Bay, for the purpose of forming a Dutch Colony there.   This having come to the knowledge of Andreas Shilling, and Humphrey Fitzherbert, the commanders of two English ships, likewise there, they determined to anticipate the Dutch.

* This incident is thus described:—"On his way to Portugal, returning from India, after having doubled the Cape of Good Hope, the Viceroy, Francisco d'Almeida, stopped at Saldanha Bay to procure a supply of fresh water. The soldiers disputing with the natives, an affray ensued. Mello (one of his officers) seeing the venerable old man alone in the midst of that inhospitable country, observed to him in a sarcastic manner, 'Here I should wish to see by your side one of those whom you favoured in India.' Almeida's composed reply was. 'This is not the time to think of that; think rather how to save the Royal standard; as for me, I am old enough, both in years and in sins, to die here, if that be the will of the Lord.' From this moment Mello never abandoned either the standard or his general, until Almeida fell, pierced by a lance. Thus, the man who had trampled over countless thousands of the Asiatics, who had humbled their sovereign princes, and annihilated in the seas the power of the Egyptian Soldan, perished on an obscure strand, by the hands of a few savages."

Accordingly, they took immediate, and formal possession of the place, in the name of their sovereign, James I., without any molestation however, from the Dutch. They altered the nomenclature of the several surrounding mountains; calling the Lion's-Rump, James' Mountain; the lower portion near Green-point, Prince Charles' Mountain; the Lion's Head, they christened the Sugar-Loaf; and the Devil's Head was dignified with the name of Captain Fitzherbert himself; the Table Mountain was permitted to retain its own appropriate designation. No further steps in this matter were, however, taken, nor do the English Government appear to have recognised it.

"In the fulness of time," (to quote from Chase) "*Van Riebeck*," a surgeon and botanist, touched at Table Bay, in his homeward voyage, in 1648. The excursions he made into the country, in the prosecution of a delightful and bewitching science, probably inspired him with the first desire to revisit this richest, and most splendidly adorned, temple of Flora; some lovely flower, perhaps, whose predecessor had been

> "———born to blush unseen,
> And waste its fragrance in the desert air."

may have thus been the trivial cause of this important settlement. Whether this be the case or not, being a man addicted to speculation, and enthusiastically devoted to the service of his country, Van Riebeck, having, with others, represented the advantages to be secured by forming a general rendevous at the Cape, for the united Chartered East Indian Company of Holland, was selected, as the founder of the new Colony.   On the 23rd of December, 1651, he launched on the ocean, in three vessels freighted with precious seeds of civilization, to the celebrated promontory of the Cape of Good Hope; where he arrived about sunset, on the evening of the 6th of April, 1652, and immediately afterwards commenced his little settlement."

The Colony, thus began, soon spread; and, within eight years, a treaty with the natives, gave the new possessors a rayon of territory of three Dutch miles beyond the original fort. Ten years more incorporated the whole peninsula of the Cape, including Saldanah Bay and the Hottentot Holland.   In 1672, two other contracts with the Hottentot chiefs, (signed on the 19th of April, and the 5th of May,) witnessed the sale, in full, perpetual, and hereditary property, of the land around the Cape.   "The consent of the chiefs," (says Mr. Moodie, the collector of the Cape Records) "and their contentment with the price paid, was testified, by the members of the Cape Government, and by the Admiral of the fleet as Supreme Commissioner; and this purchase appears to have been *quite as complete, as that concluded between William Penn and the North Americans.*

A few years more sufficed to see the Dutch colonists spread along the Eastern slopes of the dividing range of Hottentot Holland Mountains; and soon afterwards, they descended into the fertile valleys of Stellenbosch and Drakenstein, carrying with them their industrious habits and religious faith.

The Swellendam, (then called the "*far and out-lying*") district was appended to the Colony in 1742, and that of Graff Reinet, in 1786, *when the Eastern frontier of the Colony was fixed at the Eastern bank of the great Fish River.* Nor is it to be discovered, by any record on paper whatever, that the Chamtoos River, then or ever, was a permanent boundary in this direction. This *has been stated* as being the case, and has been *unjustly* made a proof of the *late* deprivation of this part of Africa, from the native tribes; but which, in truth, they never have had possession of since this year here named; viz., 1786.

The Dutch appear to have retained peaceable possession of this Colony for 143 years, when they were deprived of it, A. D., 1795.

On the 10th of June, in that year, an

English fleet arrived in Simons' Bay, bringing letters from the Prince of Orange, enjoining the Cape Government to place the Colony under British protection. This advice being disregarded by the French party then at the head of affairs, a forcible possession of the Colony was taken, on the 16th of September following.

At the signature of the treaty, at the peace of Amiens, in 1801, the restoration of this Colony to the Dutch was ordered to take place, on the 1st of October of that year. This was, however, delayed until the 20th of February, 1803; when its inhabitants were "absolved from their allegiance, to his Britannic Majesty."

On the recommencement of hostilities in Europe shortly afterwards, the British Government, knowing the utility of the Cape as a depôt, determined again to resume possession of it. After some slight resistance on the part of the Dutch troops at Blauwberg, Cape Town capitulated on the 10th of January, 1806, and the Colony was finally ceded to England, at the congress of Vienna, in 1815. From that date to the present, it has remained, as we hope long to see it, a colony of the British Empire.

Thus far we have sketched the early records of this part of the world, including its geographical discovery, first colonisation, and early history; let us next turn to its records, as viewed *in connection with Europeans*, and employ another chapter to detail its past and present history, as a Dutch and British colony.

ISLAND OF SANTA CRUZ, IN ALGOA BAY.

CHAPTER III.

THE CAPE COLONIAL HISTORY, UNDER THE DUTCH AND ENG-
LISH GOVERNMENTS.

THE colonial history of South Africa, under the Dutch Government, presents to our notice little that is either interesting or important, if we except the long disputed question of their first occupation of its various districts, together with the modes employed by them for procuring them from the aborigines.

On these points, a few remarks may not be altogether misplaced, although the question is one which has caused such angry discussion already, that it demands a cautious treatment, and very serious attention.

Those who have charged the first colonists with the injustice of having forcibly deprived the native tribes of their land, and who urge on those of the present time an inclination to follow in the same road of encroachment, seem on the one side, (*on careful examination* of the documents extant, which bear on this subject,) to have been rather hasty in forming their conclusions, and preferring their serious charge.

Those, again, on the other side, who *vindicate the colonists against the natives*, appear to be over prejudiced in some of their statements. Faults being very likely to occur in such cases, on both sides, an impartial observer may be, perhaps, over-cautious in touching such a matter. For, whilst trying to avoid the grievous error of wishing to hide, or even excuse, any cruelties or acts of injustice that may have been committed by the first settlers at the Cape, he may, on the other hand, fear lest he should fall into the far worse error, of painting the savage in the untrue colours, and false lustre, of a misguided philanthropy. This latter fault may be far too easily (and we cannot but fear has far too often been) committed lately by persons describing an ignorant, brutalized race of savages, little removed from their pristine barbarism, as "a well-disposed, peaceful, honest, and happy people." *This is pleading for the conservation of heathenism, to the hinderance of the spread of the blessings of civilization and religion, through the means of the extended colonization of enlightened and Christian nations.*

But, turning to the colonial history of the Cape, and referring to the oldest records of the Colony, we find the first proclamation of Van Reibeck, when founding it in 1652; and, in reference to the aborigines, he prescribes that "should they be detected in theft, they should on no account, without his previous knowledge and consent, be pursued, beaten, *or even be looked upon with anger*:" further, that any European "that illuses, beats, or pushes any of the natives, *be he in the right, or in the wrong*, shall be punished with fifty lashes:" and again, that "every friendship and kindness shall be shewn to them."

That the first contracts, for *the conveyance of lands*, were regularly signed and testified by the natives, has already been stated, and with the price paid they expressed themselves content. No doubt (as is the case in all transactions of a like nature,) the advantage must have been in favour of civilization. The prime cost of the articles, delivered by William Penn to the North American Indians, most possibly bore the same proportion to the value of Pennsylvania in its present improved condition, as did the tobacco, beads, buttons, brandy, and other trifles, to the value of the land at the Cape, now that it is cultivated and built upon.

The numbers of the aborigines, at the first advent of the Dutch, have been stated at 200,000. The colonists are accused of having reduced and *cut off* these, to the present population of 32,000, "by a continual system of oppression, which, once begun, never slackened."

This seems to be a severe assumption. Judging from the records of the Colony, at that period, the one fourth of 200,000, viz., 50,000, (according to Chase,) appears certainly to be nearer the original estimate of the population of the native tribes. Nor can we but believe, that *disease* and *intestine warfare* had much more to do than *oppression*, with accounting for their gradual, and still progressive decline. This also is deducible from facts; for, in the years 1663, 1666, 1674, 1713, and 1767 successively, we read of small pox, measles, and other infectious and *indigenous* diseases, cutting them off by thousands. Whilst only, in 1659, and, again, from 1673 to 1676, are there records of feuds between the Dutch colonists and natives. On these occasions, but twenty-five of the latter are said to have fallen, while 1765 head of horned cattle, and 4930 sheep were taken from them. The *causes* of these wars are most circumstantially made out as aggression—*always on the part of the natives.*

And when they were at peace with the colonists, continual hostilities between themselves and the Bushmen, or (Soaqua or Vischmen, as they were then styled,) were going on.

Mention of these internal engagements, and the casualties caused by them, is frequently made by Van Riebeck in his journal, and also in other authentic documents, still preserved in the Colony, which amply prove, not only the likehood of diminution in the numbers of the native tribes, but also the actual existence *then* of the Bushmen family, as distinct from the Hottentots, and at enmity with them.

This allusion is here noticed, because these people are said to have been descended from Hottentots; who, *from the oppression of the first colonists*, were driven out from them to live in the caves.

But, speaking of these people even then, Van Riebeck remarks in his journal, "They never had any other means of subsistence than plunder; and their stock was not their own property but plundered from the Saldanhars, who, on that account, pursued them on every opportunity, and, on coming up with them, put them to death without mercy, and threw them to the dogs." They were subject to no other power than that of the arrow and the assegai, upon which they chiefly depended, and they treacherously plundered many people of their cattle and women; which robbery and abduction of women is much practised in war by all these tribes.

From these observations, it may be gathered that the Bushmen were then in existence, as a *distinct tribe*, amongst the aborigines of Africa, and were possessed then of the same habits of life which distinguish them still.

But, resuming the controverted history of the Dutch colonists and natives, we find that the latter were, almost universally, the *first aggressors.* This is corroborated by reference to several public letters, and other papers extant, bearing dates in the years 1663—65, 1770—72, 1778 —80. Mr. Patterson, the traveller, bears his impartial testimony to the same fact. Governor Plettenberg constantly complains of " their habitual disregard of their promises, and their carrying off the cattle, and killing the inhabitants of the Colony, without any cause."

It may, consequently, be asserted, that the Dutch colonists are extensively exonerated from the charge of being the *systematic oppressors* of the aborigines. At the same time, there are doubtless very many *individual* cases, which may be proved against them, where they certainly did enslave many of those, whom they, at different periods of their history, succeeded in capturing.

This fact, together with the charge of intrusion upon the lands of the aborigines, cannot be *wholly denied, or disproved* by them; although, at the same time, it may be palliated, in some small measure, by the plea of necessity. For the wandering habits of life of the Bushmen and

Hottentots, and their custom of choosing their more settled locations in the caves and mountains, would, by consequence, lay them particularly open to the temptation of theft, and of secreting therein the stolen property.   This would account for the severe treatment they received from the colonists, whom they had robbed and plundered; whilst the lowlands, appearing thus to be *unoccupied*, might, on the other hand, naturally tempt the first Dutch boers to settle themselves in comfort on them; and the neighbourhoods of the springs of water would not fail to be selected as the most promising sites—these thus becoming the objects and scenes of strife.

This, we believe, was the early history of the European colonisation of the Cape, and the way in which the land changed ownership; viz, not by any *system* of violence or cruelty on the part of the first Dutch settlers, but by the gradual absorption of the territories of the aborigines by a more settled, civilised, and industrious class of neighbours.   That the Government were partly to blame, cannot either be doubted, by reason of their not having *followed up* the example, precepts, and orders of Van Riebeck, of always acquiring the lands *first by treaty*, or *by purchase*, before allowing any individual colonist to settle thereon.   But, even had this been attended to, the result still would, in all human probability, have been the same, according to the experience of other nations; for, as is everywhere the case, the industrious would have secured the most fertile soil, whilst the Karoo and the desert alone would have been the portion of the indolent and barbarous aborigines.

In the hands of the Dutch, however, the Cape certainly soon developed its resources; while the edict of Nantes, and the persecution of the Protestants in Europe at that period, sent a number of French refugees to this country, who at once began the cultivation of the vine, and the manufacture of wine, which, at the present day, forms so important and extensive an article of its export commerce.

If we except the establishment of the laws and the religion of Holland; the building of the castle and barrack at Cape Town; together with the organization of the four primitive districts of the Colony; viz, the Cape, Stellenbosch, Swellendam, and Graff-Reinet: no event of any great importance to history occurred during the remaining period of the Dutch occupation. In the formation of these districts, each was placed under the charge of a Landrost, or chief magistrate, who had six Hemraaden, or Burghers, to aid him in the administration of justice;

while the law employed by them was that of Holland, founded on the Roman Dutch Code, and which they had patiently to extract from the ponderous tomes of Grotius, Voetius, and Vander Linden.

The effect of the first great French revolution was felt in the Eastern, as well as the Western world, and reached even to the Cape. For, in 1795, the British Government resolved to take possession of this Colony for the Prince of Orange; and, accordingly, an English fleet appeared off the Cape at the very moment when the inhabitants were about to declare themselves (after the manner of the Parisians) *a free and independent* republic. The troops, on this occasion, consisted of the 78th regiment, some marines, and two battalions of seamen, in all amounting to 1600 men. These, landing after a few ineffectual attemps to resist them on the part of the Dutch, soon forced the outworks. At the same time, reinforcements of English, under Sir Alured Clark, appearing in Table Bay, a capitulation ensued, and, for the first time, the Cape became a colony of England. It was then retained but seven years; and by a most mistaken policy, it was, at the end of this period, injudiciously restored, *nominally* to the Dutch, but, *in reality*, to the French, who made use of the Hollanders as best suited their own convenience.

On the renewal of the war with France, however, its recapture was amongst the first steps then wisely adopted by the British Government. This was accomplished, as soon as contemplated, by the well appointed force, which, under the united commands of general Sir David Baird and admiral Sir Home Popham, appeared off the Cape in January, 1806. Scarcely had the Highland brigade, on that occasion, advanced, with general Ferguson at their head, before the Dutch gave way, retreated, and offered terms of surrender. Since that period, it has been permanently under British control, and has been steadily and progressively advancing in civilization and commercial importance. Nor is it yet, we can clearly foresee, mid-way towards the zenith of its glory.

In extent it has been materially augmented. At the period of the transfer of the Colony from the Dutch to the British Government, it included simply the four districts of the Cape, Stellenbosch, Swellendam, and Graff-Reinet; whilst Worcester, Clan William, George, Beaufort West, and the others now existing, were subdivisions of these, thus extending on the Eastern boundary to the Great Fish River, and on the North to the Roggeveld and Niewveld ranges of mountains. Since that time, these several divisions have not only been, as described, subdivided into the more numerous districts that now exist, but its boundaries have also been extended, at various times, to their present locality.

Under the Dutch, the old Colony was, in extent, about 600 miles in length, by 320 in breadth; and its inhabitants were reckoned at 60,000, of whom 22,000 were Europeans, and the rest natives.

It now encloses, within its extended boundaries, upwards of 190,000 square miles of country, and in this territory the population according to the last parliamentary returns published, amounts, at the present, to 285,279 souls; of this number, two thirds are said to be coloured, still leaving the Europeans to number 95,093.

Of the present population of the Colony, however, rather less than half are Europeans, but principally of Dutch extraction. The whole increase of numbers, since it has become a British colony, has been from 60,000 to 220,000; and, among these, the disproportionate growth of Europeans, from 22,000 to upwards of 100,000, has required, of necessity, the extended territory before named. This has been obtained by gradual, but progressive enlargements, until the limits were fixed as now they exist.

Its boundary (as shewn in our map) is, at present, a line running on the North-west, from the mouth of the Koussie or Sand-river; South-east along the Western coast, to the River Zak, and thence to the North point of the Graff-Reinet district at the Karree-Berg. It then takes a North-east direction, until it meets the Zwart, or Black Gariep River, about 30 miles above the little town of Cradock, and passing along the banks of this, until it meets the junction of the Wonderboom River, it again turns and descends Southwards; then, crossing between the Zunreberg and Stormberg mountains, it meets, and runs along the banks of, the Zwart or Black Kei River until it comes to the little Winterberg mount. Thence it goes Eastward as far as Eland Post, near which it meets the Keiskamma River; and, passing along its Southern bank, it joins the sea on the East coast.

The " Cape Colony " has thus been formed and determined; not at once, but by very slow degrees, and at various periods in its history, in a manner which it may not be inapt here to point out in a condensed form.

The Kaffir tribes and their aggressions have ever been the main reason for these fresh annexions. The Amakosa tribes of these people, who dwell nearest to the present eastern colonial border, and extend from that to the Great

Kei River, form one of the three great branches of that nation, who have appeared in Southern Africa, who migrated thence from Northwards; and succeeded, about the year 1760, in subjugating the aboriginal Hottentot and Bushmen possessors of that part of the soil. These latter then dispersed in various directions, with the exception of the Gonas, (such as the chief Pato,) who still remain and maintain their independence among them. With these latter, also, we have now a treaty, offensive and defensive.

These Amakosa Kaffirs continued, from that time, to spread rapidly over the country, along the banks of the Great Fish River. And, the game being plentiful in the very extensive bush surrounding that locality, they attempted to settle on the South-west of that river, being a part of the district originally ceded to the first Dutch settlers, and which was claimed, and had been partly taken possession of, by them.

In the year 1780, their governor, Plettenberg, then at the head of the Colony, succeeded in fixing formally, and with the consent of the Kaffirs, the colonial boundary at the Fish River; and the district South of that river, now known as "Albany," was colonized by the Dutch boers, who hired the Kaffirs to live among them as cattle-herdsmen and servants.

A quarrel, however, arose between them, and ended in an insurrection of the latter. Having expelled the Dutch from their farms, and taken forcible possession of them, and of the adjoining country to about a hundred miles inland, the Kaffirs commenced and extended their predatory devastations throughout its whole extent; that is to say, so far south as the Gamtoo or Sunday River, 38 miles North of Algoa Bay. The revolutionary war, which was being carried on in Europe at this period prevented the Dutch home Government from sending out troops to the aid of their colonists at the Cape, and likewise deterred the local legislature there from sparing any far from Cape Town. And, when at length the English attacked and took the Colony, in 1795, no permanent measures were adopted by them against the Kaffirs, as the intention of holding the Colony was so soon afterwards abandoned. When, however, the Colony was recaptured by the British, in 1806, it was with very different intentions. More active measures, consequently, were speedily adopted, and set on foot, for freeing the country from these Kaffir freebooters and invaders, and for driving them back beyond the Eastern boundary line, as first permanently fixed in the year 1780, by the Dutch governor, Plettenberg: viz, the Great Fish River.   These measures were commenced in the year 1811, but were not finally successful until 1812.

Still the love of marauding and robbery, inherent in the Kaffirs, soon induced them to re-cross the boundary, and commence pillaging the Colony. And at length they became so daring, that, in the year 1819, they once more crossed the Great Fish River in force, and attacked Graham's Town in immense numbers.

They were, however, repulsed with some loss, and were so disheartened thereby, that, soon afterwards, Lord Charles Somerset, (then governor of the Colony,) was enabled to conclude a treaty with them. By this treaty, the colonial boundary was again fixed at the Fish River: but the country lying to the North-east, between that and the next river; viz, the Keiskamma, was, in addition, to be considered " a neutral territory." It was further also provided that the English, if they should consider it necessary, might build forts, and establish military posts along the line. This treaty was made between Lord Charles Somerset, as British Governor of the Colony, on the one side, and Gaika, regarded as the great paramount chief of the Amakosa tribes, on the other.

In the course of the next year, 1820, a grant of £50,000 was made by the English Parliament, to encourage and establish emigration to the Cape.   Accordingly, with this money, five thousand families, principally of Scotch extraction, were sent out to the Colony. These, having been landed at Algoa Bay, were located on the Eastern border, along the South-west banks of the Fish River, in the district of Albany.

To these British settlers, grants of land were given; every encouragement was held out to induce them to fix their locations as permanently as possible; and a promise of future protection was likewise stipulated, as not the least of these inducements. Accordingly, with true British energy and industry, they commenced farming the land, building dwellings, and rearing stock; and a few years saw them prospering beyond their own most sanguine expectations. The rapid increase, and improved breed, of their cattle, (always a tempting bait to the Kaffirs,) soon led these latter over the colonial line once more, and pillage again began —each year adding fresh instances to the list of thefts and robberies, perpetrated by these savage free-booters.

To endeavour to put a stop to these thefts, in the year 1830, the chief Macomo, the eldest but (according to Kaffir law) illegitimate son of the paramount chief Gaika, was deprived of a portion of land, in and about the Waterkloof and Kat river, within the neutral ground; the possession of which, it was believed, facilitated them much in secreting their booty. The pillaging, however, still continued; and Macomo, having been proved accessory to it, was further deprived of, and driven from, that other portion of country (likewise within the neutral ground,) to which he had been permitted to retire after his expulsion from the former part. Both of these removals were in accordance with an order from the Government; and such an order was certainly warrantable, because Macomo and his followers occupied both these places *only by agreement, during pleasure and good behaviour.* But still the last removal was effected under circumstances which gave much alarm to the colonists at the time; and there is every reason to suppose that the general conclusion of the community was correct, in believing that this chief, incensed and exasperated by this step, was principally instrumental in inducing the rest of the Kaffirs again to revolt, and invade the Colony. This they did towards the end of 1834, when the second Kaffir war commenced.

Then the assegai and the torch began their deadly work along the whole Eastern border of the colony. The unfortunate frontier farmers, (most of whom were the original settlers of 1820,) were pillaged of their flocks, herds, and property. Their homesteads were burnt over their heads, and, in many instances, their lives were lost whilst they were endeavouring to save those of their relatives. The total loss of this luckless community at this period has been rated, and, we believe, not over-rated at £300,000.

This war continued to ravage the Eastern frontier of the colony until the year 1835, when it was at length terminated by the then governor, Sir Benjamin D'Urban, who concluded a second treaty with the Kaffirs. This he had written out, and regularly signed and executed by them; judging that one, so agreed to, and put on record, would be more binding upon them. By the terms of this treaty, the Kaffirs agreed to admit military possession of their country, and to become, henceforth, "British subjects." At the same time, Sir Benjamin D'Urban recorded his firm opinion to be, "that the expulsion of the Kaffirs from their fastnesses in the Amatola Mountains was *indispensible* to the safety, and permanent peace and welfare, of the Cape Colony." He further stated, (what the late governor, Sir Harry Smith, eventually found to be correct, and was endeavouring to effect when he was recalled home; viz,) that the Great Kei River would form the best and only secure frontier boundary for the Colony.

Towards effecting this desired end; Sir Benjamin, previous to drawing up the second Kaffir treaty here alluded to, made proclamation, as governor, on the 10th of May, 1835, in these words: " *The eastern boundary of the Colony of the Cape of Good Hope is henceforward extended Eastward to the right bank of the Kei River.*" This he did at the Kei, where he drew up his army, and fired three cannons.   In the wording also of the treaty itself, which bore date the 17th of September, 1835, it was provided that " the chiefs and their tribes became subjects of his Britannic Majesty."   Thus far the sword and the arm of power were employed to hold these savage tribes in check: and there are fair grounds for supposing that they would now have been in a very different state of control, had the same line of policy been unremittingly carried out.

Instead of this, however, a change was soon made.   A new governor appeared on the arena: and, yielding to what has since proved itself to be very fallacious and injudicious advice, he determined to try the power of concession on the Kaffirs; conceiving, philanthropically, that possibly they would be more contented and peaceable, if they were given back their fastnesses.

Accordingly, Sir Andreas Stockenstrom, then

lieutenant-governor on the frontier, cancelling Sir Benjamin D'Urban's former plan on the 5th day of December, 1836, by proclamation "*renounced* the allegiance of the said chiefs and tribes:" and in a third treaty with the Gaika chiefs and tribes, bearing the same date, agreed "that *the boundary* between the said Colony and the territory restored to the Kaffirs by proclamation of this day, is, and shall be understood to be, that which was agreed upon in the year 1819, between the then governor, Lord Charles Somerset, and the Kaffir chief Gaika, "viz, a line drawn along the Keiskamma River, and so across the North-west. The fourth article provided that this territory between the Keiskamma and Kat Rivers was to be held by the Kaffirs as a *loan;* and the next article enacts that the "territory shall never be reclaimed *except in case of hostility committed, or a war provoked by the said chiefs and tribes, or in case of a breach of this treaty.*"

This territory, then and thenceforth, was styled the "ceded territory;" and, no occupation of the land by Europeans being permitted, the Great Fish River once more became the actual colonial boundary line. So far all seemed well; the act of concession was on the side of mercy, and had it succeeded, as was anticipated by some, in making the Kaffirs content, and so stopping this continual border warfare and bloodshed, a great object would doubtless have been gained. Such, unhappily, was not the case; for the policy of concession, formed without knowledge of the native character, proved a failure.

The Kaffirs are by no means a dull, though a savage people; and they had sufficient penetration to canvass, most shrewdly, our line of policy towards them. While firmness and control kept them in awe, concession was looked upon as either vacillation or cowardice. They at once concluded that we could not hold what we had taken from them, or else that we were afraid of them, and that they could frighten the white man out of the country altogether; if only they persisted in their invasions and pillage, and in waging periodical wars whenever they found their strength sufficiently recruited to commence and prosecute one. Being, however, weakened by that of 1835, which had but then ended, they were content to "sit still" (as they style it in their Kaffir phraseology) for a while, and enjoy their lately acquired spoil. Moreover, a strong military force was retained in the country, such as they were unable to compete with, until the rising generation should come to manhood. Accordingly, no actual outbreak took place until 1846, when another war was opened with the Colony. During the eleven years, however, from 1835 to that time, continual Kaffir aggressions and petty thefts were being carried on along the Eastern frontier. This is most fully borne out by the several official documents of that period, which also bear numerous testimonies to these aggressions being invariably on the Kaffir side, and never provoked by the colonists; who, on the contrary, are throughout fully and amply exonerated from all or any such accusations.

The dread of inability, to maintain and defend these extended possessions, has lately led to an effort to reduce them, by abandoning the Orange River Sovereignty—the most impolitic step, it is to be feared, that has ever yet been taken with respect to this country. This may seem strong language to use; but, nevertheless, it is both just and true, and such, moreover, as can easily be supported, not only by reference to the colonial history, but, also in the evil effects already arising from the measure.

Undoubtedly this colony—although, as above shewn, a rapidly increasing, and, comparatively, a flourishing one within itself—is not a *satisfactory* one to the home country. The constant demand for troops to protect it from its border tribes; the "two millions" required periodically for the expenses of "Kaffir wars;" the small returns of export produce; the outcry of the colonists against the introduction of *unre-*

strained convicts: all these matters have tended to make "the Cape" no favourite dependency of late. But, it may be asked, why has this dissatisfaction arisen? We fear it must be honestly allowed, by every impartial observer of the past history of this colony, that it owes its origin, too much, to mis-management, and vacillation in the policy adopted there from time to time.

For instance, let us only glance at the sketch of the past history of the last twenty years. During this period, we find three Kaffir wars rapidly succeeding each other; seven Governors, each trying different "theories of administration;" whose various experiments at *concession* and extermination, respectively ended in the adoption, and re-establishment, of the policy for which, in 1837, the wise and good Sir Benjamin D'Urban was recalled. Scarcely has this been effected, by the late lamented Sir George Cathcart, when another, duly authorized, arrives in the Sovereignty, to nullify once more the advantages gained. Not, this time, by *concession* to the natives, but by *abandoning* British subjects, and denying them their rights as such—thus sowing in their minds the bitter feelings of distrust and republicanism.

These colonists have been hitherto most *unjustly* charged with disloyalty to England. We say unjustly, because we have lived long amongst them, *know* them, and their feelings, intimately, and we can most conscientiously and impartially assert, that *they are not disloyal* to their native land, its sovereign, or its laws. But if, eventually, they were to become so, (which God forbid) how could we blame them without taking equal blame to ourselves; if, after being permitted to locate in the Colony under British protection, and having scarcely parted with, and sunk their capital there, *they are abandoned* to the ruthless mercy of the barbarians. Surely this *must* tend to cramp enterprise; to stay improvement; and to weaken every effort for social advancement within the Colony. It must retard commerce, and lessen thereby its exports; nay more, it *may* tend to unhinge the loyal affections of Englishmen in Southern Africa; and it now *does* give renewed energy, not only to the disaffected and rebellious colonists, but to the native tribes also, and stimulates and *encourages* them to a fresh outbreak, and renewed warfare.

The least false step in the government of the Colony, and its dependencies, at the present time, will be of the most material injury. Never, in its history, was there a better opening for amending the errors of the past, and permanently securing its welfare, than that now presented.

The boundaries for the Kaffir tribes are fixed at the Eastern bank of the Great Kei River, the best, and the *only secure* one for the Colony; British Kaffraria is steadily advancing in civilization : the colonists are yet loyal, energetic, and enterprising; and the local Government of the country is vested in a local Parliament. Let this be but followed up, and extended; divide the Colony, by giving to each province its own local houses of assembly; increase the population of the Eastern province by emigration; oppose British industry to savage indolence, *by filling up, compactly*, the whole of "the Royal Reserve," in British Kaffraria, with these immigrants; encourage the extended organization of a colonial militia and yeomanry force; and, at the same time, keep a sufficient body of British troops in British Kaffraria—the Colony paying for them; and then no more Kaffir wars will occur; then the colonists will *remain* loyal; commerce will *increase;* civilization will become *established*, and, as a necessary consequence, it will extend among the natives, and, in its wake, Christianity will *enter*, and, it is reasonably to be expected, take possession of their hearts.

This is not the mere theory of invention, but it is the confirmed conviction of our mind, after many years sojourn in South Africa, together with very close and silent observation of the working of society there, and the rights and requirements of *all classes* of its inhabitants.

The abandonment of Kaffraria, has also (we are aware) been largely and widely spoken of, in England, of late. It has been asserted that this may be effected without the least detriment to our retention of the old Colony, and therein of Cape Town and Simon's Town, as military and naval depôts.

Nothing could be more fallacious than this supposition! *Wherever* the colonial boundary is, *there* the Kaffirs will be; their inherent love for plunder being too strong, not to keep them always as close to the colonist's cattle as they can be.

If Simon's Town was our only possession in Africa they would be located in Hottentot Holland mountains, and our colonists and settlers would one and all be sacrificed. Such injustice to them should not be contemplated; when by maintaining the present connections, and *working out steadily* the policy so well and so energetically re-established by the late Sir George Cathcart, a *permanent* peace, may, we sanguinely believe, be secured. But, unless *emigration* into British Kaffraria and Victoria *be at once adopted*, no policy, troops, or any laws whatever will prevent another renewed Kaffir inroad on the Colony.

The maintenance of troops, on the frontier for some years yet, is indispensibly necessary;

nor can we but believe, from the salubrity of this climate, and other local resources, that this might most advantageously be made a large central and invalid depôt for regiments in India and the East, both cavalry and infantry.   But let it ever be borne in mind, that indispensible as military men, and cordons of military forts are, (just such as have been lately erected) in Kaffraria; still the paramount requirements is an *increased European population*.

We know of passes in the Amatola mountains, through which we have often walked and ridden, while hunting after the objects or beauties of nature, by which 5000 Kaffirs could be led back into those fastnesses in one dark night; while ten times the number of troops, now garrisoning the forts around, if there, could not prevent them.   And this is no error in military tactics, or want of foresight.   Far otherwise, the frontier lines of the Colony never were better placed, or organized, than at the present; we do not know that they could be so.   But, say that forts are placed, not every forty, but every ten miles, along the border; those who have seen and lived "in the bush," know full well, that still, with the greatest ease, Sandilli, Macomo, and Anta, with all their warriors at their backs, could soon, if they wished it, elude all discovery, *and be entrenched in the Amatolas*, before it was even known to be their intention to leave their present locations.

Hence, the only secure mode of preventing these recurring inroads, is by filling up unoccupied ground with industrious immigrants. These, by agriculture, felling wood, and other occupations, would never want means of support, nay, even of affluence, for themselves and their families, if they were only once located there; and their presence, *on their own farms*, would do more, as burgher militia-men, for the defence of the Colony, than the vast number of regular troops, employed in the late war.

Together with this, the abolition of the illicit sale of gunpowder to the natives, in the Colony, is most important. The present order for restricting its sale, has done much towards stopping this iniquitous practice; but it has not done all, nor nearly so. On the contrary, we know one honorable, upright man, a merchant on the frontier; who, seeing the likely means there were for evading this ordinance, and unable to *detect* or *stop* it, (even although it was suspected,) prohibited it altogether as an article of sale in his stores; thus proving the yet existing abuse of the ordinance. Hence, to effectually put an end to this fatal mal-practice, the sale of gunpowder should be a Government monoply. It should be placed in the charge of ordinance officers, appointed specially for that purpose, who alone should be allowed to dispose of it: and that only by Government permit, and with strict, and searching personal and individual enquiries, relative to those to whom they give it. A few strict, energetic, and decisive measures of this nature, adopted speedily, to confirm the present revived policy on the frontier of the Cape, would, it is most sanguinely and justly believed, place South Africa beyond the power of the savage; and, opening up her internal and extensive resources, would expand and develop her true and full capabilities, for becoming one of the richest, if not *the richest*, of all territories of our British Colonial Empire.

A MALAY FAMILY.

CHAPTER IV.

THE PHYSICAL GEOGRAPHY, TOGETHER WITH A TOPOGRAPHICAL SKETCH, OF THE WESTERN PROVINCE OF THE OLD CAPE COLONY.

WE next turn to a sketch of the physical aspect, and geographical formation, of South Africa, together with an outline of its territorial divisions, products, and commercial statistics.

Ere touching these, however, the peculiarities of the atmosphere attract our attention, and, in this, nothing more, perhaps, than the noted phenomenon of "The Table Cloth," which is viewed with wonder by all strangers, who sight the Cape—spreading, over the summit of the Table Mountain. This is a large cloud; formed, apparently, by the S. E. wind which prevails at the Cape, and generally blows, a very few days excepted, for the whole of the summer months, appearing to be generated by the neighbourhood of the mountain. A few hours after this wind commences, the vapours, in the upper region of the atmosphere, become condensed, by striking against the cooler surface of the mountain, and roll forward in large masses; on which, the sun shining brightly, gives them the appearance of opacity, and so arose the phrase of "The table cloth being spread on the mountain." This vapour rolls on, in increasing volumes, until it comes to the precipitous termination of its mountain career; where it falls over the precipice in masses; until, in its descent, it meets with the denser atmosphere below, in which it is quickly absorbed, and disappears.

It is a very curious sight to observe this process going on. As the vapour, in its fall, gets under the shade of the perpendicular wall of rock, it assumes a dark and threatening appearance, as if this great body of cloud was about to pour a deluge on the devoted town beneath. These fleecy-looking masses, however, are rather the bales than the bags of Æolus, which send forth wind instead of rain. These sudden and overpouring gusts overturn everything in the streets; blow trees up by the roots; and drive clouds of sand and gravel from the shore, as far as the ships at anchor in the Bay. We have known, on such occasions, persons blown off their saddles, when riding near Cape Town, and carriages and horses turned completely round by its force.

On another occasion, we were much amused, by a pair of gold spectacles being blown from the nose of a very short-sighted person, who was thus completely incapacitated from even *trying* to recover them, if such had been possible. In connection also with this, we remember once hearing the simple question put at Capetown, "What is the meaning of all those different coloured badges, worn by the gentlemen of the Cape round their hats?—some blue, some brown, some green;" alluding to the different coloured veils, worn for the purpose of shielding the eyes from the gravel during the South-Easters. It is, of course, needless to say, that the first of these which occurred afterwards, fully explained, not only the meaning of this practice, but likewise the laugh with which the interrogation had been saluted.

This S. E. wind at the Cape extends to the Northward and Westward; whilst, out of its focus, the winds are moderate and variable. It has been supposed, that the winds at and off the Cape, are less boisterous now than formerly: this, however, is a fallacy. They blow there now with such force at times, that the largest and best sailing ship known could not beat up coast against a full South-easter.

This wind is certainly local, and has its origin very near the Cape; most possibly, some peculiarity, in connection with the formation of the Table Mountain, turns it into this peculiar channel. That it is a local wind is certain, from the fact of its being hot and dry; for, did it come up from the sea, it, on the contrary, would be cold; since that is the direction of the large masses of ice of the Antartic regions, and all vapours which originated there would, consequently, when condensed, be more or less impregnated with moisture, as well as cold. From the registers, kept in the immediate vicinity of Cape Town, it has been ascertained that, when the Table-cloth has been spread on the mountain, and this wind blowing hard there, a North-wester, accompanied with heavy rain, has been local at Hottentot Holland, which is only at the opposite side of False Bay.

It is also known that, a hundred miles to the Southward of the Cape, the wind is always from the Western quarter; while, even after sighting it, although the wind has been W. S. W., the Table-cloth has been seen on the mountain, indicating a South-Easter at Table Bay.

During these gales, the thermometer usually rises gradually, and gains the highest point of graduation immediately preceding their close. The North-Westerly wind, on the other hand, which generally prevails through the winter, brings the quicksilver down, and is usually accompanied with rain. This latter is called at Cape Town "the Kloof wind," because it rolls over the town from "the Kloof" or ravine situated on that side. It is not considered conducive to health; while the South-Easter, from blowing all pestilential vapours and effluvia out to sea, and purifying the streets and avenues by their overpowering currents of air, has obtained the local epithet of "*the Doctor.*"

The "hot," or "desert" wind, of Southern Africa, is another atmospheric visitant, occasionally to be found. This is simply the expended force of the Sirocco of the Zahara desert; which, having spent its main strength there, comes to die at the Cape.

It has somewhat of the nature of the "*Simoom,*" inasmuch as it comes silently along, and is loaded with a dry scorching heat, which is a death blow to all vegetation, and is not agreeable, for the time, to any branch of nature's creatures. It is viewed, in the South of Africa, as a scourge—yet it is a blessing. Where frost seldom comes to absorb the caloric from the face of nature, nor yet to check over abundant and decaying vegetation, this answers the purpose; and although, during the time of its visit, its presence is not appreciated, yet its utility is soon felt and acknowledged after it is gone.

It differs from the Simoom, however, in that it is colourless, and although charged with heat and aridity almost amounting to suffocation, it does not appear to possess the pestilential properties, with which the former is freighted.

On the whole, the atmosphere of Southern Africa is very healthy, temperate, and pure. Its changes are accompanied by various indicators, which give warning of their approach, and so enable all to prepare against their effects. The upper currents of air are rare, and seldom bedimmed by clouds, vapours are soon absorbed or dispersed, while the temperature averages, during winter, from 50° to 60°; and in the summer, from 70° to 80°. The mean of the barometer is 30·18.

The climate appears, however, to possess a manifest difference in the East and West of the Colony. The winter of the West side is wet, inclement, and disagreeable; while, on the Eastern frontier, it is cold, dry, bracing, and delightful; the summer, again, of the Eastern province, is wet and stormy; whereas the Western is pleasant, dry, and salubrious. There is also a full month's difference in the advent of the seasons. The commencement of winter, for instance, at Cape Town and the surrounding districts, is in June; while, along the Eastern frontier of the Colony and in Kaffirland, it does not begin until July.

Thunder storms visit, with great violence, the mountainous districts in the interior of the

Colony and in Kaffraria; whilst, along the coast-line, they are less frequent. They also invariably follow the "hot winds," but these again seldom appear near the sea.

The nocturnal beauties of the heavens, here, are indisputable, and the frequency and grandour of meteoric appearances, is imposing in the extreme. We believe we do not say too much, when we describe a moon-lit landscape, in Southern Africa, as "the most perfect prospect of nature.

But, descending thus to speak of the land, reminds us, that the terrane structure, and aspect of this territory, is also immediately before our notice.

The outlines of this country, towards the sea, are formed of a few prominent points, separated by large sweeps of the ocean. The leading features, in the aspect of the Cape, consist in three successive ranges of mountains, running parallel to each other, and to the Southern coast. The first range which, at least in a great part of its line, is called "*the Lange Kloof*," or "Long Pass," runs parallel to the coast, at a distance of from 20 to 60 miles, widening towards the west. The second range, called "*Zwart Berg*," or "Black Mountain," is considerably higher, and more rugged, than the first, and consists often of double and triple ranges. The belt of land, interposed between the Zwarte Bergen and the Lange Kloof, is nearly of the same average, as that between the latter and the sea, and it is of considerably greater elevation. Beyond the Zwarte Bergen, at an interval of 80 or 100 miles, rise the "*Niewveldts Gebirge*" or "Snowy Mountains," the highest range of Southern Africa, the summits of which are generally covered with snow. They have never yet been accurately measured, but are not supposed, in their greatest height, to fall short of 10,000 feet. The belt or plain interposed between these two last chains, is considerably more elevated than either of the two others, so that Southern Africa, forms, as it were, a succession of terraces rising above each other.

The plain next the sea is covered with a deep and fertile soil, watered by numerous rivulets, well clothed with grass, and with a beautiful variety of trees and shrubs. Rains here are frequent; and from its vicinity to the sea, it enjoys a milder, and more equable temperature than the interior and remoter parts of the Colony. The second terrace contains a considerable portion of well-watered and fertile lands; but interspersed with large tracts of the arid desert, called Karroo. The third belt, called "the Great Karroo," is composed of one vast plain, 300 miles in length, and nearly 100 in breadth; occupying, therefore, a space nearly equal to the whole surface of Ireland—the soil of which is of a hard and impenetrable texture, destitute of almost any trace of vegetation.

Having thus described the general outline, we shall present the minuter details respecting this country, in an equally instructive and more pleasing form, by sketching a tour through the various districts and divisions of the Colony, beginning with that of " *the Cape*."

This district, in extent, is the smallest subdivision of the Colony, being only 190 miles in length, by 30 miles in breadth; and containing an area of about 3,700 square miles of country. It extends from the Cape of Good Hope, Northwards along the Western coast, to Point St. Martin, on the N.W. of St. Helena Bay. But, although the smallest, it is perhaps, *at present*, the richest and most productive district of the Western province of Southern Africa; yielding as it does, under the European culture of about 50,000 acres of ground, the largest part of the colonial produce exported from Table Bay; the average annual amount in value of which is about £220,000. This produce consists chiefly of grain, fruit, wood, wool, and wine; together with some few articles of manufacture, such as hats, candles, soap, snuff, and

View of Cape Town and Table Mountain from Table Bay.

Page 67.

other articles. The richest localities of this part, are about Wynberg and Constantia, situated ten or twelve miles from Cape Town. The ground around here is thickly planted with oak, fir, and vines; the whole landscape, also, is one expanse of the most pleasing and beautiful vegetation, clothed, as it is, with a variety of tints of green; while, in the more Northerly division of Malmesbury, (lying along the coast of Saldana Bay, and styled the "granary of the Cape,) the fields display the more mellowed tones of the ripening corn.

The Table Mountain is, perhaps, the most remarkable feature in the terrane structure of this locality. Its tabular surface, (lying 3,582 feet above the level of the adjacent ocean,) extends in a horizontal plane for nearly two miles, and contains an area of about ten acres. It is flanked on the N.W. and S.E. sides by two buttresses of rock, called the Lion's Head, 2760 feet high, and the Devil's Mountain, 3315 feet above the level of Table Bay. At their bases these are still united, although the constant torrents of rain and tempests have worn them into three detached masses towards the summit.

The formation of this mountain is very singular. The upper face of the rock is interrupted, midway downwards, by heavy bold buttresses, composed of granite, in which large blocks of *quartz* and *mica*, together with pieces of *felspar*, appear through. These rise from the plain below, at an angle of 45°, and are then split vertically by deep chasms, which divide them into a long row of rugged supporters to the face of the rock. On the North side, towards the top, it is perpendicular in appearance, although it is composed of *horizontal* strata of *red sand-stone*, which varies, in its degrees of tenacity, as it ascends towards the summit. This also is thinly interspersed with small pieces of *quartz*, which are embedded in it; and are seen only where the weather appears to have worn away the superincumbent stratum of sand-stone.

Professor Playfair's theory for the original formation of this most peculiar mountain, seems undoubtedly the most feasible one yet advanced. He is of opinion "that the structure of the peninsular, points out two separate epochs, distinguished by very different conditions. It appears, at the present time, to be composed of a wall of *granite*, highest at its Northern extremity, and lowering gradually to the South; faced at its base with *schistus*, *killas*, or *granwacke*; and covered at its summit with a platform of horizontal *sand-stone*. The penetration of the *killas*, by veins from the mass of granite (which it surrounds) proves that the *killas* through the superior rock, is of older formation than the *granite*. The granite, therefore, is a mineral that has come up from below into the situation it now occupies, and is not of the materials which have been deposited by the sea, in any shape—either mechanical or chemical. It is a species, therefore, of subterraneous lava, and the progeny of that active and powerful element, which we know, from the history of the present and the past, has always existed in the bowels of the earth. The introduction, therefore, of granite into the situation it now occupies, must have taken place while the whole was deep under the level of the sea, previous to its elevation, or the subsidence of the surrounding waters. The granite may thus be considered as *newer* than one of the rocks incumbent on it, and *older* than the other—thus highly favouring the opinion that granite does not derive its origin from aqueous deposition." With the exception of *coal*, *iron*, and *copper*, (indications of which have been discovered in various parts of this continent,) no ores or minerals have yet been found in the adjacent country.

In the village of Malmesbury, however, distant about 40 miles from Cape Town, there is a warm mineral spring of water forced up. It is highly impregnated with sulphurated hydrogen, and is in some request as beneficial in the cure of cutaneous diseases. It is said to contain lime, soda, and magnesia, and its temperature varies from 92°. to 96°. It is used also, medicinally, as an aperient.

Travelling towards the interior, we next come to the *division of Stellenbosch*, which is so called, from a small picturesque town of the same name, situate about 30 miles from Cape Town. This is one of the oldest villages in the Colony, dating its foundation in the year 1681. The name was derived from its founder (then Dutch governor of the Colony) Simon van der Stell, together with that of his wife, whose aristocratic maiden name was Bosch.

It is a pretty, but not very striking, locality. The soil appears rich and productive, and is principally laid out under vineyards. The chief produce is wine; although wheat, oats, and potatoes, are also raised in some parts. The scenery is varied near the mountains, and many localities are thickly wooded with oak. The formations under, and of the earth, are granite, iron-stone, and clayey alluvial mould. Near the Paarl, which is also situated in this division, another mineral spring of warm water, similar to that at Malmesbury, has been lately discovered, which is said to be very efficacious in liver complaints. The attraction of this, together with the acknowledged salubrity of the climate, and the superiority of the growth of the orange and lemon trees, makes this district a favourite resort for invalids and visitors from the East.

At the South of the district, and on the extreme North of Simon's Bay, lies Groote Drakenstein, which is noted for some large and deep caves. They were excavated, upwards of 100 years ago, (by order of the Dutch Government,) in search for silver.

Several small rivers rise in the mountains, situated in the S. E. of this district, and flow through the valley beneath, supplying the various farms with adundant irrigation. These streamlets are not, however, confined to this district, but extend throughout the undulating lands which stretch along the whole Southern coast of Africa, and are bounded on the North by the long coast-chain of mountains; which, running East and West across the continent, (at about 30 miles distance from the ocean,) forms that first terrace which is presented to the mariner's eye.

The Zwaarte Bergen, or *Black Mountain*, as has been said, rising yet higher, and branching out into double and treble ranges, is the next chain of elevation to this, that is noticeable. These are more rugged and uneven than the first, and, in their nature, partake much of the barrenness and aridity of the *Karroo*, lying at their base; which is composed of long thirsty plains of naked clay and sand, with stunted shrubs, and tufts of sour grass, sprinkled sparingly over its surface.

These mountains extend through the districts of Swellendam and Worcester, from the East towards the North-west; retaining, in their geographical position, a similar curvature to the coast line of the promontory; and finally falling in with the Bokkeveld, and Ceder-Bergen ranges, at the extreme North-western extremity of the latter district. These, together with the Karree-Berg, and Kamies, or Lion-Mountains, then take up the highland chain along the Western coast; which, running Northwards through the division of Clanwilliam, passes into Namaqualand, and finally vanishes at the mouth of the great Gareep, or Orange River, in latitude 28°. 40'., longitude 16°. 30'.

The character of the country met with, as we proceed towards the more inland and Northerly districts of the Western province, is decidedly mountainous. The Onder-Bokkeveldt, and Roggeveldt-Berg chains in the South of Clanwilliam; the Middle-Roggeveldt on the North-east of Worcester; and the Niewnveldt-Bergen ranges running East and West through the centre of the Divisions of Western-Beaufort, and Graff-Reinet, carry on the other terrace of highlands. This, passing through the more Easterly districts of Cradock, Colesberg, and Albert, in the Rhinoster-Berg, Zuure-Berg, and Storm-Berg ranges, and so meeting the Draken-Berg or Quathlamba mountains stretches North and South through Kaffirland, and reaches nearly to Delagoa-Bay on the Eastern coast of Africa, and South-western to the Mozam-bique Channel. In rear of these, again, are other chains lying more inland, not of so enor-mous an elevation, indeed, as this last mentioned one; but of considerable importance, although no accurate survey of their true geographical position and extent has yet been obtained.

The internal and subterranean formation and compositions of these various mountainous dis-tricts have, as yet, been but little explored: but judging from the few metallic mineral samples, which mere accidental research has already brought to light, in various parts of this continent; there is more than sufficient grounds for assuming them to be largely impregnated with iron, copper, lead, and coal, if not indeed with the richer and auriferous species of ore.

Beyond the Kamiesberg, in the division of Clanwilliam, (latitude 30°. 50'., longitude 18° 45'.) on the South-western coast, considerable quantities of copper were found, so far back as the year 1751. Want of local capital and energy has, however, hitherto allowed it to remain wholly undisturbed, until but very lately.*

In these localities, the ore is found lying in granitic beds, and there are large and extensive amalgamations of *gold* and *silver*, as well as other metals, to a considerable extent, to be met with. These materially increase the intrinsic value of the copper ore; irrespective, of course, of their own exclusive working, which might not, at the first, be sufficient to encourage the miners.

It is well known, that in Japan, which produces as its commonest mineral, the finest and most malleable copper in the world, gold, in a very considerable quantity, is blended in the ore. And also, in the lead mines of Upper Louisiana, in North America, the ore is said to yield frequently as much as fifty ounces of silver to the ton. Let us sanguinely hope that those who are now making the enterprising effort, of laying bare these hitherto hidden riches of Southern Africa, may be amply rewarded for their exertions, by the mines of wealth; which, it is but reasonable to believe,

---

* Messrs. Phillips and King, of Cape Town, are now actively employed in working some of these mines, which have repaid their energy, not only with copper ore, but also large amalgamations of silver and *gold*.

lie beneath its surface, throughout this and all its districts; and only require the unconquerable energy, and indomitable perseverance, of Britain's sons to bring to view, and render useful.

The surface productions of the lowlands, throughout these districts, seem at present, however, to satisfy the industry of the inhabitants; who leave unexplored these mountain localities, or only visit them in search of pasture for their flocks and herds of cattle.

But besides the Cape and Stellenbosch divisions, which have been already noticed, there are those of Swellendam, Worcester, George, Beaufort, Caledon, and Clanwilliam; which, in the Western province of the Colony, are nearly, though not equally, productive with the former in agricultural and mineral products.

Of these, the divisions which lie towards the South, are the richest in soil and vegetation: such as Swellendam and George, the latter especially bidding fair to rival the Cape; while those on the North are of a richer geological structure. Wool, butter, aloes, grain of all kinds, and salt are among the commonest articles of export, from this division. The latter is gathered from a few salt-lakes, situated near the mouths of the Gouritz, and small brack rivers. The heat of the sun, evaporating the water in these lakes, leaves the saline particles encrusted along their edges, which are then gathered and stored; and thus form a leading article of trade in this, as likewise in other parts of the country, where these lakes or "salt-pans" as they are styled, are situated. The large and extensive forest of the Knysna, also growing in this division, provides the colonial markets with a plentiful supply of excellent timber; and even furnishes sufficient to make it an article for the export trade of the locality. This is the most notable forest in the country; but there are others which require only the same notice and labour to make them equally productive. At about 30 miles East of Clanwilliam, for instance, are large plantations of cedar, and there are similar ones of poplar and oak in Worcester; while, in the Eastern district, extensive forests of every kind of African timber are available.

Swellendam and Worcester are both worthy of notice, as regards their fertility and commercial importance, but they are devoid of any objects of special interest to the eyes of a traveller. The former contains an area of about 7700 square miles of country; while Worcester includes 20,000 square miles; but, of this, a large portion is mountainous, and covered with Karroo, which necessarily compels the in-

SCENE IN THE KNYSMA FOREST.

habitants to be graziers, of migratory habits of life.

Almost the only fresh-water lake in South Africa occurs in one of the wards of this division. It is situated on a high elevation of the Bokkeveld, and is called the Verkeerde Valley. It contains numbers of a species of fish, called by the Dutch the Witte-visch.

The climate of these districts is rather cold and sharp during the winter, the mountains being constantly covered with snow, and frost lying heavily on the ground. In the summer months, however, it is cooler and more agreeable than in the lower localities.

Several hot mineral springs exist in various parts of these districts; those at Caledon being in great repute, as efficacious in the cure of cases of chronic rheumatism, diseases of the skin, and scorbutic ulcers. Their heat is 92 degrees, and their waters contain muriate of soda.*

The climate throughout Swellendam is very salubrious—the average of the thermometer in the summer months being 76°. Its principal commodities for trade are grain, dried fruits,

---

* Of all these baths, which are exceedingly numerous, and diversified in their ingredients, throughout the Western Province of the Colony, the most important is that situated in what is called the Brand Valley, about 10 miles from the village of Worcester. It issues from a calcarious bottom, and always possesses an unvarying temperature of 140°.

soap, aloes, butter, tallow, wine, and brandy. To these may also be added skins, feathers, and wool, which are exported to a considerable extent, for England, from a Port called St. Sebastian's Bay, or Port Beaufort, situated on the line of sea coast within the district.

The more Northern divisions of Beaufort West, and Clanwilliam, which have been named in common with these others, partake of a different character of soil, and are more adapted for grazing and cattle breeding, than for agricultural products.   In Beaufort, "the Gouph," an extensive tract of undulating country, interspersed with wide plains, covered with heath, spreads out over 6000 square miles of country, lying between the Zwartzberg and Nieudweldt mountains, and supports about 200,000 sheep, 8000 head of horned cattle, and 600 horses. Throughout this division, it has been estimated that about 200,000 acres of land lies unappropriated—the cause of non-occupation, being supposed to be the great want of water.   The average price of land here is from sixpence to five shillings the acre.

Another large tract of country, used as a sheepwalk, is the Nieudweveldt, extending to the Karee Bergen, and covered with flocks and herds of cattle, of the finest and most approved descriptions.   The Beaufort division thus yields the largest supply of live stock sent to the colonial markets; while Swellendam exceeds all others in agricultural produce—its annual average being about 30,000 bushels of grain.

Clanwilliam is the largest division of the Western Province of the Colony. It contains 22,111 square miles of country, but most of which is bleak and mountainous, and is also unproductive, owing to the scarcity of water.

Many districts in it are solely supported by breeding cattle, (principally horses and sheep) and the smallest amount of agricultural produce, is received from this division, if that of Beaufort be excepted. Tobacco and rice, of a good quality, have been raised on one farm within one of these districts; and the ready and remunerative market, found for them amongst the people of the neighbourhood, amply repaid the enterprising cultivator. The forests in the cedar mountains, have already been noticed as belonging to this division, with which is comprised all that is worthy of note.

To the North, again, of Clanwilliam, lie Little and Great Namaqualand; which, at the present, contain one of the few remnants of the pure Hottentot race. In itself, it is an uninteresting land; very hot, oppressive, and unhealthy in climate; and covered with wide plains of Karroo and desert, on which rain seldom falls, and not sufficient to enable the inhabitants to raise enough grain for their own support. In extent it stretches Northwards along the Western coast, until it joins the country of the Damara tribes, about 200 miles above the Gariep, and about the same distance Eastward from the coast line. It is separated from the Bechaanas land by an immense desert, is wholly uninhabited, and quite devoid of water. The soil is a loose sand, occasionally tufted with patches of grass.

On the Eastward, again, of Little Namaqualand, and North of the divisions of Beaufort and Clanwilliam, extends the Koronna country, and Griqualand; which former is bounded on the north by the Gariep; the latter stretching across it. These tracts take their names from their present tribes, of whom we shall have to treat more minutely hereafter. Their soil, however, first demands attention. It is here more verdant than in Namaqualand, although partaking of the Karroo character; but, as we proceed Northwards, it is covered with long rank grass, and thinly planted with acacia trees, and mimosa thorns. The fact of the inhabitants rearing cattle in abundance, and of an approved description, is a sufficient proof of the better description of land.

Ere leaving these several Southern divisions of the Cape, however, one object is well worthy of special and minute description, as being, in all probability, the most astonishing and extensive specimen of the kind in the world—we allude to the great Congo grotto in the Southern division of George. Adequately to describe this wonderful and truly grand spectacle is impossible; we therefore gladly adopt the language of another eye witness, Lieut. Sherwill, of the H. E. I. C. Service.

"We soon found ourselves," says that writer, "at the mouth of the Cave; not, as I had expected to have found it, a low narrow entrance, but a vast arched opening, a suitable approach to such a place. At the portal, which is about eighteen feet high and wide, is a vestibule, in which preparations were commenced by lighting torches, and divesting ourselves of all superfluous raiment, as the boers, who were to be our guides, assured us we should find it pretty warm below. They endeavoured also to persuade us to join them in their *soopje*, or dram of brandy before commencing operations, which being refused, they fortified themselves, and we started, each man with a light in either hand, except the torch-bearers, who held a bottle of oil besides their torch. The procession, as it moved off, had a curious appearance and looked like a legion of Efreets about to celebrate some dreadful orgies. We wound our

way for about one hundred paces, through a
narrow passage excavated by nature in the
living rock, (which was of a dark pitchy hue,)
until arrested by a precipice at our feet. Before
us stretched a thick cloud of darkness; and all
around us, in spite of our torches and candles,
wore the same aspect, the gloom appearing
literally impenetrable and tangible. A stout
ladder was lowered down, and we descended to
the depth of about thirty-three feet, and found
ourselves standing in a vast hall of six hundred
feet in length, about one hundred in breadth,
and from sixty to seventy feet high. In the
centre of this magnificent cave stands a colossal
stalactite of seventy feet in height, white as the
purest marble, and sparkling as if strewn with
diamonds. From the roof depend enormous
masses of lime, gradually growing into stalac-
tital columns; whilst, on the damp ground, rising
to meet these pendant masses, are huge stalagmites, formed by the continual filtration of lime
through the superincumbent rocks. Some have
nearly met, and formed columns, others are but
commencing to form; in fact, the whole floor
of the cave is strewed with stalagmites of
various growths, and on the roof opposite to
each hangs a corresponding mass. The work
of filtration of calcareous matter is proceeding
steadily, and in time, this vast hall will become

a labyrinth of pure alabaster-like columns. This cave is known by the name of Van Zyl's Flak; after a Dutch boer, who discovered these caverns whilst hunting in the mountains.

"Leaving this hall, we entered a small cavern, about forty feet square, and thirty feet high. This is called the Registry, from the practice of visitors writing their names on the pure snow-white lime walls. Here I discovered several names of our Indian community, and, amongst them, that of an old college companion. I was surprised to see that of a lady, with whom I afterwards became acquainted. How she ever managed to descend the green, damp, and slippery ladder, to me is wonderful, but descended she had, and there was her name to prove the fact. As we proceeded, the soil under foot began to get gradually moister, until it turned into downright mud, which gave us much annoyance, by insinuating itself into our shoes. A few more yards brought us to the most beautiful and most wonderful part of the caverns. Whilst writing our names in the Registry, all the boers except one, who had delayed us, purposely, by pointing out various names and superscriptions, had quietly slipped away, but on passing from this spot through a narrow passage, and entering the next cave, we soon perceived why they had left us. For a sight, at once beautiful and astonishing, now burst upon our view. We stood in a vast cave, one hundred and forty feet square, and about fifty in height, the whole of the most dazzling and sparkling whiteness. Columns and pillars of snow-white, and some of transparent crystalized lime, stood on all sides, the roof being covered with innumerable small and delicate icicle-looking stalactites. Each of these had a drop of pure water pendant from their extremities; and as each drop parted company with its filter, and fell to the ground, it had the appearance as of a shower of diamonds falling from the roof. The boers had all taken up positions with their lights, to enable us to see the whole of this fairy-like cavern at one *coup d'œil* and, I stood bewildered and astonished at the wonderful sight. In the centre of the cavern stands a column, as pure and as white as alabaster. It is the height of the hall, fifty feet, and about nine feet in circumference, and worked in the most minute manner. It is formed of crystalized lime, surrounded by horizontal bands, or raised divisions, at every three or four feet. These divisions are filled up with a minute filigree work, and vertical lines; in fact, the column appears, to use a borrowed expression, as "if raised by a giant and finished by a jeweller." At either end of the hall, are groups of the same substance, resembling bed-curtains and flowery drapery, running into the elegant arabesques. All around the sides of the hall the lime has also taken grotesque forms, amongst which fancy may discover the high altar of a Roman-Catholic Church, decked out with all the paraphernalia of a high mass. Stalactites, resembling high and lofty candelabra, cups and goblets, steps and censors appear in one direction; whilst, in another, is represented a collection of elegant drapery, flowers, trees, and animals—one deposit bearing the exact resemblance to the head of a gigantic bull. Being continually saturated with water, the groups appear semi-transparent. The hanging and falling drops of water also, reflecting the torchlight, gave to the whole a dazzling and sparkling appearance. The spar, however, when broken off, dies, and loses all its transparency—becoming a dull and opaque body.

"Leading out of this hall are innumerable passages, the extent and termination of which it is impossible to determine. The walls are pierced, in every direction, with dark looking openings; and, on entering any of them, it is immediately found that *their* sides are perforated in the same manner, each passage leading into other caverns; thus making the whole mountain one vast subterranean net-work of caves, grottos, and caverns. We entered several of these, but were obliged to desist from proceeding far, in consequence of the heated state of the atmosphere. A small low cave with a slooping roof, named the "Yskegal Kamer" (or icicle-room,) deserves special notice. Although itself small and low, its roof, closely studded with the most minute stalactites, presents one of the most striking sights I have ever witnessed *under ground*. The small *icicles* really appear as if cut from solid pearls, their colour is so exquisitely beautiful and soft. A constant distillation of water goes on in this room, which is received into deep natural reservoirs in the floor; the water being so pure, that it is impossible to distinguish it, until immersed up to the chin, which happened to many of our party. I was the first victim, being plunged over head and ears, torch and all, into a deep pool.

"We here asked the boers to conduct us to the long room, mentioned by Mr. Thompson in his work on South Africa. One and all, they declared that no such place existed; nor was it until they saw that we were determined to find it, unaided, that they confessed its existence; but urged that it was a great way off, through the most intricate passages, and over a most uneven and broken surface, where we were very likely to get a broken limb, or head. This, however, only made us the more anxious to reach the "Lange Kamer:" so off we started, and found what the boers had represented, to be most true—the ground being slippery, rugged, and difficult. Loud was the merriment at the numerous mishaps and tumbles; and, as no one escaped, the laugh was mutual. We proceeded through narrow passages and archways, up and down hill, over rocks, stones, sand, mud, and various other impediments; dropping a boer, here and there, to shew us the way back again. At length we arrived at a small descent, of about fourteen or fifteen feet, but very steep, and faced with a deep covering of soft loamy mud, down which it was impossible to walk. Throwing down a torch, therefore, to show us the bottom, we commenced our descent in rather a novel manner. Each man sitting down on his heels, and allowing himself to shoot down with a velocity almost equal to that attained on a Russian ice-hill, forward we all went, one after the other, waving our torches over our heads, and each clearing away a formidable portion of the mud. Could any of our friends *on earth* have seen us, as we reached the bottom, we should have been fit objects for their mirth; for the mud, being of a bright orange colour, had imparted its hues to our dorsal habiliments, and most of us were without shoes or stockings—my own, for instance, having been left, long before, in the icicle-room.

"We now stood in the "Lange Kamer," or Thompson's hall, so called because he discovered it, in the year 1822. Mr. Thompson describes its length as five hundred feet, but I should have thought it nearer eight hundred; and from twenty to forty feet high. The sides are of a dark earthy hue; the floor, very uneven and broken, and rising and falling as much as forty feet into deep pits: the whole being devoid of any particular interest, save its immense length. We proceeded to the end, and found it terminated by a solid wall of sandstone; beyond which no passage has been discovered, though several diverge to the right and left of the cave. We were now, by calculation, about two thousand feet from the entrance of the caves. How much further we could have gone, I know not; but, by this time, we all had had enough of subterraneous wanderings; beside which, the heat was becoming quite intolerable, and the offensive smell, caused by the torches, together with the numerous bats which infest the innermost caves, rendered it highly advisable that we should begin to retrace our steps. We accordingly retreated, and all our mirth was renewed, when we commenced our abortive attempt to re-ascend the slope of slippery mud, across the entrance of the hall. One of the boers, by great exertions, did effect the ascent;

but, in trying to aid the next person up, he was dragged from his high position, and rolled to the bottom with his protegé, both covered with the yellow mud. At length, by cutting holes for our feet, we reached the top; not, however, without much mirth and merriment.

"On our return to the outer cave, we commenced exploring amongst the smaller chambers, and after a variety of plunges into the deep pools, falls and bruises, we found ourselves in a curiously excavated room, with a round hole pierced through one of its sides. Through this I thrust my body and torch, and endeavoured to reconnoitre, but without success, the darkness spreading itself out on every side. I could just discern the bottom, about fifteen feet below me, but the wall between it and me, was perfectly perpendicular, and the air was close and unwholesome. I have little doubt, that this cave, extends far away into the heart of the Zwarte-Bergen. Several of our torches being, at this juncture, extinguished by a rush of bats from the interior; and as our oil was beginning to fail, in consequence of some of the bottles having suffered in the manifold falls and slides, we deemed it advisable to wend our way towards the daylight. When we reached it, the first encounter was painful in the extreme to our eyes; and the roars of laughter from the boers, made the caverns ring with echoes; and it was little wonder that their mirth was excited, for the daylight discovered us to be an odd collection of yellow monsters. The uproarous mirth of these good-natured, happy, light-hearted fellows was quite enlivening to us, after the heat and fatigue we had just gone through, during our lengthened sojourn underground; and wet as we were from the continual dropping from the roof.

"After paying our small fee, we parted company with these jolly boers, and returned on our way to George, much pleased, and highly gratified, with our subterranean ramble.

"As a specimen of natural excavation, I much doubt if these caves are equalled by any in the world, both for beauty, *height*, (that usually deficient quality in natural excavations,) or in extent. And, compared with artificial excavations, they are gigantic—the most wonderful of this latter description, being those of Ellora, Adjunta, Karlie, and Elephanta, in India. There, the whole mountains are excavated by the hands of men, and finished with a minuteness quite astonishing: but, although I have seen them all, they did not so much gratify me, as the sight of these Congo caverns of Southern Africa."

In closing (with this intelligent account of

the Congo Caverns,) this notice of the Western Province of the Cape, we are constrained to say, that, whilst this territory is undoubtedly the richest and most fertile surface portion of the Colony, we do not consider it to be either the best, or the healthiest. On the Eastern frontier, the climate is far more enjoyable and more equable; less visited by prevalent high winds; and with less variation in the temperature. The further along the Eastern coast the traveller goes, the more forcible this remark becomes. We have known sailors of delicate health, sailing along this coast, who have told us, that, although they were invariably ill in Table Bay, Mossel Bay, or Simon's Bay; yet when their ships came off the coast of Albany, (in the Eastern district of the Colony) or neared Kaffirland, they at once recovered their energy and elasticity of spirits, and were ready and able to endure any hardship. The same observation has been made by those who have travelled on shore.

The commercial importance of this province, at the present, makes it the best known, and most appreciated: but, as the internal resources of the continent open out, and become more cultivated, we feel fully convinced, that the Eastern one will completely supercede it; and, ere long, it will not only equal, but surpass it, in the actual aggregate amount and value of its export and import trade.

At the same time, in these lower divisions of Africa are localities, which, in the salubrity of their climate and fertility of their soil, are not surpassed by any *out of Southern Africa;* for, where the whole surface is covered with such delightful prospects and temperature, people often become fastidious, and leaving spots which they would seek for in vain in other lands, they go in quest of something yet better.

In speaking of any of the districts of Southern Africa, the best recommendation that can be given for the country is the fact, that *no one who once settles there, ever cares to leave it.*

A MALAY COOLIE OF CAPE TOWN.

CHAPTER V.

" ALBANY " opens the sketch of this part of the
Colony; which, with the exception of the Cape
district, is the most populous in it, although
being far from the largest in territory. In its topographical description, it is divided into Upper
and Lower Albany, the latter part also being
known as " *the Zuureveld.*" This was the immediate location of the British settlers of 1820,
who may be said to have founded and formed
this division of the Colony, and well indeed
they have done so. The farms and homesteads
do credit to their industry and perseverance,
their cheerful contentment, and unshaken loy-
alty to the religion, government, and sovereign
of their fathers, notwithstanding their continual losses from the Kaffirs and Hottentots,
does equal credit to their piety. We know
not that we ever were more impressed, than
by the unflinching confidence, which these settlers of Albany and their children possess, in
their certain success as a Colony. Notwithstanding the most trying obstacles, no matter

how they were defamed, or their best efforts mis-represented, and though war or blight stripped them of their property, still they would begin over again. And with the true determination of those from the highlands of North Britain, and the hardihood and endurance of her best sons, they still continued to work; of which exertions, Albany, as it now stands, is the lasting memorial.

The soil of this district does not materially differ from that in the other divisions. In Lower Albany the pursuits of the inhabitants are in agriculture; while, in Upper Albany, they are in grazing—sheep being generally kept.

The chief town in the Eastern Province, is Graham's Town, which is situated in the centre of this division. The approach to this from the Colony is very picturesque, passing through what is called "Howison's Poort." This is a long narrow defile of about ten miles in length, which appears to have been formed, by some violent disrupture of the earth. The rocks overhang the sides of the road, throughout the ravine, and their faces and fissures are clothed in the most diversified canopies of aloes, lichens, ferns, orchidacæ, and floræ. By the side of the road a little gurgling rill of the clearest water runs, completing the wild, and almost fairy, beauty of this lovely spot.

VIEW OF GRAHAM'S TOWN, FROM THE GROUNDS OF OATLANDS.

Page 95

The town itself is a pleasing and cheerful spot, situated on the declivity of a small hill, which is surrounded with others of greater elevation. The streets are wide and airy, and the houses surrounded with gardens, which are well watered, and abounding in fruit trees. There is a *freshness*, consequently, engendered about the place, which is not to be seen in other parts of the Colony.

Graham's Town is now a rising and rapidly increasing place. It contains upwards of 1000 houses; and its population exceeds 5000 persons, of which about 1000 are coloured. It possesses two churches, a grammar school, a library, two banks, a court-house, and large barracks, in which, at present, the head quarters of two regiments are stationed. Amongst its inhabitants, are numbered two bishops, one of the English, and one of the Roman Catholic Church. It is likewise the site of a nunnery, as well as of various imposing edifices, used as dissenting places of worship. The shops are decidedly better here, than in any part of the Colony, not even Cape Town excepted. And, as a general rule, there appears to be more unanimity and public spirit prevailing in this community, than elsewhere. The town is governed by a municipality ; who endeavour, to the best of their ability, to improve and extend its importance.

The market is good, large, and always well stocked and attended. It frequently presents a display of ivory, ostrich feathers, wild beasts' skins, antelope horns, and other promiscuous curiosities, brought from the interior of the African continent, which are not perhaps to be seen any where else in the world.

About a mile from the town, is situated on the north-west side, the pretty house and grounds of " Oatlands," formerly the residence of General Somerset, but now that of Walter Currie, Esq., the Commandant of Albany, the representative of one of the settlers, and one whose name is well known among his fellow-colonists, as one of their bravest burghers.

It may not be here misplaced, to include the notice of the rest of this part of the division, (all of which is intimately known to the author,) in the more informal shape of

A RIDE THROUGH LOWER ALBANY.

To this end, we started from Graham's Town, well mounted and supplied, and turned our head in the direction of Bathurst, the Cowie, Southwell, and Lushington Valley, which form its richest locations. Passing the large barracks of Fort England, and leaving Graham's Town behind, the first ten miles of our road were through a fertile and picturesque valley, studded with luxuriant farms and gardens.

The road, as it here winds along through the valley, presented to our eye one of the richest scenes of South African *cultivation*. The farm house and pleasure grounds of Belmont, reflect the most unbounded credit to the intelligence, persevering industry, and taste of Mr. John Carlisle, their possessor; who, as one of the first and most enterprising of the frontier-men of Albany, located himself here. Notwithstanding the most distressing losses, and continued encroachments, from the Kaffirs, he has yet resolutely maintained his ground; rebuilt his homestead after each war; and held his own plough. And whilst thus, by his example, he stimulated all near him to active personal exertion, he also proved himself possessed of that true taste, and practical knowledge of husbandry, which enabled him to add to the richness of the scene we are now describing, by the picturesque and valuable grounds of Belmont.

This is a fair specimen of a frontier settler's farm; and, although possessed, certainly, of more taste, in the disposition of the gardens and pleasure grounds, than the generality of them; we think that it is not so extensive as some.

Near this, on both sides of the valley, as the traveller proceeds, he is pleased with the diversified landscapes of nature, as well as the signs of industry and husbandry which are displayed everywhere around him. Market gardens, small farms, and well-built ricks of corn, meet his eyes on all sides; and, through the whole district of Lower Albany, this still continues to be the character and description of the surrounding lands, for nowhere in the Colony is there a better and more practical system of farming established than there. The cattle are well-bred and cared for; the land is tilled in a business-like way; the farmers personally superintend their land; and the produce, when brought to market, is such as none of the best farmers of England would be ashamed to present as an evidence of their knowledge and industry.

Oats and barley appear to be the principal grains propagated—the soil not suiting the growth of wheat. Potatoes and vegetables of all kinds, as well as fruit and flowers, are most prolific, and are universally fine.

Proceeding through these fertile vales for about ten miles, we reached a very comfortable house, by the road side, known as "Manley's Inn." This farm, during the war, was formed into a "largaar," or place of rendezvous, for the burghers of the surrounding district, and, from its central position, it appeared well suited as such. After refreshing ourselves and our horses here, we remounted, and proceeded to a large farm belonging to Walter Currie, Esq., the commandant of Albany. This was formerly his residence, but, successive wars having driven him from it, he determined not to rebuild the house or offices, which were destroyed during that of 1850—52; and, consequently, purchased Oatlands, near Graham's Town, where he and his family now reside; still, however, retaining, for farming purposes, this place, which is called Langholm. It is situated about nineteen miles from Graham's Town, and five from Bathurst, on the expanse of a large elevated tract of ground or common, which is known as "Currie's Vlaakts." In some parts, the ground undulates considerably, and, everywhere, it is sprinkled with tufts or clumps of evergreen bushes, disposed in so perfect and picturesque a manner by nature, that, on first viewing the effect produced by the vistas of deep blue hills, and distance which appear between them, the beholder is led to suppose it to be the work of art —such is, however, not the case. From some of these positions, the most exquisite views of landscape appear through, as if framed in a trellis work of foliage, and containing all the pleasing variety of the distant hills of Southwell; the dense bush which clothes the banks of the River Cowie; or, again, the village and church of Bathurst on the neighbouring hill.

On one side, the boundary line of this extensive farm reaches far into the thickest parts of the Cowie forest: and here the stately buffalo, the graceful dyka and blue-buck, as well as the wild-boar and other savage denizens of these glades, roam in all their native ferocity; still constantly affording an exciting day of sport to the worthy lord of the manor.

The main supply of water, on this farm, is now obtained from a large artificial tank; which, planted around with willows, and kept in good repair, forms a pleasing object to the eye, as well as affording all the convenience and utility of a plentiful supply of the pure element. Even the shy and wary buffalo does not disdain, during the heat of summer, to leave his forest retreat, and creeps, in the depth of midnight, to its side to quench his thirst. It cannot but be a matter of regret that this praiseworthy example, of forming dams and tanks, is not more largely followed among the South-African farmers. Thousands of tons of water are allowed yearly to go to waste; which, if thus husbanded, would irrigate their parched crops during the heat of the dry season. This large tank, at Langholm, was the sole work of Mr. Currie, who graphically described the hours of toil which he had expended on its excavation. The house, which was placed on a commanding, yet sheltered, position, was in ruins, and formed one of *seven*, which could be seen on the neighbouring hills around—monuments of the devastating work of the brand and the assegai of the ruthless savages, whose love of rapine and plunder had (during the late frontier wars) levelled them to the ground. This one had twice been destroyed, and the inmates driven in terror from its walls; the last time under such distressing circumstances of death, pillage, and bereavement, that it could not be a matter of wonder that it was not again to be rebuilt.

Leaving this pretty spot, (but not until we had inspected a large and well-stacked rick of oats, together with an amply stocked garden and several acres of rich land laid under the plough,) we wound our way towards the adjoining location of "Lushington Valley." This luxuriant vale was part of the original land apportioned to the settlers of 1820 on their first arrival, and yet displayed many traces of the taste and industry, which they and their children had expended on it. Here, however, traces of the torch, and the savage hands that wielded it, were visible; dwellings in ruins, and hedge-rows and gardens trampled down, being the sad remnants. Notwithstanding all these disheartening drawbacks, we were pleasingly surprised with the active and cheerful assiduity, with which their possessors were everywhere working to amend the damages, and restore the appearance of peace and plenty. The farms seemed smaller in size here than elsewhere through the district, although richer in soil. Wheat, oats, maize, potatoes, barley, beans, and other plants were flourishing on all sides; while the road, by which we crossed the valley, was over-hung by large peach and quince trees— other fruit also growing around.

Quitting this beautiful spot, and crossing the bed of the Blue Krantz river, we ascended a steep hill; and, after a pleasant ride of a few miles across the townlands, we reached the little village of Bathurst, the belfry of whose unpretending church stands, as a prominent landmark, in the centre.

At first sight, the arrangement of this place appeared disorderly and irregular; but, on closer acquaintance and inspection, we found this to arise from the alleys or lanes of the village being all covered with grass. The hedge-rows were formed of fruit-trees; the little gardens were neatly kept, and full of flowers; the jasmine and creeping clematis, everywhere supplied the places, which, in England, are filled by the woodbine, sweetbriar, and dog-rose. Each time, afterwards, that we beheld this quiet little spot, the impression more forcibly intruded itself upon the mind that we were riding through some sequestered, rural village in Northamptonshire, Somersetshire, or Shropshire. During our stay here, we were most hospitably received and entertained by the worthy and primitive pastor, Mr. Barrow, who spared no pains or trouble to make us acquainted with every object and locality of interest. This is one of the healthiest spots of this continent, life being longer here, by several years, than in most other parts. The field-cornet * of the district informed us, that, during the last year, (1853) there had been, in the whole district of Bathurst, containing a population of 1200, but five deaths; on three of which he had held inquests—leaving but two arising from natural causes, which were an infant a week old, and a young female.

The next point that we visited was the mouth of the Cowie river—proceeding from Bathurst by the main road. We thus traversed for a few miles through very picturesque scenery, which skirted the town; and then, emerging from this, passed over a long plain, covered with light sandy soil, and thin grass. This was

---

* A field-cornet of the Cape, or more properly, according to the Dutch phraseology, veldt-cornet, is a petty officer, who is appointed to settle disputes, act as a magistrate, and keep the various registers for a portion of country 15 or 20 miles in extent. There are several to each district, and they answer to our parish officers in England.

principally used for grazing, and the herds of cattle looked sleek and fat. One or two mills varied the monotony of the view, which, in crossing the plain, partook of sameness. This, however, terminated at the end of about seven miles, by the ascent to the highlands, which overhang the mouth of the Cowie. On reaching this, we were much pleased with the sudden change in the prospect. As we advanced up the sides of the hill, the whole landscape became clothed in tangled bush and underwood; wild flowers carpeted the sward; while the numerous indigenous climbing plants of Southern Africa matted the foliage overhead into a dense natural umbrella. Passing, in file, through these overhung avenues of forest scenery, we suddenly immerged from the thicket, unwilling to quit its romantic jasmine, and geranium scented glades. We found ourselves now standing on a spur of the Cowie hill, which was sloping down to the side of the river, dotted, on the way, by pretty little cottages and gardens. Immediately above the banks, stood the hotel and its grounds, which certainly did due credit to the taste and industry of its host and hostess. We were much struck and pleased, by the honest joy which the people everywhere evinced at seeing their pastor; who, like other Clergy in that land, was deservedly loved and respected.

Having crossed the river, we inspected the large steam mill on its opposite bank, the property of Mr. Cock—busily employed in grinding flour and other avocations. Immediately above the mill, on an elevation of the ground, stood the castellated house and gardens of the proprietor; where we were hospitably received, and urged to remain. Declining this kind offer, we pressed on towards Southwell, which was our next halting place. As we proceeded towards this, we passed along the banks of the Cowie, until nearly abreast of the Mansfield. This is a location, about ten miles from the mouth, and seven from Bathurst; and up to which the river is navigable, if only the formidable bar of sand across its mouth were once removed. This the proprietors are energetically attempting to effect, and, lately, a grant of £50,000 has been obtained for the purpose. We sincerely wish well to this laudable undertaking; which, if accomplished, will tend to double the importance of this district.

Advancing towards Southwell, we passed several large farms, all maintaining the high character of Albany for agriculture and industry. The crops appearing good and abundant, and the tillage and stowage of them managed in a practical manner. At the location itself, there is nothing very remarkable at the present;

but, shortly, a church and school-house is expected to rise there; for the erection of which, Mr. Waters, a deacon of the Church, was zealously labouring amongst his surrounding flock, by all of whom he is equally beloved and deservedly respected.

Crossing from Southwell back to Langholm, our road lay through the Cowie bush, having first crossed the ruined remains of another large farm, once the property of Mr. Phillips, also one of the settlers of 1820. In our ride through the bush, we visited the noted pass in this neighbourhood, so poetically described by the traveller Barrow; and then, after exploring all the beauties of these forest scenes, we retraced our steps towards Graham's Town.

This visit was an ocular demonstration of the *perfect success* of the effort made by England, in the immigration of 1820, sent out to these locations. Nor can we but feel convinced that a repetition of the same policy, at the present time, is the best measure that could be effected towards securing and extending peace on our South African border. Between Southwell and Graham's Town, proceeding through the Zuureveldt, are Cuylerville, Theopolis, and Salem. The former of these was the *first village* established by the settlers, the other two are Missionary locations, one belonging to the London

VIEW OF ECCA PASS, UPPER ALBANY, WITH QUEEN'S ROAD PASSING THROUGH IT.

Page 107.

Missionary Society, the other to the Wesleyans; these latter likewise possess other smaller locations in different parts of this district.

The geological structure of this division partakes much of the nature of the other parts of the continent. The cliffs belong, generally, to the sandstone and quartz formations which are so predominant in South Africa. Graywacke, quartz, schistus, and clayslate are common. In the formation and cutting of the Queen's-road through Upper Albany, some few years ago, large organic remains, and a few fossils, both of the animal and vegetable kingdom, were discovered in a fine state of preservation, and have, we believe, been since sent to England. Along the coast of the Indian ocean, there are various descriptions of soil, chiefly sand mixed with shells and vegetable matter. Further inland there is much clay, interspersed with sandy flats, and patches of rich vegetable mould, resting upon a stratum of iron-coloured clay, or upon beds of limestone and sandstone. Throughout the districts of Upper Albany along the Great Fish river, and the more remote ones of Lower Albany, as well as near the Bushman's River and in the Zuureberg, the face of the country is extremely rugged; it is, however, studded with farms, and these are well stocked with sheep.

In travelling over these districts, it may not be unacceptable to notice, in a slight sketch, one of the new villages which was lately established here by the late lamented general Cathcart, for the defence and strengthening of the colonial border.

This has been a most successful stroke of policy, and one which cannot be too extensively copied. *Towns* not straggling villages, *houses* not huts, are what are required by those who would make head against barbarism; and the enterprising · spirit, with which those few attempts lately made have been carried out, only the more plainly shows, that the loyal hearts and industrious hands, necessary to the formation, are not wanting when once the project be started.

Having lately visited the one at Waterloo Bay, called New Town, we shall endeavour to give some description of it, and also of the line of road and surrounding country.

On leaving Fort Beaufort, we passed through the old Missionary institution, called "Birt's Station," now granted to a number of Dutch farmers, under Mr. Hartman. Preparations were already making here for the erection of a Dutch church, and, from the numerous families already occupying the Keiskamma, there is every reason to believe that a good congregation will assemble here. Continuing the route, we next came to Post Victoria, travelling over some good road made by the 74th Highlanders. Here we observed three extensive stone defences; which, had the stones been of better quality, would have bid defiance to time, and proved most useful rallying points in times of danger. A small party of the mounted police are stationed here, and are surrounded by Fingoes, composing numerous villages. About five miles beyond this station, we came to Foonhah's Kloof. This extensive valley forms a portion of the land so recklessly sold before the war, or rather put into the hands of land jobbers. At the present time, only one solitary farm is occupied. Proceeding onward, we passed numerous farms situated along the banks of the Keiskamma; while the country, lying between the Rand and the Fish River, is thickly populated with Fingoes, with farms at intervals. At this point the country assumes the most beautiful park-like appearance—the scenery being equal to any to be met with in South Africa. The old ruins of Fort Wiltshire stand here. At the various windings of the road may be seen the beautiful Keiskamma river, and in the other direction the windings of the Fish river, with the lofty Chumie and Amatolas extending to the Tabindoda, which is seen in the distance; whilst the long range of the Botha Hills are observed, stretching away to the sea. Thus, after travelling through forty miles of the most superior pasture land, well-wooded and watered, a change of country takes place—the Mimosa becoming more thinly scattered, and the grass more adapted for horned cattle than sheep. This continues for about 15 miles, when we reached Fort Peddie, a small but clean and neat village, with a good hotel and accommodation.

On quitting this, you cross the main road from Graham's Town to King William's Town. At a short distance further, the Gualana stream is forded, where hundreds of acres of maize and millet are seen, growing luxuriantly in a fine open undulating country. The next place, on the route, is the Missionary station, called Newtondale, surrounded by an extensive Fingo population. About ten miles from this, we arrived at the village of New Town, where two hundred erven are laid out, and several houses in progress, and erven fenced. The situation of this place is well chosen, commanding a full view of Waterloo Bay and its anchorage; and, at no distant period, it must become what Green Point is to Cape Town, with the advantage of having an extensive pasture commonage, as well as being surrounded by many agricultural farmers. The terms upon which the erven are granted, are occupation, with about a £5 fee towards a fund for making aqueducts. Those that are bought, cost about £13, with a stipulation of their being fenced in. There is every probability of these erven falling into the hands of *bona fide* occupiers, as no person can possess more than one erf. This effectually puts a stop to land jobbing, and gives strength to the frontier. The country, lying between the Fish river and the mouth of the Keiskamma, has been allotted to industrious hands—most of them large farmers of grain, having a port at their doors, from whence to ship to all parts of the world.

In noticing the approach to Waterloo Bay, on the land side, it may be said that it is not surpassed by any port, or projected one, on the frontier; as the whole line of road to the beach is composed of good hard soil. Thus the drag through miles of sand, so much complained of on other roads, is entirely avoided. In describing the bay, it certainly cannot be said to be land locked; still it offers good anchorage, and is decidedly superior to Madras Roads, which form one of the most frequented ports of the East. The bay may be said to be about three miles from point to point, with an indentation of two miles. Vessels may ride here at anchor and discharge, and, if three or four moorings were to be laid down, the advantages of the harbour would be much increased.

In remarking on the advantage of Waterloo Bay, in discharging cargo, as compared with other ports on the coast, it is a well-known fact, that there is none of them with so little surf. This is attributed to the power of the Fish River, collected from all its tributaries, such as the Little Fish, the Konap, the Kat, and numerous others. This, coupled with a strong influx of sea tide, gives an irresistible power at the mouth, so as to resist the surf. Owing to the situation of the bluff and reef, which extend out into the sea, and form an indent, this powerful stream, instead of being carried along the shore, (as is the case with most of the other rivers,) runs directly into the sea, and thus all the cross surfs, so much dreaded by boatmen, are completely beaten down. At the same time, the three or four regular rollers are so far diminished, as to offer little danger to boats.

With regard to the advantages to be derived by the Eastern districts:—It opens out the whole heart of the country, and brings no less than fifteen towns and villages within easy distance of a port; added to which, are the great facilities of transit offered by the roads being naturally hard and good. Independently of this, there will be, by next season, about 2000 producing farmers located within two days' easy ride. And be it remembered, that all these will be seeking an outlet for the products of their industry.

In treating of the advantage of Waterloo Bay to Graham's Town, I am fully aware that the merchants met with many obstructions, when it was formerly frequented; but it should be borne in mind that this was in time of war, and the want of competition led to most exorbitant charges in getting their goods across the Fish River. At the present time all such difficulties may be obviated—an enterprising colonist having established a punt to ferry waggons and goods over, at a reasonable rate.

With Waterloo Bay as the landing port, the following towns would be within the under-mentioned distances; computed, in time, by the transit of waggons:—Graham's Town, two; Fort Beaufort, three; Somerset, five; Cradock, six; Colesberg, ten; Graaff-Reinet, eight; Queen's Town, seven; and Burgher's Dorp, eleven days.

Thus much for local description. The area of the division of Albany comprises 1792 square miles, and contains a population of 19,777; of which, about 1710 are whites, and 12,067 of the coloured races. Without any exception, it is the most densely populated district of the Colony, having $11\frac{1}{4}$ souls per square mile.

The chief products of Albany are cattle, sheep, and grain, together with a very improving, and rapidly increasing, trade in *wool*. It is estimated to contain 10,000 acres of ground which is under cultivation, and 1,200,000 acres of pasturage. The main portion of these latter lies in that part of the district called Upper Albany, extending along the banks of the Great Fish River, past Forts Brown and Beaufort, as far as the Kat River mission-station, the Blinkwater, and the Winterbergen. This last-named mountain is the highest in this part of the Colony. It forms the North-eastern angle of Albany; and, from its table summit, it commands an extensive view, not only of the whole of this district, but also of those of Somerset, Cradock, and Graaff-Reinet, together with parts of Kaffirland. From its sides flow the Konap, and other small streams which are tributaries to the Fish River; and which, from the elevation of their sources, are easily led out for irrigation, and thus add to the luxuriance of the adjoining farms. The country through and around the Zuureberg, (in the district of Uitenhage) has lately been much improved, by the cutting of a new road through this district, from Port Elizabeth to Burgher's-Dorp. Other similar works are also progressing through Kaffirland; and, in a few years more, we trust to hear of the whole of these districts being intersected by main roads—thus cutting out the bush, and opening up easier commerce with the upper, and more interior, districts.

Albany, on the other side of Graham's Town, presents little of interest. The farms are good and valuable, but not particularly picturesque or striking to a travellers eye; perhaps by reason of his being engaged, when seeing them, in his long ride of 90 miles through Sidbury, Quagga-Vlaats, and the Addo-bush to Port Elizabeth, and thus is thinking more of his road and journey's end, than the surrounding districts, or their productions. Suffice it, however, to say that the occupants of them are as industrious as their compeers; quite as hospitable; and their houses as open to travellers as those in other parts of this division.

" *Uitenhage*" is the next portion of the Eastern Province deserving notice. It lies between Albany and the Western Province, and was originally part of the latter—incorporated as a portion of the old Dutch district of Stellenbosch. In 1804, it was established as an independent division. It is divided into eleven wards or "hundreds" as they are called, and each of these into two veldt-cornetcies.

Its area extends over 8960 square miles, and it contains a population of 11,019; of which, 4628 are whites, and the remainder, of the coloured races. Its principal productions in grain are wheat, rye, oats, and barley, but *butter* is its staple commodity in the market. This is very deservedly prized, and is much sought after. The soil varies materially—in some districts being much richer than in others. Olifant's Hork is the most highly cultivated part of the division, where the soil consists of a clayish mould, which is well calculated for all kinds of horticultural productions.

The town of Uitenhage is a pretty, secluded spot; well laid out, and profusely supplied with water from a spring, which is situated in the Winter-hoek mountains, about six miles distant. From this it flows through a stream four feet broad and fifteen inches deep, and supplies, it has been ascertained, 2,512,632 gallons in 24 hours. The consequence of this, in conjunction with the salubrious climate, and rich soil, of the locality, is a profusion of fruits, trees, and flowers, of the most luxuriant growth—adding considerably to the beauty of this part of the country. At about seven miles from the town, on the Eastern side, are mineral springs, one of which is tepid.

The mountain scenery of this division is very fine. The Zuureberg and Winter-hoek ranges are boldly formed in outline, and the rarity of the atmosphere giving them an areal tinting, softens down the view to a most pleasing effect.

The "Cockscomb" craggy mountain, or, as it is also sometimes called, the "Grenadier's Cap," rises, in this latter range, to an altitude of 5400 feet, the Winter-hoek peak itself, to that of 2752 feet; these, consequently, form conspicuous land marks to mariners to and from India, as they are visible, from the ocean, at the distance of several miles.

The geology of Uitenhage is very interesting, and the district appears rich in ores and minerals. Lead is, in many places, apparently close to the surface, and, in others, it has also been discovered. Copper, of a fine description, is largely scattered through the mountains, and has been made, to a considerable extent, the subject of examination, and even speculation, as an article of commerce.

In this Eastern district of Uitenhage, at about thirty miles distance from Port Elizabeth, the "Maitland lead and copper mines" are situated, where these ores were first discovered, some years ago. A mining company was then formed to work them; but, from want of geological knowledge, and competent directors for the miners, they have, as yet, been unproductive. They are not, however, wholly abandoned, and there is a possibility, even now, of the speculation not only succeeding, but realizing a profit. With regard to past efforts, the following statement of these "Maitland mines" was given seven years ago :—

"In November, 1845, a commencement was made with working the old vein of lead, and 10 cwt. were sent home to England, to be assayed; the result of which is, that one ton of ore gives 11 cwt. 3 qrs. 5 lbs. of lead, and 26 ozs. 5 dwts. of fine silver, being nearly the same proportions given by Major Van Dehn, some fifty years ago. The veins have been followed to the depth of twelve feet; here the ore is twelve inches thick, and much purer than near the surface, and will probably yield seventy or seventy-five per cent. The silver is more than double the average of the English ore, which only gives 11 oz. to the ton.

Since commencing the above, a series of veins of lead, and lead and copper combined, in a highly metaliferous formation, have been discovered; where the indications are even better than at the original mine, from which it is distant about half a mile, and separated by a river. The veins, in this place, cross out on the side of a steep hill, and dip, in an opposite direction, into the other veins, forming what geologists call a fault, (quite common in metaliferous formations). Where the strata has been raised in the form of an immense basin, there is every probability of the veins extending for miles.

nearly East and West, as the metaliferous limestone, in which the ore is found, can be traced to a considerable distance.

A little of the copper has been analyzed at Cape Town, which gives upwards of thirty per cent. of copper, and a little arsenic; but the quantity was small, and cannot therefore be taken for a just estimate. Twenty tons of lead and copper ore have been sent to England to be analyzed. There are also several other metals, which have not been analyzed, but they are not yet found in sufficient quantity to become a special object of working."*

* The Author, whilst at Port Elizabeth in 1854, personally visited these Maitland mines, and can accredit the truth of the above statements. That ore, to a very large extent, exists there there can be little doubt: if it lies too deep, to *pay* for excavating it, is another question. Not professing, however, any *accurate* knowledge of such matters, he has pleasure in inserting the opinion respecting these mines of a scientific person fully competent to judge—It is as follows:—

"The lead ore, in the Maitland mines, is in the form of a sulphuret disseminated, in greater or less manes, through a crystallized carbonate of lime, in a layer parallel to the stratification of its matrix, which is a semi-crystalline limestone, lying conformably on the quartzite rock of the country, at an angle (I believe) of about 65°. The Galena (Sulphuret of lead) is found, crossing out on the top of the hill which faces the lodge, and also on the eastern extremity of the same. It was stated, that, on the top of this hill, it was found, when examined, to become richer the deeper the exploration was carried.

"From this circumstance, (supposing it to be correct) one would be led to hope that the adit, facing the lodge, would prove highly productive when the lead-bearing-spar was reached. Although the fact, that the same layer, examined on the Eastern end of the hill above-mentioned (*if it really was the same*, a fact which I think of the highest importance to be determined) did not prove rich in that situation, would not lead to so favourable an augry.

Near this same locality, a small vein of coal has also come to view; it is inconsiderable, however, and may rather be taken as the indication of larger streams of it being near at hand. The mineral that has been already analyzed gives the following result:—Colour, dull grey

"The copper ore is the yellow, and variegated sulphuret. It occurs in a vein of quartz, parallel to the stratification of the chlorite schist, a rock dipping nearly at the same angle as the limestone, but in an opposite direction.

"The quartz vein is traceable for some miles through the country; now, on the top of the hill, then, in the bottom of a deep glen, and again, on the sides of a ravine.

"In many of these localities, the pyrites appear in the quartz vein, but no where in very great quantities: nor does it appear that there is any decided increase of richness with the increase of depth. At one spot, viz, "Andrew's Shaft," this certainly does appear to be the case, and, it seems to me, that if further examination proves it to be so, that there is good prospect of ultimate success in the search. If the adit into the lead-hill proves that the ores are richer, when followed to a depth, I shall have better hope of the copper-veins.

"With regard to the discovery of *gold*, Sir R. Murchison says, "that gold has never been found in the metallic state, in any quantities where there were not metamorphic rocks lying on granite, with a strike varying but little from North and South in direction." These are what he calls the "constants" of gold. Now there is *no granite* at the Maitland mines, nor, in fact, *any igneous rocks of any kind*, and the few rocks which, presenting *some* traces of the action of heat at a depth, may be called *metamorphic*, have been already sufficiently explored, to make it *very improbable* that gold may be found, in the metallic state, in that neighbourhood.

"With regard to the grey sulphuret of copper, in the Western adit, I believe it to be a mere concrete manes of copper ore, aggregated together in the decomposition of the limestone, through which it was originally disseminated in small quantities, as it is now, on the hill facing this adit.

"I have heard it stated, that these Maitland mines *must* be productive, because sulphuret of copper is always found in large quantities. To those who entertain this opinion, I would recommend a reference

—when fresh broken, inclining to grey with some lustre—contains in 100 parts:—

> Carbon, or charcoal .... $37\frac{1}{4}$
> Volatile, or earthy matter........ $37\frac{3}{4}$
> Ashes, or earthy matter.......... 25

It is also impregnated with magnetic iron.

In the same vicinity, about ten miles inland from the ocean, several small fossil shell-fish have been found; together with large beds of sea-shells, which are now frequently collected and burnt for lime.*

to Avermon's "Practical Mineralogy," p. 40, in which the following passage occurs, relative to this ore of copper, as found in North America; 'There are very few instances in which the ore in these veins will *pay* for the labour and expense of excavation and transportation.'

"I record these few observations, merely for my own satisfaction, to show what my opinions really are, and the ground I have—or fancy I have—for entertaining them. I have not, hitherto, and I do not now conceal that my opinions of the *paying* qualities of these mines are *not* favourable: but I shall be most happy to find that I have been mistaken. I believe a very erroneous notion is widely prevalent, to the effect that men, who take an interest in science, are so tenacious of their opinions, as to wish to support them through right and wrong. I *totally* disclaim any such feeling for myself, and, I believe, may safely do so for the majority of my brother amateurs in science. I have often had to change, and to modify, opinions on points of science, and would always rather be convinced that I am wrong, than remain in error."—R. Roubridge, M. D., Algoa Bay.

** The above, as here inserted, was presented to the Author, for use, by the Hon. W. Fleming, of Port Elizabeth, South Africa, to whom his best thanks are due.

* Many of the shells, both as fossils and in their present perfect state, belong to that species of the miocene formation in the tertiary deposits, which geologists style the *Cardita Ajar*. It is worthy of note, that this shell, in its fossil state, is largely found throughout England and France at the present day, although it exclusively belongs to Africa, in its animated and inhabited form.

Throughout the upper districts also, iron largely preponderates; and, in the division of Graaff-Reinet, cornelians, topaz, and bloodstones are occasionally picked up. Fossil remains have been found, both in these parts, and at Beaufort, where a skeleton of an antediluvian quadruped, in a perfect state, was discovered some few years ago.

In proportion to the small extent, to which subterranean research has as yet been carried in Africa, the knowledge and indications of metallic and mineral products is very great; and sufficient encouragement is, at least, given to induce further examination. Nor is it possible fully to estimate, at present, the amalgamations which may be discoverable in the ores of this continent.

Salt-pans also exist near Uitenhage; one situated near Bethelsdorp, which belongs to the London Missionary Society's Institution there, being said to yield, in good seasons, 316,000 bushels. This quantity, sold at the market price of 6*d*. per bushel, thus realising, alone, an income of £7900 per annum to that Institution.

The soil, around these salt-pans, consists, generally, of a sharp gravel, formed of decomposed schistus. In some parts, however, it appears to be of a calcareous stratum, strewed over with flints. The "pans" then spread out over an immense tract of ground, and may be better imagined when described as " *Valleys of salt.*" These are thickly covered with a coating of very fine, dry salt, of a dazzling and brilliant whiteness. The origin of them yet remains a mystery. The simplest, and not the least improbable, of the many conjectures and surmises advanced on the subject, seems to be the theory of Mr. Chase. He supposes them to be formed by large beds, or deposits, of rock-salt, being placed below the surfaces of these " pans," and saturated by the heavy rains of the winter season, descending through the soil, and reaching the fossil. The evaporation of them, during the succeeding hot season, thus forms the crust of salt that is collected on the bed or floor of the "pan." This, again, cracking from the heat, becomes disconnected, and being carried about by the wind, is formed into the small particles, in which it is collected as an article of commerce.

Besides the town of Uitenhage, that of Port Elizabeth is also situated in this division, on the shores of Algoa Bay.

This may be described as the " Liverpool," or, more properly, the " Boston " of the Cape. In commercial importance, it is daily increasing; large stores and mercantile firms are springing up; and the bay is always well stocked with vessels. A thriving independent trade, direct from this to America and England, is maintained, and there is every appearance of prosperity there at the present. We are not sanguine, however, of the stability of this. As a port, it is by no means so superior as to command a monopoly; and, if the Eastern Province continues to increase in the present ratio, in its upper districts, the advantages of the Kowie, Waterloo-Bay, and East-London, as outlets for the commerce of the interior, must become more apparent, and will, eventually, be certainly adopted.

There is also a want of public spirit, unanimity, and right feeling, about this place, which by no means augurs well for its importance or stability; while the bleak, uninteresting aspect of the surrounding country, it being totally devoid of trees, together with the present limited supply of bad fresh water, and the little prospect there is of finding it purer, further tends to strengthen our belief that Port Elizabeth will decrease, as the Eastern Province and Albany steadily rise to prosperity as now they must do.

We next pass through the old Dutch division of the Colony, called *Graaff-Reinet*. This is now subdivided, in addition, into those of Colesberg, Somerset, and Cradock. We shall give a condensed notice of each of these.

The first formation of this division was in the year 1806, by the Dutch governor Van der Graaff, and was so named after him and his wife Reinet. Originally, this location was supposed to contain 50,000 square miles. Since its sub-division, however, into four, Graaff-Reinet numbers but 8000 square miles; Somerset 9000; Colesberg 11,654; Cradock 3168; while the remaining portion was annexed to Uitenhage.

The village of Graaff-Reinet is a pretty little place, regularly laid out, and planted neatly with lemon trees, acacias, and oleanders; the Sneewberg mountain forming the background. The soil varies much in its nature. It, however, may, in many places, be called *very rich*, especially near the Sunday-River. Large tracts of the lower parts of this division are covered with a small succulent shrub, called "Speck-boom;" which is botanically described as the "*Portulocaria Afra*," and affords excellent food for sheep and goats. The Elephant was said to live upon it, hence it has likewise been styled in Africa, "Elephant's-food." The sap has a slight acid taste, very refreshing in the heat; the leaves are also agreeably used for pickling, preserving, and in tarts.

This locality is now one of the principal ones for the produce of wool, the farmers having lately consented to improve their breed of sheep, by the introduction of the merino and other wool-bearing animals. According to the last statistical return of this division, the population was 10,736—the coloured races exceeding the Europeans in this calculation by 1330. The value of horses alone, within the district, was £36,238, cattle, £55,361, and sheep, £337,572. To this were added £22,986, in goats, and £339, in pigs; thus making the aggregate value of live stock to be £444,816.

The quantity of wool, shipped for the market, from the Eastern port of Algoa Bay, during the year 1852, amounted to nearly 6,000,000 lbs.; of this large quantity, this district yielded *one seventh*.

The landed property here is estimated to be 1,615,178 acres; on this, 1077 houses and 990 huts have been erected. The commercial importance and value, of this district, is very great. Besides wool and cattle; tallow, butter, soap, hides, and skins are produced. Also a small proportion of wheat, oats, rye, and barley.

In several parts of the district, the country is wholly destitute of wood—the farmers using cattle-dung for fuel. This is dug out of the cattle-kraals, when softened by the rain. It is then cut into square pieces and stacked in a similar manner to turf or peat in England, Ireland, and Scotland; when sufficiently dry, it burns well, and is there preferred to wood as fuel, giving a stronger heat, and causing less trouble. For this reason, it is frequently used by blacksmiths at the forge instead of coal.

Game, of all kinds, is here abundant and plentiful. Sometimes, indeed, it may be said to be superabundant; long droughts, in the interior, often compelling the spring-bok to forsake the extensive plains, which are there its favourite haunts, and to migrate into this outlying district of the Colony. This they do, in such *incredible* numbers, that their visit is felt by the farmers to be a serious calamity—the herbage being entirely consumed by them.

Somerset is a part of this *old* division. It is a rich agricultural locality, but, otherwise, uninteresting. The soil, and general character of the country are diversified. The Great Fish River runs through the centre, and receives, as its tributaries, nearly every stream which waters the district. In dry seasons, the valley, running along the bed of this river, is arid and parched; whilst, immediately after rain, it becomes clothed in rich and sweet grass, and this, interspersed with a luxuriant supply of succulent bushes, makes it a good cattle-grazing country, and very valuable as such.

Cradock adjoins Somerset on the N. E. boundary, and possesses a population of 6491 persons. It is not suited to the maintenance of a large population; although there are scattered through it some highly valuable, and productive, farms. In the Brack River district, large quantities of corn are produced; also a great abundance of various kinds of fruit. The Achter-Sneewberg is famous for the size of its cattle, and the Tarka for sheep. A large proportion of this division, however, is *Karoo ;* which, during the dry seasons, is arid and sterile; although, when well supplied with water, (which it is periodically) it is prolific.

The principal town, which bears the same name as the division, is a thriving little place, situated on the left bank of the Great Fish River. The main road to the interior of Africa passes through it, and thus accounts for its possessing, though so inland a spot, so considerable a trade.

In the immediate vicinity of the village, are cold and tepid châlybeate springs, which are held in much repute for the cure of rheumatism and cutaneous diseases.

Colesberg forms the district lying farthest to the North of the Colony, being bounded by the Orange River, for a distance of 200 miles. The total area of this division is computed at 11,654 square miles. The population numbers 6765 souls.

The main road, leading to the fording place on the Orange River, and from thence to the Griqua and Bechuana tribes, the great lakes, and other interior localities, passes through the centre of this district, and gives it great importance in a commercial point of view—a considerable trade being carried on with the several tribes of the country towards the North.

In cattle and sheep, this is considered to be the richest division of the Colony; while, in the field-cornetcy of Hantam, a race of the hardiest horses, that can be obtained in the Eastern Province of the Colony, are bred.

The general appearance of the district is monotonous, arising from a great scarcity of wood. Many extensive tracts scarcely produce a bush, and the farmers are dependent upon the manure of their cattle and sheep kraals, for their necessary fuel. This want is the more severely felt, as the country lies high, and the cold of winter is often extremely severe. Sharp frosts and violent snow-storms are common; at which seasons the cattle and sheep suffer greatly, and many even perish, for want of shelter.

Although the district contains extensive plains, yet these are broken by numerous lofty hills and detached ridges; all of which supply abundance of excellent pasturage. The country is seldom intersected by kloofs or ravines, and the main roads preserve, with slight deviations, the level country, keeping along the base of, or winding amongst, the hills and ridges, and but seldom passing over them.

The Orange-River is here the most remarkable geographical object of notice. It takes its rise amidst the great chain of mountains which stretches across this part of Africa to the East; and, along its course, it is fed by countless tributaries, all flowing from the same locality. When swollen by the rain in the interior, the aspect presented by this river is certainly magnificent; it being, in some places, more than 3000 feet broad, with considerable depth, and a full and rapid current. At other seasons it is easily forded, the water at the usual drift being shallow, and the banks of the river declining, by an easy gradation, to the water's edge.

The village of Colesberg (named after Sir Lowry Cole, a late governor) is situated near the base of a hill, called the Zooverberg, at a distance of about ten miles South of this river. It may be described, in general terms, as "a narrow valley, enclosed by rocky hills," with little to commend it to notice, save its utility for trading purposes.

Viewed as an entirety, this division of the Colony may also be said to possess a want of interest; the scarcity of water obliging even the farmers, who inhabit it, to have no settled location, but rove about with their flocks in quest of this indispensible element. An effort towards locating them, however, has lately been made, by the formation of a new town in this district, called " Middleburg."

Contiguous to this division, lies that of *Albert*, which was annexed to the Colony in 1848. It contains an area of about 1,643,960 acres. The chief town is entitled Burgherdorp. This is a rising place, but the district, itself, is the contrary, owing to the great scarcity of water, and herbage for cattle ; the latter in the summer is sour, and in the winter the climate cold and bleak, hence beasts do not thrive well here.

Next crossing the North-eastern extremity of the Colony, we close our tour of the Eastern Province, in the districts of *Beaufort* and *Victoria*.

The former of these contains about 1,000,000 acres of land, and a scattered population, chiefly of Fingoes and natives. It is a rich locality, in which sheep and cattle thrive well. The land is open and good for agriculture, possesses a luxuriant sward of grass, and fine perennial streams issuing from the mountains. The chief-town, Whittlesea, is so called after the birth-place of Sir Harry Smith, its founder. Here an extensive coal deposit has lately been discovered, and fine building stone is abundant.

This division possesses thirty-five miles of sea-coast, and lies between the Great Fish river, to the point of its junction with the Kat river—and the Keiskamma river, to the point where it is joined by the Chumie. Its Southern part is then continued between the Kat river and the Chumie, to Macomo's Hill, and further by the foot of the Chumie mountains, and the Kat Berg, to Gaika's Hill. Beyond that, again, it has a detached piece of territory, beyond the Winter-berg, which is bounded by the Zwarte or Black Kei, and the Klip-Plaats rivers.

The chief-town in the division of Victoria, Alice, is situated on the banks of the Chumie, about sixteen miles from that of Beaufort, in the adjoining district of that name.

This latter division is a tract of country striking and interesting, and well watered by the Kat River. It forms a basin, encircled by a chain of mountains, from which issue numerous streams that give fertility to the soil. These mountains are of considerable altitude, and present, from their summits, magnificent views of the surrounding country. In many places their sides are clothed with gigantic forest trees of the most useful description. Amid the dense kloofs of these rugged and frowning mountains, the valley of the "Blinkwater," and the dark and precipitous "Waterkloof" are situated, telling the tale of many a hard fought struggle between Macomo, the rebel Hottentots, and our gallant troops.   Here fell the gallant Colonel Fordyce, and many other brave officers and men of his spirited 74th regiment of Highlanders.

To prevent the recurrence of such painful scenes as those amid which these sad casualties occurred, an opportunity is now offered.   The disaffected having been expelled, this land now lies waste and unoccupied; an opening is thus afforded for a large population of immigrants to be located there.   This will effectually protect these fastnesses; for it will deter the savages from again trying to occupy them, to the constant ruin of the industrious colonial farmers. And by this alone can the evil be prevented.

THE WEARY AT REST.

CHAPTER VI.

THE HOTTENTOT TRIBES.*

KORUNNAS, HOTTENTOTS PROPER, NAMAQUAS AND GRIQUAS.
THEIR DISTINCTIONS, MANNERS, CUSTOMS, AND LANGUAGES.

TURNING to the tribes and retracing our steps to the South of Africa, whilst assuming that the "Old Cape Colony," (comprising the present Eastern and Western Provinces,) was originally peopled by the primitive aborigines, the "Hottentot" and "Bushmen" families, we now present the reader with an outline of these races. To say that this was *wholly* their territory, or that they *exclusively* inhabited it, can be but conjectural. All that is practicable towards elucidating these points, is to gather up the few authentic historical records extant, and then endeavour to trace the analogy between these and other more Northerly tribes of the African continent.

---

* The meaning of the term *Hottentot* is involved in some obscurity. It seems to be of Dutch extraction (Hot-en-tot,) and was probably given in reference to their language, which might have appeared to those who first heard it, as consisting of little better than an assemblage of such unmeaning monosyllables as "*hot*" and "*tot*."

By the Kaffirs the Hottentots are called *Amaqeya* and *Amalau.* The latter is properly a nickname. It signifies 'those who prefer eating their cattle, to keeping them;' and may be regarded, therefore, as a Kaffir stigma on the proverbial improvidence of the Hottentot race.

That the Hottentots are the aborigines of South Africa, is as certain as that the Kaffirs are foreigners and intruders upon its soil. And that nearly all the districts, which are now exclusively in the hands of the Kaffirs, were originally in the possession of the Hottentots is deducible from the fact, that several of the mountains, rivers, and passes in Kaffraria, and on the frontier, still possess Hottentot names: such as "Bushman's river," "Oliphant's Hoek," "Vische, or Fish river," "Huish Doorns," &c., &c.

How far interior this nation spread at the period when the country first became known to Europeans is uncertain, as few of the first settlers were explorers far into the land. Most possibly, however, the districts now within the Cape Colony, were then inhabited by these people, and this we gather from the following gleanings from authentic documents :—

When this Southern promontory was first colonized by Europeans, A.D. 1652; (as has been already stated,) these Hottentots were found resident on, and around, the present site of Cape Town. After some little litigation and resistance, having ceded the lands there to the Dutch settlers, they retired from them towards the interior of the continent; travelling along the Southern and *Eastern* coast; but returning, in gangs, at intervals, to traffic with them, and exchange cattle for brass rings, wire, and beads. About the beginning of the eighteenth century, on one of their visits, they reported having met with another tribe of blacks who were coming down the Eastern coast, but a considerable distance from Cape Town. They reported these people as cruel and barbarous; and added the account of various encounters they had had with them; in which their people had always been vanquished and many killed. When thus their Northerly and Easterly advance was retarded by the Kaffirs, the Hottentots had doubtless returned to the Cape, to try what possibility there was of their driving out the Dutch. Soon, however, convinced of the fallacy of such an expectation as this, and thus dwelling, as it were, between two fires, they finally decided on migrating towards the North-west; and, keeping on the North side of the Dutch boundary, they moved towards Namaqualand, about the year 1760.

In this exodus, it is more than probable that the natural boundaries of the country, viz, mountain ranges and long wide rivers, would have influenced them much in locating themselves.* The Dutch boundary extended then

* Speaking of the Hottentot tribes and their ancient localities, Mr. R. Moffat in his " Missionary Labours and Scenes," says :—" At all

along the Fish river on the East, (or as it had been first named by the Portuguese discoverers, Rio d' Infanta,) and, from it, along the Nieuweveldt and Roggeveldt ranges of mountains toward the West. This territory having been thus ceded by the Hottentots, must have originally belonged to them: but, further, when relinquishing it, they would, as a natural consequence, have been conversant with other interior districts, to which they knew they could retire, on evacuating this one. For it must ever be borne in mind, that this *first* grant of land to Europeans, at the Cape, was, on the part of the natives, (as has been shown,) not compulsory, but optional, and was arranged in good faith by these aborigines. And hence, any claims which the Hottentot tribes may *have had*

events, it is evident that they have arisen from a race distinct from that of their neighbours, and extended *inland*, inhabiting the most fertile spots, till their course was arrested on the East by the bold and warlike Kaffirs, and, on the North, by the Bechuanas and Damaras. It is probable that they stretched out into Great Namaqualand, along the Western divisions of the Colony, till prevented by a desert country, beyond which lay the Damaras; and then, again, they proceeded from Little Namaqualand Eastward, along the cooling banks of the Gariep or Orange River, richly fringed with overhanging willows, towering acacias, and kharree trees and shrubs, umbrageous at all seasons of the year. Thus, *by the localities of the country*, they became separated into the three great divisions of Hottentots, Korunnas, and Lesser and Greater Namaquas. From time immemorial, these have been the boundaries of their habitations, while the desert wastes, and barren mountain ravines which intervened, became the refuge and domains of the Bushmen, who are, emphatically, 'the children of the desert.'"

to the South African soil, they have voluntarily relinquished years ago ; and they have *now* no grounds for reclaiming it.

All internal evidences shew the *Kaffir* nation, as *not* indigenous to these districts, but as having worked down from North to South, meeting on their way with various located tribes, which they either exterminated, subdued, or expelled —being always victorious when brought into collision with them.

Amongst these were the Hottentots, whom they dispersed to the Western part of the continent. And, in so doing, the Kaffirs gained but a victor's right to *their* present districts. Hence this question, so often argued and con-tended for, respecting the injustice of our pos-session of the soil in Southern Africa, is but an assumed one. That land having first been *voluntarily ceded* by the aborigines, to the Dutch, and taken from these by the British in war, brings it but to the right of tenure of all the national possessions. And further, when the Kaffirs, having wrested the country from the Hottentots, crossed the colonial boundary, and there met with those whom they could not expel or conquer : the land taken from them, by our force of arms, was a conquest of that *which ori-ginally did not belong to them.*

When thus conquered by the Kaffirs, and

Griqua Hottentots at their Recreations.

Page 139.

refused re-entrance into the Southern districts, by the Dutch, the Hottentot tribes passed out, as has been observed, towards the North-west, about the year 1760, and, dividing into three tribes, they located themselves as we now find them; Korunnas, Namaquas, and Bushmen.

The Griqua tribes are, *indirectly*, of Hottentot extraction, being an intermixture of Dutch and Hottentot blood. They are also styled "bastards," of which appellation they are extremely proud.

Another bastard tribe, belonging to this family, are the Gonas, or Gonaquas, formed by the union of the Kaffir and Hottentot races. They assimilate, however, more to the Kaffirs; although also resembling the Hottentot in physiognomy.* They adopt the Kaffir language, and being so few in numbers, and so like that people in their various habits, manners, and customs, they are considered, and treated, as *bona fide* Kaffirs.

"The Korunna tribe," is the pure Hottentot; or, as they are sometimes called, "Hottentots

* In conversiug with a very intelligent resident in Kaffirland respecting this tribe, he mentioned that his *first* impression, on viewing them, shortly after his arrival in the country, was, that they strongly resembled the inhabitants of China; and, having named this to a person familiar with that country, his observation was, that they bore more resemblance to the natives of the islands in the Chinese ooas, than to the actual residents on the mainland of the celestial empire.

proper."* In appearance and stature they are most singular, approaching, in every particular, to a caricature on the contour of the Egyptian copts. They average in height about four feet five or six inches, and are small boned, and and very sinewy. Their hands and feet are long and thin, and their nails almost resemble claws. Their arms are long in proportion, reaching far down their side; the chest and shoulders are narrow and contracted; the head long and compressed, and sloping from the top of the cheek-bone (which projects far out and close under the eye) towards the chin, which is also protruding and pointed, thus giving the face the form of an inverted isosceles triangle, of which the chin forms the salient angle. The forehead recedes from the eyebrow to the top of the cranium, at a considerable inclination, this latter being thinly studded over with small tufts of black wool, about the size of peas. Their eyes are dark, small, and stealthy, and wander frequently. The ear is very long and large, and stands out from the side of the head; the cheeks are sunken and wrinkled; the nose quite

---

* The "Hottentots proper" are, however, a distinct tribe from the Korunnas, although the former are now but limited in numbers. It has been supposed that the Korunna tribes were an integral part of the common nation who remained behind in the interior districts, while the others pushed on toward the South; from which they again, however, receded on the arrival of the Dutch.

flat and broad toward the base, extending nearly as far across the face, at the nostril, as the extremities of the lips, which are also very flat, large, and projecting. The short indented end of the nose, and the flat fleshy fronts of the lips being nearly in the same perpendicular line, form the most prominent point of a physiognomy which, being of a copper-coloured tint, is neither handsome, intellectual, or engaging ; indeed, on the contrary, it is revolting and disagreeable even to look upon.

The costume, usually adopted by these people in their savage and wild state, is simply a skin tanned on the inside, and well rubbed with a mixture of melted fat and clay. This they swathe round their bodies, and attach to it such ornaments as they may possess, consisting of beads, buttons, curb-chains, or whatever else they may chance to find or steal. They usually wear a handkerchief bound round the head, if they can obtain one ; if not, a strip of skin or fur is substituted. Those now resident within the Colony, whether of this tribe, or the others belonging to the Hottentot nation, readily assume the European costume ; and the women, in particular, are vain and ostentatious in dress, usually selecting the gaudiest colours, and display as little taste or judgment in the harmony of their arrangement, as in their selection. In this they manifestly differ from the Kaffirs, who avoid and shun the adoption of European costume which is forced upon them; pertinaciously retaining their national, graceful, and well-arranged garb, viz, the kaross, or else the tinted blanket.

These *Korunnas*, or, as they are at times styled, *Koras*, are, except when excited, misled, or urged to the contrary, a quiet, unassuming race, who lead an erratic life, along the banks of the great Gariep or Orange River. They dwell by tribes, which are very numerous, though they are, in themselves, small. Their mode of architecture is well explained, when we say the villages resemble clusters of gigantic beehives. These they cover with leaves, grass, and mats, and are thickly lined with rushes, and vermin of all kinds and sizes.

Their food consists chiefly of roots, berries, curdled milk (supplied sparingly by their flocks) honey, and locusts. The honey they gather periodically, being cleverly guided to the wild bees' nests, by the little sparm or honey-bird; while the locusts are killed during their flight in autumn,* and stored in large quantities.

* For a more lengthened account of the sparm, and its wonderful powers of instinct, in guiding the Hottentots to the wild bees' nests; together with the migratory locusts, and their periodical flights through Africa, &c., the reader is referred to a small work by the Author, entitled "Kaffraria and its Inhabitants," lately published by Messrs. Simpkin, Marshall, and Co., London.

These stores are then deposited in holes in the ground, and are used with much economy, as a very recherchè repast, but only occasionally to be indulged in during the privations of the winter months of the year, when fruit or berries are not to be gathered, or game to be found.

The actual extent of population, of this people, is not correctly ascertained, but is supposed to be about 10,000 or 15,000. They have been described by T. Pringle, Esq., in his " African Poems," pleasingly and graphically :—

> " Fast by his wild resounding river,
> The listless Coran lingers ever;
> Still drives his heifers out to feed,
> Soothed by the gorrah's humming reed;
> A rover, still unchecked will range
> As humour calls, or season's change;
> His tent of mats, and leathern gear,
> All packed upon the patient steer.*
>
> Mid all his wanderings, hating toil,
> He never tills the stubborn soil;
> But on the milky dame relies,
> And what spontaneous earth supplies.
> Or should long parching droughts prevail,
> And milk, and bulbs, and locusts fail;
> He lays him down to sleep away,
> In languid trance, the weary day;
> Oft as he feels gaunt hunger's stound,†
> Still tightening famine's girdle round;

* Wife.   † A sharp pang.—*Spencer*.

> Lulled by the sound of the Gareep,
> Beneath the willow's murmuring deep.
> Till thunder-clouds, surcharged with rain,
> Pour verdure o'er the panting plain;
> And call the famish'd dreamer from his trance,
> To feast on milk and game, and wake the moon-
>   light dance.

Their principal weapons are the bow and poisoned arrows, and a javelin or spear, which they use only for hunting; as they are by no means a warlike tribe, and offer no resistance to those who attack them.

Religion they have none—a kind of wild traditionary superstition holding its place in their stunted and obscure minds. Little progress seems to be made either among them by Missionary enterprise; as those of their tribes professing Christianity are not to be relied on, while the great majority refuse to hear. The difficulty of attaining their language, and the diversity of dialectical divisions and forms throughout it, also seem to be great obstacles to the progress of knowledge.

Amongst these divisions of the Hottentot dialects, little is known respecting that of the Korunna tribes, except by one laborious Missionary, the Rev. Mr. Wuras, of the Berlin Society; who, it is said, has not only mastered the language, but is compiling a grammar of the Korunna dialect in European characters, while

a catechism and explanation of the Apostles'
Creed have already appeared. To this pioneer
of civilization and Christianity among them, the
greatest praise is due, for his untiring and unwearied efforts; and, it is to be hoped, that others
may be found, who will not allow his labour to
be lost amongst this degraded and degenerated
people. We insert from Mr. Appleyard's book,
p. 14, a specimen of the Korunna language;
viz, a translation of the "Apostles' Creed."

Koemreha Tshu 'koab üm, 'keisa 'koerroe
aul 'hoemmidi 'hoeb dikakje dihaamb.

Koemreha Jesip Christip, Tshu 'koab di'koei
oaain, sida 'goeb 'koh 'oaaekjeha *Heilige Geest*
ga, oaaekjeha oageis Maria sa, thoe 'kamee
ibkjeke ha Pontius Pilatus i 'eebga ibjekeha
ibjeke 'kaneha, ibkjek 'ooea, ibkjeke 'naneha,
ibkjeke hellega 'oa koeaha, ibkje 'nona 'eib
i'eebga keiha 'oobgoe 'hummiga 'oa ibkjekeh
'awaha, ibje Tshu 'koab di am 'ooam 'na 'noa,
'naba goe ibkje ta 'kawaka, koeeha di 'oosa
dina 'koorahka. 'koemreh *Heilege Geest*, 'an-
noem Christen di *kerk*, 'annoenn di 'koeib *zonde*
di oeroebaab, oob di kei'm i "ammo koeem.

The Hottentots proper, are, in every respect, so
nearly affianced to, and so much resemble these
Korunna tribes, that a separate description of
them is unnecessary. They are now not nume-

rous, and appear to be still gradually decreasing. A few remnants of them are to be found along the Northern border of the Colony, and also thinly scattered throughout the Western districts. But although thus disappearing from the country, and becoming amalgamated with the European races; it is more than probable that this people once possessed the whole South-eastern territory of Africa, even up to the river Kei. This conclusion is arrived at from the fact that the rivers in this district chiefly retain their Hottentot names, altered only to conform them to the laws of the Kaffir language.

Their language is now also nearly extinct, being superseded by the Colonial Dutch and Kaffir dialects. Those within the Colony, who are usually denominated Hottentots belong properly speaking, to the *Griqua tribe*. These have already been incidentally noticed, as also bearing the appellation of "*bastard*," and being an intermixture of Dutch and Hottentot blood. The Bergenaars (or mountaineers) who were nearly annihilated, some years since, on the borders of the Bechuana country, by the Kaffir chief Umzelekazi, and also *the Newlanders*, (who take their name from living in the Newlands district,) are amongst the tribes denominated Hottentots. Their main body, however, dwell in various thickly populated parts of the country beyond the Gariep or Orange river, living in clans or tribes under different chiefs. They also form a very large portion of the population residing at the various Mission-stations at Gnadenthal and elsewhere throughout the Colony. The probable numerical strength of the entire race is from about 20,000 to 25,000 souls; the majority being females, which remark may be applied to all the coloured tribes of Africa; while the contrary is the case with Europeans.

As an evidence of this, we have but here to introduce the parliamentary return, laid before the House of Commons, on the motion of Sir James Graham, within the last year.

Population Return of the Cape of Good Hope. 1852.

WESTERN DIVISION.

Area in Square Miles.	White Population		Coloured Tribes.		Total.	
	Males.	Females	Males.	Females	Males.	Females
72,682½	21,724	20,294	25,563	23,546	58,804	56,082

EASTERN PROVINCE.

Area in Square Miles.	White Population		Coloured Tribes.		Total.	
	Males.	Females	Males.	Females	Males.	Females
45,574 (Without Kaffraria.)	18,116	16,356	64,689	71,148	82,805	87,588

GRAND TOTAL OF THE COLONY.

Area in Square Miles.	White Population		Coloured Tribes.		Total.	
	Males.	Females	Males.	Females	Males.	Females
118,256½	39,840	36,650	90,252	94,694	141,609	143,670

Total Males and Females, White and Coloured......285,279

By this return, it will be seen that, in the Western Province, where Malays and Mosambiques constitute a large portion of the population, the majority is in favour of the males; while, in the Eastern division, where the coloured tribes *of the country* principally dwell, it is in favour of the females. In Kaffirland this is still more discernible.

From this table may further be adduced, that, of the total population of the South African Colony, two-thirds are coloured tribes. It may also be noticed that in *all the districts* the proportion of males to females, among the whites, has the advantage of about five per cent; but, among the coloured races the females have a decided majority in numbers. The census of British Kaffraria is 67,358, of whom 700 are estimated as white people. In this, however, are not included the numbers of troops employed in the defences and wars.

The average population of this country per square mile is about $1\frac{75}{100}$. How different is this from the recent overstocked state of Ireland, where the average was 300 per square mile; and how advantageously might both have been equalized by a transfer from one to the other, and thus have been mutually benefited.

Griqua-Town is the principal location of this race, situated about fifty miles to the North of

the Vaal river, in the very centre of Southern
Africa. It is now a town of considerable importance; the elders of the tribes dwelling there,
together with two or three Missionaries of the
London Missionary Society. It is reported that
these people have lately been taught the use
of fire-arms and powder, to a great extent, and
that as many as 5000 of their numbers are
regularly armed with musketry.

They assume a regular form of government,
handed down to them for some years past; and
which was first formed under the chieftainship
of Andries Waterboer. This person was elected
to his office by their own voice, and proved
himself, in every respect, worthy of the dis-
tinction. He had been originally educated by
Mr. Anderson, the first Missionary there; who,
for twenty years, laboured with praiseworthy
zeal, and was deservedly popular amongst this
people.

Waterboer's government being strict and
well-regulated, drove from amongst these Griquas all the disorderly and ill-affected; who
banding together, and swelling their ranks from
the neighbouring Bushmen and Korunna tribes,
by those of a similar disposition, commenced
marauding among the mountains, and so arose
that tribe already named—the Bergenaars or
mountaineers. They have now, however, dis-

appeared—the remnants of their number becoming Bushmen of the wildest kind.

Besides Waterboer, Cornelius, and Adam Kok, are others who have assumed chieftainship among the Griquas, and may be named as exercising considerable influence and power among them. From its isolated position, this tribe of the Hottentot nation has, throughout the years of their early history, been the best organised, and well-disposed, of the number. Recent colonial events, however, have induced all parties to look with very great and *well-merited* suspicion, on every branch of a nation, whose ingratitude, love for political agitation, and universal democracy of principles, united with their determined, and, in too many instances, late fatal resistance to all proper and military control, have been the main cause of the last outbreak of the border tribes of the Colony. The last race belonging to this part of the Hottentot family worthy of note here, is *the Namaqua tribe*, which dwells in Great and Little Namaqualand, on the Western extremity of the Gariep or Orange river.

To give, in a few words, a clear idea of the topography of this district, I quote the account of Mr. Moffat, who visited it, so far back as the year 1806, when the first Missionaries of the London Missionary Society entered on

their work in this part of Africa.   After many
years of apparent trial and difficulty, they
abandoned it, however; and the Wesleyan Me-
thodists have now, we believe, the sole super-
intendance of this people

Writing of Namaqualand, Mr. Moffat says;—
"Great Namaqualand, as it is usually called,
lies north of the Orange river, on the Western
coast of Africa, between the 23° and 28° of
South latitude; bounded, on the North, by the
Damaras, and, on the East, by an extensive sandy
desert, called, by Mr. Campbell, the South Zara,
or Zahara.   As an inhabited country, it is
scarcely possible to conceive one more destitute
and miserable; and it is impossible to traverse
its extensive plains; its rugged undulating surface; and to descend to the beds of its waterless
rivers, without viewing it as, emphatically, "a
land of droughts bearing the heavy curse of

> "Man's first disobedience, and the fruit
> Of that forbidden tree, whose mortal taste
> Brought death into the world, and all our woe."

Meeting with an individual on my journey thither, who had spent years in that country, I
asked, What is its character and appearance?
"Sir," he replied, "you will find plenty of
sand and stones, a thinly scattered population,
always suffering from want of water, on plains
and hills roasted like a burnt loaf under the

scorching rays of a cloudless sun." Of the truth of this description, I soon had ocular demonstration.

It is intersected by the Fish and Oup rivers, with their numberless tributary streams, if such their dry, and often glowing beds may be termed. Sometimes, *for years together*, they are not known to run; when, after the stagnant pools are dried up, the natives congregate to their beds, and dig holes or wells, in some instances, to the depth of twenty feet; from which they draw water, mostly of a very inferior quality. They place branches of trees in the excavation, and, with great labour, under a hot sun, hand up the water in a wooden vessel, and pour it into an artificial trough; to which the panting herds can approach, partially to satiate their thirst. Thunder storms are eagerly anticipated, for in these only rain descends; and frequently they will pass over with tremendous violence, striking the inhabitants with awe; while not a single drop of rain falls to cool and fructiy the parched waste.

When the refreshing and restoring element, however, *does* descend, it is generally in a partial strip of country, which the electric cloud has traversed; so that the traveller will frequently pass, almost instantaneously, from ground, on which there is not a blade of grass, into tracts of luxuriant green, which have sprung up as the result of a passing storm. Fountains are seldom to be met with, the best being very inconsiderable; frequently very salt; and some of them hot springs; while the soil contiguous is so impregnated with salt-petre, as to make it crackle under the feet like hoar-frost, and it is with great difficulty that any kind of vegetable can be produced. Much of the country is hard and stony, interspersed with plains of deep sand. There is much granite, and quartz is so abundantly scattered, and reflects such a glare of light from the rays of the sun, that the traveller, if exposed at noon-day, can scarcely allow his eyelids to be sufficiently open to enable him to keep the course he wishes to pursue."

The recent accounts furnished of these tracts, by Sir J. Alexander, Mr. Archbell, and others, who have visited them, from time to time, all coincide in confirming this parched character and sterility, as belonging to Namaqualand. They also represent it as one of the least inviting, and most uninteresting parts of Southern Africa.

The banks of some of the rivers in it, in which water seldom flows, may be traced, in their winding courses, by acacias; the timber of which is of the poorest description. Ebony trees also grow, thinly scattered in the immediate neighbourhood of the Orange river; but neither there, nor in the open country, is anything like timber to be found, which would authorize commercial speculations, such as have been recommended by a person travelling there some few years ago. If such efforts are to be put forth in Africa, let not energy or capital be wasted here, when far more promising fields for their employment can be easily found, nearer the navigable rivers, and frequented sea-ports of the Colony, along the Eastern coast.

The climate here (as shewn in the extract quoted above) is intensely hot and oppressive, the average of the thermometer, during the summer months, being 120°. This intense heat, combined with the aridity of the soil, causes it to abound with the various species of reptiles; amongst which, the hooded snake, or Cobra-di-capella, is conspicuous; it being frequently seen in this district of the length of fifteen feet. In addition to which may also be enumerated the Puff-adder, (the *Vipera-berus* of Southern Africa) the Scorpion, Tarantulas, and several other equally poisonous and venomous insects.

The tribes who inhabit this country are a collateral branch of the Hottentot family, from whom they do not materially differ, in their personal appearance, manners, habits, or customs. They are a pastoral people, and lead a migratory life, wandering over the vast sandy plains in search of food for their cattle, whose milk forms their principal means of subsistence. They are governed by chiefs, and their mode of life, in every respect, resembles the Korunnas. They are not a numerous race, although their country is of such extent. This is, in all probability, to be accounted for by the extreme unhealthiness, want of water, and consequent scarcity of vegetable food for man and beast, throughout the district. Their tribes or families are but small, and are very thinly dispersed over the country.

Their language is a dialect of the Hottentot, or as it is styled by Mr. Appleyard, the " *Click-class.*" This is an appellation which he gives to the language of the Hottentot and Bushmen family, in contradistinction to that spoken by the Kaffir, Bechuana, and other tribes, which he styles the " *Alliteral class.*"

Of the Click dialects there are three :—viz, those spoken by the Namaquas, the Korunnas, and the Hottentots proper. This classification is adopted, in consequence of the peculiar nasal, guttural, and extremely harsh and clicking sound given, by these various branches of the Hottentot family, to the pronunciation of different sounds and letters. This language,

throughout its various ramifications, is so un-
couth and unharmonious, that very little has
been accomplished by Europeans, in acquiring
it. And, on the other hand, the tribes themselves are vanishing and decreasing so rapidly
before the advance of other native races, as
well as before the march of civilization, that
it is very sanguinely to be hoped and desired,
that it will eventually disappear and become
obsolete.

Its existence, however, and common use,
throughout its dialects, by these three tribes,
affords sufficient evidence of their common origin, if, indeed, similarity of personal formation
and appearance, were *insufficient* to shew it.

As regards the formation of *a literature* for
the Hottentot language, little or nothing has
been done. Dr. Van der Kemp has published
a part of a catechism in the dialect of the Hottentot proper; it is, however, nearly obsolete.
The four Gospels were translated into the Namaqua dialect, several years ago, by Mr. Schme-
len, a missionary, assisted by his wife, who
was herself a native. Since then, a Rhenish
missionary has translated the Gospel of St.
Luke, and, it is believed, that the whole New
Testament is shortly to be published. Mr.
Wuras has added a catechism, containing a
brief exposition of the Apostles' Creed, in the

Korunna dialect, together with a grammar of this dialect; which has not yet, however, appeared in its printed form.

A specimen of the Korunna dialect having been given in the Apostles' Creed, we further subjoin, for the curious in philology, the "Lord's Prayer" in the Namaqua Language,

Matt. vi., 9—13. Zütaa up, nanoepna hap, zaa onsta annoe annochü. Zaa koeoep ha, zaa kaup (9) nü ü, nanoepna koemmi, 'natszü oonna ho- (10) epy. Neezeep zütaa beeree ba maataa. (11) Ore zütaa zuritin oennübataa, zütaa zuri- (12) tiaum nataara oennüba koemmi. Taa 'ayg (13) ga oaapua kay kwütaa, gawee 'ayggapgoe ooreetaa. Zaap ke koeoeba, ore kayp ore kay kayp tazeekatip na ammap.

To display also, at a glance, the variation, and, at the same time, the agreement, *verbally*, between the dialects of this language, we also subjoin (from Mr. Appleyard's grammar) the following list of words.

English.	*Hottentot.*	*Namaqua.*	*Korunna.*
Father	üp : abob	üp	üm : abob
Mother	,kus	üs	üs : kus
Son	oaap	oaap	oaam
Man	Koeep	kooin	koeeb [koees
Woman	tarakores	tarrass	trakoees :
Head	dannap	tannas	bïkam
Hand	'oemma	'oemma	'oemma

Eye	moep	moes	Moemp
Tooth	'koep	'koes	———
Fire	eip	eys	eip
Water	'kamma	'kamma	'kamma
Sun	sorrees	tsorüs	sorrees
Moon	'kaap	'kaap	'chaam
Great	kei	kay	kei
Little	'karri	'kalli	———
Bone	'koop	'kooe	———
Yes	a	a	a
No	ha a	heei	ha a
I or Me	tire : tita	tita	tire : tita
God	Tshoei 'koap*	tsoei 'kwap	tshu 'koab

This Hottentot language is undoubtedly the lowest and most inferior mode of articulation employed by the human race; and yet, gutteral and inarticulate as its sounds are, its general grammatical construction resembles that of other languages; and, in refined distinctions in one or two of the dialects, it surpasses those of Europe. It is a very likely, and a very natural, supposition, that, as it now exists, it is

---

* "The Kaffir word "*u Tixo*," is, (says Mr. Appleyard) most probably derived from this word; and which, like the Hottentot, is universally applied to designate the Divine Being, since the introduction of Christianity. Its derivation is curious. It consists of two words, which, together, mean "the wounded knee." It is said to have been originally applied to a doctor, or sorcerer, of considerable notoriety and skill among the Hottentots, or Namaquas, some generations back, in consequence of his having received some injury in his knee. Having been held in high repute for extraordinary powers during life, he continued to be invoked, even after death, as one who could still relieve and protect; and hence, in process of time, he became the nearest, in idea, to their first conceptions of God."

but similar to the tribes themselves, by whom it is used; viz, not as it was, the original language of the nation, but the degraded remnant of what both once were. The people, it appears, have arrived at their present condition, by a gradual process of innovation which had been going on for centuries past, during the long period which the several Hottentot migrations are conjectured to have occupied. In the course of this, they appear to have descended from one stage of intellectual degradation to another, until they finally arrived at that extreme point of barbarity, in which they were first found by Europeans. Their language, partaking of the same degeneracy, may reasonably be assumed to have lost much of its original symmetry and harmony, and to be now recognized merely by the skeleton of its form, expressed in the most disagreeable and unmusical manner.

Such, throughout their tribes, is the *senior* branch of the aboriginal South African family of Ham—"the Hottentots." Despising themselves, and still more despised by others; degraded and debased even by the approach of civilization; drunkards, and idlers; they wander over the land as outcasts upon it: and, until Christianity assumes among them *a form* of organization and regularity, and a discipline more tangible than at present, we fear but few permanent results from its introduction can ever be expected.

To the second, and yet wilder branch of this race, we now, however, turn our attention, and scan, at times with awe, the little distance that lies between man, in his lowest state, and the brute, in his most exalted one, approximated and assimulated so closely as the two are, in and throughout the various tribes of the "Bosjemen," or, "Bushmen Family," who inhabit the deserts and caves of this continent. Of their peculiar history we give a detailed account in the following chapter.

HOTTENTOT WOMAN OF ALGOA BAY.

CHAPTER VII.

DESCRIPTION OF THE DISTRICTS, MANNERS, AND CUSTOMS OF
THE BUSHMEN FAMILY.

TRAVELLING far into the barren interior, over
the thirsty plains of the African desert, and
leaving behind by hundreds of miles, the haunts
of civilization, and even those of the less barbarous nations also; now the straying Bushmen, scattered over the wild and dismal scene,
are here and there descried, wandering from glen
to glen, or bounding like the ape from one rock
to the other. As a species of the human genus
it is revolting in the extreme, and indeed degrading, to have to depict or describe them.
Hunger and cold, and every description of privation and distress, seems to have cramped the
growth of life within, and to have left them a
caricature on our humanity too painful to contemplate; resembling, in fact, animated skele-
tons, or mummies raised from their tombs. In
appearance, they are as ugly as anything, in
human shape and feature, can be conceived.
Their stature is dwindled down to the diminutive average of, for men, about *four feet*

two inches; and, for females, about *four feet.* Many, however, are considerably below this standard, amongst both sexes. The outline of the physiognomy is triangular and concave; the cheek bones very high; the chin sharp and prominent; the nose flat; the lips thick; and the eyes, which are very small, narrow, sunken, and keen, are set obliquely in the head, the interior corners being the lowest. They are situated far apart in the face, and are always in motion. The colour of their skin has been well described as that of a withered leaf of tobacco; but they are so completely clothed in coats of grease, filth, and ochre, (with which they smear their bodies) that, except where or when this peels off, it is never visible. Their legs, thighs, and arms, are lean, withered and divested of all appearance of muscle. The joints are large; the bones long; and the body protuberant and mis-shapen.

Such, in appearance, is that miserable, needy, hollow-eyed, sharp-looking creature, called a Bosjesman, or Bushman of Southern Africa. It is impossible adequately to describe these creatures, so as to give an idea, to European minds, of the *wildness* of their looks, as they appear in their desert haunts. They wear no clothing, except part of a raw skin, generally that of a sheep, goat, or antelope, hung loosely over the shoulder. To this the women add a belt, or strap of hide, fastened round the loins, with shells, or a piece of leather cut into narrow strips so as to resemble a fringe, attached to it. This, hanging in front of the body, forms the only cover to their person; and from their savage, untutored state, even this appears to be viewed by them more as an ornament to the figure, than as an article of clothing.

The Korunna-Bushmen, who have latterly fallen in more constantly with European traders in the interior, and have become more docile and less wary, have obtained from them beads, shells, and bits of copper wire, which they wear round the ancles and arms, like the other native tribes. They sometimes also attach them to the little pellets of wool that grow scantily dispersed over their heads. This wool (for it is not worthy of the name of hair) they rub into little round knots with a mixture of grease, filth, and red ochre, which does not tend much to add either beauty to their appearance or sweetness to their odour.

Their *weapons* are bows and quivers full of poisoned arrows; the bow is usually two feet six inches in length, and is formed of some kind of hard pliable wood, found and selected in the interior forests. They string them with a thong of twisted hide well saturated with grease. The quiver, which is bound upon the back, is composed of bark or rushes, interwoven with narrow thongs of hide, or the intestines of animals. Each of these contains from two to three dozen of reed arrows, about eighteen inches long, and pointed by a piece of barbed flint, or sometimes bone, placed in a notch at one end of it. This is strongly impregnated with poison which they extract from the juice of the *Euphorbia*, the *Amaryllis Toxicaria*, or the *Illiteris* bulbs, and also, it is said, from the fangs of the viper.*

When preparing for war or plunder, the Bushmen draw forth all their arrows from the quiver; and, fastening a fillet of skin round the head, they stick them round it in a kind of coronet or diadem; for the twofold purpose, it is supposed, of rendering their appearance more terrific, and of having the arrow placed so as to be ready for speedy use. In addition to this, they usually carry a piece of thin stick, or a porcupine's quill, thrust through the cartilage of the nose; similar war ornaments are also worn attached to their ears.

Their *dwellings* are varied in form, according

* Mr. Moffat, in his account of the Bushmen of the desert, says :— "They cut off the head of the poisonous kinds of serpents; this they dissect, and carefully extract the bags or reservoirs of poison, which communicate with the fangs of the upper jaw. They mingle this with the milky juice of the *Euphorbia*, or with that of a poisonous bulb. After simmering for some time on a slow fire, it acquires the consistency of wax, with which they cover the points of their arrows."

to their grades. The Korunna-Bushmen who dwell on, and around, the Karoo country, South of the Vaal and Caledon rivers, usually live under mats, which they roll up in the daytime, and are carried, by the women, from place to place. At night they tear off two branches or sticks from the bushes, and, bending them into a semi-circular shape, they suspend this mat from them, above some natural cavity in the ground. Into this hole they creep, and, coiling themselves up like animals, they lie down to sleep during the darkness of the night. These mats are usually made by the women; long rushes or grass being platted together, and anointed, like all the rest of their gear, with thick coatings of clay and grease. These habitations are, however, only indulged in by the Korunna-Bushmen of the lower districts; and are luxuries of civilization wholly unknown to the Namaqua Bushmen, or those of the South Zahara desert.

Amongst these latter, a cave, or a deep fissure in a rocky precipice, is sufficient shelter from the atmosphere; and these they endeavour to render as warm as possible, by lining them with leaves, grass, and skins, the cold of night being all that the Bushman dreads, in the climate of his native wilds.

"It is impossible," says a traveller, speaking

of the dwellings of these latter, "to look at some of their domiciles without the enquiry rising, involuntarily, in the mind, Are these the abodes of human beings? In a bushy country they will form a hollow, in a central position, and bring the branches together over the head. Here the man, his wife, and, probably, a child or two, lie huddled together on a little grass, in a hollow spot not larger than an ostrich's nest. Where bushes are scarce, they form a hollow under the edge of a rock, covering it partially with reeds or grass; and they are often to be found in fissures and caves of the mountains. When they have an abundance of meat, they gorge and sleep, dance and sing, by turns, till their stock is exhausted. But hunger, that imperious master, soon compels them to resume the chase. It is astonishing to what distance they will run in pursuit of the animal which has received the fatal arrow. I have seen them, on the successful return of a hunting party, the merriest of the merry, exhibiting bursts of enthusiastic joy: but this momentary happiness, contrasted with their real position, produced on my mind the deepest sorrow. Many suffer great distress when the weather is cold and rainy, during which their children not unfrequently perish from hunger. A most inhuman practice respecting children also prevails amongst them. When a mother dies, whose infant is too young to supply its own wants, it is, without any ceremony, buried alive with the corpse of its mother."

Respecting their domestic habits, if indeed they can be said to have any, little is known, except from Missionaries who have been amongst them. Polygamy is universal, while conjugal affection seems totally unknown. They appear to care little for their children, seldom correcting them for offences, and when they do so, it is merely in a fit of passion, when they nearly kill them. The children appear to be the scape-goats on which are visited their parents' offences; for when a father deserts the mother, or in the case of a quarrel between father and mother, or the several wives of a husband, the deserted and defeated party always wreak their vengeance by murdering their opponent's child. "There are even instances," says Mr. Kicherer, a most zealous Missionary, who lived for some time amongst them, "of parents throwing their tender offspring to the hungry lion, who stood roaring before their cavern, refusing to depart till some peace-offering be made to him." "In general," he adds, "their children cease to be the objects of a mother's care, as soon as they are able to crawl about in the field. In some

few instances, however, you meet with a spark
of natural affection, which places them on a
level with the *brute* creation."

These creatures are altogether the slaves of
passion; and even the females seem as barbarous as the men—no softness of heart or nature
appearing to characterize their sex.   They are
wanting, as above described, even in what we
term the common instincts of a fallen, vitiated
nature; for, from equally authentic sources, as
those from which we have already quoted, we
have heard, that on the *least* pretext they will
murder their offspring without compunction
on their own part, and without any crime
being imputed to them by their companions.
If pursued by enemies, if in great want of food,
when the child is born deformed or ill-shaped,
or in cases of spite or revenge to the father,
the mother frequently has been known to smo-
ther her infant, strangle it, bury it alive, or
casting it from her, leave it exposed, to perish
of famine or drought, or, perhaps, to be devoured by the wild beasts, in the scorching
plains of their desert habitations.

They, not unfrequently also, forsake their
aged parents and relatives, when obliged to
move their location; and, making "the trouble
of carrying them," or "their uselessness," the
frivolous excuse for their brutality, they leave

them to perish by slow torture, sometimes merely giving them the shell of an ostrich's egg filled with water, and a small piece of meat to support life, and sometimes nothing at all.

To the other coloured races around them, they seem to bear a more deadly hatred than to the white man; for if, perchance, an isolated and unprotected Hottentot or Fingoe should fall into their hands, they subject them to the most cruel torture, putting them to a slow and lingering death, in the most excruciating manner. Mr. Shaw in his " Memorials of Southern Africa," gives the instance of a Hottentot, who had the misfortune to fall into the ruthless clutches of a party of these wild people. " They placed him up to the neck in a trench, and then wedged him in, on all sides, with earth and stones, so that he was incapable of moving. In this dilemma he remained all night, and the greater part of the next day; when, happily for him, some of his companions, passing that way, effected his release. The poor fellow stated that he had been under the necessity of keeping his eyes and mouth in constant motion during the whole day, to prevent the birds of prey from devouring him."

As may be inferred from the general description of their habits, agriculture or cattle breeding are wholly unknown to them. The patience required to wait for the product of their labour, or the tardy paces of cattle, obliging them, of necessity, to remain longer in one locality than they would desire, or even deem safe, prejudices them against either.

They live by hunting and thieving, and, in the failure of these, on the larva of ants and grasshoppers, ostrich's eggs, locusts, roots, or indeed, almost anything; for no kind of food, from the largest quadruped of the plain to the most disgusting reptile that crawls through the rocks, is disregarded by the cravings of a Bushman's hunger. And, in the sorest extremities of famine, when even these objects fail, "the girdle of famine," a belt of hide, drawn closely around the person, still enables them to cling to life, without experiencing the more acute agonies of gnawing hunger and privation.

Mr. Thompson, of Cape Town, described to the author the use of this most necessary garment, as he had seen it amongst these people, during his travels in the interior of Africa, in the year 1827. He spoke feelingly of the conclusive answers in the negative, the poor Bushmen gave to his enquiries after game, viz, "by exposing their persons and pointing to this strap pulled tightly round their emaciated bodies."

Neither will it be thought so repugnant to our

feelings, that these barbarous creatures should thus be found trying to support existence, by feeding on reptiles and insects; if, for a moment, our readers but reflect on the tenacity with which nature inherently clings to life, throughout all her representatives.   Nor can we altogether discard their articles of diet, without remarking, that the blindness of prejudice, or, at least, the want of stimulating hunger, makes us, when surrounded with luxury, abundance, and civilization, look at such things with disgust, when necessity would oblige us to eat them with toleration, or even a relish.   Let it not be supposed that we wish to advocate the adoption of this fare by European palates, but we remember well our own feelings of gratitude and joy, when kneeling down and drinking from many a muddy pool of water in the plains of Africa, where we had to draw it through our closed teeth, to avoid swallowing the countless swarms of tadpoles, animalculæ, and insects which floated in it, and which we could see, and feel playing against our lips, and in our mouth, as we drank copiously of the refreshing beverage.   We have also seen ladies content to use a gentleman's hat as their drinking goblet, when overtaken by thirst, in the arid mountains of the African continent. Necessity is a hard master!

The locust *(Gryllus migratorius)* which the
Bushmen use for food, is, of course, only palatable to their peculiar taste—blended, as it
is, with grease and filth, and sometimes with
the reeking blood of a quagga or hyæna. We
have, however, tasted them, when prepared as
they are stored, viz, divested of the thorny
part of the leg and wings, dried in the sun,
and ground into a kind of meal or powder
between two stones. This preparation, when
mixed with wild honey, and baked, is by
no means a more repulsive repast, than the
fricasseé of snails or frogs, which our continental
neighbours consider so fine, and which even
some English connoisseurs do not wholly discard or decline to appreciate.

Hunting is the chief resource of these wild
people. And this, like all the rest of their actions, whether for war or peace, is conducted
principally by deceit and cunning. Throughout all their habits, whatever they have not
strength, ingenuity, or patience to accomplish
otherwise, they endeavour to effect, through
the medium of treachery, guile, and perfidy.
Hence, in the art of carrying off their pillage
from any unfortunate frontier farmer, whose
lands or flocks they may approach in their
migrations, they display great dexterity, and
generally decamp with the spoil, and devour

it long before the theft is even discovered.   In hunting, also, they are extremely expert, and pursue with pertinacity, and wonderful endurance and speed, the quaggas, zebras, hippopotami, ostrich, and bustard; as also the various kinds of buck and antelope, which traverse the African deserts in such numberless herds.   If they cannot succeed by their fleetness of foot, or with the aid of their wild, half-famished, and savage dogs, to come within bow shot of, or run down, their objects, they still follow them up; and then, having covered the ground, towards evening, with snares and traps, they retire to a distance, and starting off in a side-long course, they try to head the game, and drive them back over the ground prepared, with these engines for their destruction.   If they thus succeed in embarrassing any of them, before the hapless beast has time to recover itself, they pounce upon it, and a poisoned arrow sends certain death where it strikes.

Their stratagem for securing the ostrich, and also the kaop, (a species of antelope) as described by Sir J. E. Alexander, is worthy here of remark.   "I was anxious to know," he says, "how the Boschmans manage to kill the kaop; and remarking two light frames, covered with ostrich feathers, grey and black, on a tree, I asked them what they were.   The Boschman said, " With these we disguise ourselves as ostriches, and thus get near the kaop, to shoot it with our arrows."

" A present of tobacco induced a Boschman thus to disguise himself. He placed one of the feather frames on his shoulders, and secured it about his neck ; then, taking from a bush the head and neck of an ostrich, through which a stick was thrust, he went out a little way from the huts, with a bow and arrow in his left hand, and, pretending to approach a kaop, he pecked at the tops of the bushes in the manner of an ostrich, and occasionally rubbed the head against the false body, as the ostrich ever and anon does, to get rid of flies. At a little distance, and sideways, the general appearance of the Boschman was like that of the giant bird, though a front view betrayed the whole of the human body.

" Approaching sufficiently near to the Kaop, which, of course, has nothing to fear from its feathered companions of the plains, the Boschman slips the ostrich head between his neck and the frame, and, cautiously taking aim, discharges his arrows at the deceived Kaop."

Living in the wildest manner that it is almost possible to conceive, these tribes are without government, chiefs, or control of any kind. Amongst them, might makes right ! and ne-

cessity proclaims that she has no law! The
punishment of crime, if such a thing be indeed
understood by them, is necessarily very unequal; depending, as it of course must do exclusively, upon the power or weakness of the parties concerned.   Revenge and self-preservation
seem to be the two paramount feelings in each
individual breast.*

They are very cautious in their habits; flying from the face of strangers, concealing themselves amongst the rocks and bushes, or even
plunging down a precipice, rather than fall into
the hands of their adversaries.   They appear
invariably to prefer death to surrender; and
always fight with the most determined and
dogged resolution.   It has been known that,
when both their right and left arms have been
completely disabled, they have still tried with
their toes to fix the bow, so as to be enabled
to continue their obstinate defence.

They have no religion: while the vacuum
in their obscure minds, which should be filled

* Several most tragic instances of revenge, as put into execution
by these creatures, are upon record. One of the most barbarous, we
remember hearing of, was in the case of some real or supposed oppression, having been exercised over some Bushmen by a party of
Dutch Boors. The Bushmen followed them home in the distance;
and, having ascertained the exact locality of their dwelling, they then
discovered the spring which supplied it with water: this they impregnated with the poison, (which they used upon their arrows) and so
glutted their revenge by destroying the whole family; and all who
drank of it.

with it, is supplied by superstition and witch-craft, the sad fruits of ignorance and mental terror. They also possess strange traditions, which they believe, and recite to each other.

As an instance of the extravagance and absurdity of these, we again quote from the pen of Sir J. E. Alexander, whose account of this people deservedly claims credit and appreciation.

"It is believed in the land," he writes, "that some of the Bosch people can change themselves into wolves and lions when they like."

" Once on a time, a certain Namaqua Hottentot was travelling in company with a Bosch woman carrying a child on her back. They had proceded some distance on their journey, when a troop of wild horses appeared, and the man said to the woman, " I am hungry, and I know you can turn yourself into a lion; do so now, and catch us a wild horse, that we may eat."

" The woman answered, " You'll be afraid." "No, no," said the man, " I am afraid of dying of hunger, but not of you."

"Whilst he was yet speaking, hair began to appear at the back of the woman's neck; her nails began to assume the appearance of claws; and her features altered. She put down the child.

" The man, alarmed at the change, climbed a tree close by. The woman glared at him fearfully, and, going to one side, she threw off her skin petticoat, when a perfect lion rushed out into the plain; it bounded and crept among the bushes towards the wild horses, and, springing upon one of them, it fell, and the lion lapped its blood. The lion then came back to where the child was crying, and the man called from the tree, " Enough, enough, don't hurt me, put off your lion's shape, and I'll never ask to see this again."

" The lion looked at him and growled. " I'll remain here till I die," said the man, "if you don't become a woman again. The mane and tail then began to disappear the lion went towards the bush where the skin petticoat lay; it was slipped on, and the woman, in her proper shape, took up the child. The man descended, partook of the horse's flesh, but never again asked the woman to catch game for him."

Such are the miraculous extravagancies, with which they feed their wild imaginations, and wile away their tedious hours of inactivity; and, if we except sorcery and witchcraft which are common amongst them, these appear to be the only vestages of tradition or religion which can be discerned.

Their language is inarticulate to all except themselves; and, even then, one party will express themselves in a dialect which another, separated from them only by a range of mountains, or the bed of a river, cannot understand. All their articulations, however, abound in 'clicks,' and assimilate nearest to that of the Hottentot tribes. This similarity is at least sufficiently apparent, to enable us to class these people as being of common origin with the Hottentot nation. Some of their dialects are understood by the Hottentots; whilst others, again, are not. But, with regard to this, much depends upon the localities of the respective tribes. Thus, a Korunna may be able to converse with a Bushman, living in his immediate neighbourhood, though he might find it difficult, or even impossible, to converse with another, dwelling further into the interior of Africa. Their dialects are, however, perversions of those of the Hottentot; whilst, in addition to the clicks and gutteral enunciation of that language, the Bushmen, when they speak, make a still more unpleasant sound, of croaking in the throat. It seems, indeed, more than probable, that no single dialect, in use amongst them, is spoken or understood in common by more than fifty or a hundred families; a circumstance which, in itself, would be sufficient greatly to retard their general improvement, but more especially so, when combined, as it is, with a restless disposition and roving and predatory habits.

As regards *literature*, nothing has been accomplished in their language. Indeed, it is the opinion of the best authority on these dialects, that it is quite incapable of possessing any. Humanly speaking, it appears necessary to teach the Bushmen a new language, (and the same remark applies, with almost equal force, to every Hottentot tribe) in order to their Christianization and civilization.

The notice here of two more tribes of this degraded family, will suffice to complete and close their painful history. These are the "Balala Bushmen;" and, last and inferior to all, the "Zulu Bushmen," or better known, perhaps, in Europe, as the "Earthmen of Natal."

Of the former of these, the "Balala," little more has been ascertained, than that they reside on the borders of the Bechuana country, near the Mampoor Lake, 800 miles North of Lattakoo. They are more generally known as "Bechuana Bushmen." They appear to sustain a relation to that people, of a similar nature to that which the "Korunna or Namaqua Bushmen" bear to the Hottentot family.

From the isolated manner in which they live, various dialects have also arisen amongst them; and this circumstance, connected with the remote and unexplored districts which they inhabit, renders their barbarity and wildness still more apparent. No communications can be held with them, when they are approached, except through an interpreter, or by signs. The most authentic information respecting these distant tribes, is derived from the journey among them of two French Missionaries of the Paris Society, Messrs. Arbousset and Dumas; whose valuable work, published in French, will well repay perusal to those who feel a more particular interest in the interior tribes to the North-east of the Cape Colony. From their accounts, as well as that of Mr. Moffat, who has also passed through some of the districts which they haunt, it would appear that these "Balala" are used and treated as slaves by the Bechuana tribes; who, allow-- ing them to roam about at large, when they require their services, make excursions into their neighbouring deserts, and, bringing in the "Balala," they compel them to perform their work; and when it is finished, they are again turned adrift.

It is amongst these people that the mantis is said to be held sacred. They are also reported as venerating the caddisworm. They style it *N'go*, and in times of extremity or famine, they pray to it for relief.

We here insert a short specimen of one of their prayers, rendered in the dialect of the Baroas; it is as follows :—

'Kaank ta, ha a ntanga ë? Kaang ta, 'gnu a kna a sé'gè. Itanga 'kogu 'koba hu; i'konté, i'kagé, itanga i'kogu 'koba hu; 'kaang ta, 'gnu a kna a sé'gè.

The interpretation is thus :—

"Lord, is it that thou dost not like me? Lord, lead to me a male gnu. I like much to have my belly filled; my oldest son, my oldest daughter, like much to have their bellies filled, Lord, bring a male gnu under my darts."

Such is their degraded, idolatrous worship! They begin by questioning the love of their deity, and then conclude by grossly asking for flesh, and flesh only. Their mode of expression, also, is harsh and barbarous, and their croaking enunciation, when heard, is still worse. These people are, however, few in number, and their language may merely be regarded as a perversion of the Hottentot and Baroa tongues; their dialects like themselves, are, happily, fast becoming extinct.

The last notice which we shall give of these tribes, is of the lowest, most degraded, and utterly savage beings, who, bearing the term "human," are to be found on the face of our globe. We here allude to the "Zulu Bushmen," or the "Natal Earthmen."

These are but an outcast tribe, bordering on the Zulu country, and stretching far away into the continent of Africa, even to the confines of the Zahara desert.

These creatures shun all intercourse with their species, whether black or white; and their chattering more resembles that of a baboon, than any of the human dialects. Here and there, however, a stray sound betokens remnants of those of the neighbouring tribes of Zulus, and Sechuana. During rain, or any inclement weather, they hide themselves amongst the rocks, or in the branches of the giant trees; but they usually reside in holes in the earth, scraped out with their nails, or, rightly termed, their claws. If pursued, it is astonishing with what alacrity and rapidity they will excavate one of these retreats; and, disappearing suddenly, burrow along like a subterranean animal. They wear no kind of clothing, and acknowledge no government. It is said that these people have, from time to time, been devoured by the Mantatee or cannibal tribes, who reside close to them. But, however this may be, it appears now undeniable, that the poor miserable wretches have been so persecuted and hunted down by their own species, that they cease to view them except in the light of enemies and tormentors, and shun them, as it were, by instinct.

Lower than this, our races happily cannot

go; nor is it possible for those who have not personally witnessed these tribes, to imagine the extent of barbarism evinced by them; or the small degree of intellect which they possess—barely distinguishing them from the upper classes of the brute creation.

It is humiliating, in the extreme, to depict them; for though, doubtless, isolated cases of cruelty have been exercised to them by the old Dutch Boers, in days gone by; still it would be unjust to make these the sole reason for their present degradation, or keep the fact out of view that their modes of life *now* are voluntary. *They will not receive kindness*; or, if they do, they only make a return by treachery, robbery, and even murder, if the opportunity occurs to them to commit it. No presents of cattle or corn; no inducements to locate and settle (all of which have been repeatedly tried by those Boers who live nearest to them,) can induce them to relinquish their wild marauding life, or approach towards civilization. And hence, sad as it is to contemplate, the only securities to civilization, when brought into contact with such beings, are coercive measures, which, in self-defence, the Boers are compelled to adopt, and, unhappily, with no more mercy and leniency, at the present time, than of old; but such being the case, now that conciliatory and milder measures have been *first* tried; where, unfortunately, their blood is shed, it must be allowed that it is, virtually, their own deed.

Perhaps the most pleasing thought, in connection with them, is the fact of their rapid diminution in number—whether from disease or want, it is difficult to determine. They are, however, fast passing away; and it is earnestly to be hoped, that they will soon be no longer a burden to themselves, and a degradation to the human species; but that the fact of their existence will remain only as a matter of history.

It is hard to ascertain whether disease makes much havoc amongst them : it is certain, however, that they have no kind of surgery or medical treatment to counteract it. Their only attempt to arrest sickness or death, appears to be in cutting off the little fingers, which is a practice universally adopted when they become ill.

The only vestiges of civilization that exist amongst them, are their paintings; which, as the best feature in their history, may close this sketch. In these, (which, however, are mainly among the Korunna and Vaal Bushmen,) they, at times, display much ingenuity and cleverness in copying. They execute them on the walls of their caves, and with various coloured clays instead of paint. The subjects are usually hunting scenes; but, sometimes, engagements between themselves and the Boers. The accuracy with which they delineate the various species of game; the characteristic lineaments of their own people, and those of the Boers, are certainly surprising, when we consider how wild and un-tutored the artists are. Nor is their grouping, by any means, faulty; the only peculiarity being, as is the case with Chinese paintings, that they have no conception of perspective, and all their figures are in profile. Viewing them, however, as productions of art, though certainly of the lowest grade known, they still display an intuitive talent for imitation, and added to this, a considerable amount of execu-tion in depicting their grotesque conceptions. Several of these paintings still exist in caves, in various localities through Southern Africa, for-merly inhabited by these people; and, although the artists and their posterities have now all disappeared from around them, yet these traces show that they have once been there, and stand as isolated mementos of their intelligence, and rude attempts at artistic representations.

Thus far for these chronicles of the "Bushmen family;" those wildest and most degraded of all the sons of Ham: whose history must ever leave on the minds of all narrators, readers, travellers, or beholders, feelings far removed from pleasure, if not from pity, and perhaps, in some, emotions of scorn or disgust.

But while, with humble gratitude to Him "who has made us to differ," we may prefer our better lot; cast, as it may be, amid civilization and refinement, and in lands where the full lustre of Christianity is shed around; yet we still believe that, even in all their degradation, these despised Bushmen have feelings of enjoyment in their barbarous liberty, which are unknown to us.

Having travelled, for miles, through their mountain homes, and once, like them, enjoyed their desert life, we can appreciate the emotion which induced Pringle to put into the lips of the wild Bosjesmen his well-known lines :—

> "My home is 'mid the mountain rocks,
>   The desert my domain;
>   I plant no herbs or pleasant fruits,
>   Nor toil for savoury cheer;
>   The desert yields my juicy roots,
>   And herds of bounding deer."

CHAPTER VIII.

THE KAFFIRS.

THEIR COUNTRY, ORIGIN, PERSONS, TRIBES, ORNAMENTS, WEA-
PONS, MANNERS, CUSTOMS, MANUFACTURES, AND EMPLOY-
MENTS.

WE now turn to a more interesting page in
African history, the more pleasing task of depicting the Kaffirs, a people better known in
Europe by name, than understood in character,
or appreciated in worth.

Few, if any, of the barbarous tribes at present existing on the earth, surpass this people
in interest, intelligence, or talent. They are,
throughout all their tribal distinctions in perfect harmony with that wild, lovely, and romantic country which now bears their name.
Nor are their picturesque and graceful figures,
folded in their karosses, and seen scattered here
and there throughout the hills, the least attrac-
tive portion in the whole contour of Kaffrarian
scenery.

The delightful climate; the intense rarity of
the atmosphere; the perfectly cloudless sky;
together with the unequalled beauty of the

flowers, shrubs, and trees, studded everywhere (as they appear) with birds of the gaudiest plumage : all here tend to entrance the European visitant, and transfix him with admiration.

To the naturalist this country becomes a perfect paradise ; for, whichever way he turns, novelties meet him at every step ; whilst the charm of his discoveries is more than doubly enhanced by the multiplicity of objects, daily making their appearance, which hitherto were unknown to him.

The geological structure of Kaffraria, (under which title is included and known the whole tract of country lying along the South-eastern coast of Africa, between the old Cape Colony, the new one of Natal, and the Sovereignty or Dutch Free-State) is of a diversified character, but it does not differ much from other parts of the continent, except in the vast preponderance of iron-stone. This is doubtless the cause of the frequency and violence of the thunder storms in these parts ; which, in awful grandeur or destructive consequences, are nowhere surpassed.

The basaltic formation here and there appears above ground, and thus diversifies the character of the floræ ; the plants growing over the surface of these rocks, being of a more profuse and varied character than elsewhere. This formation is first discernible to the geo-

logist as he travels along the Eastern coast of
Africa, in the districts of George; then disappearing, it next rises to view in the lofty mountain above Graham's Town, known as "Governor's Kop." Traversing a few miles of
country here, it gradually falls at Frazer's
Camp Hill, and is not again perceived until he
reaches Mount Coke, a high hill situated about
three miles to the Eastward of Fort Murray;
on which is established the large Wesleyan
Missionary station, which is known by that
name. The rock here disappears as abruptly
as it rose to the surface, and is finally found to
die away into the interior of the earth, on the
banks of the Q'nahoon river, near to the old
Fort Waterloo. After being here lost, it is not
again seen anywhere along the Eastern coast,
either through Kaffraria or Natal.

Pure granite is of very rare occurrence, although a stone, not unfrequently mistaken for
it, is common. This is a kind of trap, which,
in Scotland is called when-stone, and somewhat resembles the hard blue lias of Somersetshire. A large proportion of felspar and talc
is interspersed through it, combined with a species of thin quartz.

Along the coast-line, sand-stone is largely
scattered, whilst iron-stone is the principal feature in the formation. The mountains and hills

are generally of a round form, and the valleys
of a basin-like shape. The soil is mostly a rich
alluvial mould, on a sharp gravel of decomposed
schistus; and although the indications of vol-
canic influence near the surface of the earth,
are of very rare occurrence, yet the primary
rocks are not often visible, except on the more
elevated ranges of land, as in the Wintervogee-
berg, Drakenberg, and other mountains.

The general character of the country is mountainous. The landscape scenery of which, is
more easily appreciated, when viewed, than described to those who are strangers to it. The
purest tints of cobalt could not exaggerate the
intense blue of the distance, whilst the glorious
rays of the setting sun, throw their long sha-
dows in oblique lines of crimson lake and mad-
der, which few artists can imitate or delineate
on canvass. The foregrounds of pictures in
Kaffirland, are either formed of vast plains of
unbroken pasture land, dotted with herds of
Kaffir cattle, and multitudes of wild beasts;
or else by undulating hills, covered for miles
with dense bush; whilst, here and there, large
forest trees appear. The valleys are watered
by serpentine rivers, whose streams flow, alternately, through long deep beds, overhung with
frowning, perpendicular krantzes (precipices,)
amongst rough blocks of stone, over which they

Kaffir Picquet on the Kabousie Pass.

Page 190.

break and fall in far sounding and picturesque cascades.

The two grandest, of these latter, are the falls of the T'Soma, in Kaffraria, the height of which has never yet been properly ascertained; and those of the Umgeni river, in Natal, which descend over a perpendicular precipice of three hundred feet, and fall with the full force of a large river, seventy-six feet wide, into a deep and bush-enveloped basin beneath. Several travellers who have witnessed these falls, as well as those of North America, have testified that the latter do not bear comparison with them; either for height, grandeur, or picturesque beauty.

The force of the African rivers are very much varied during the different seasons of the year; in the rainy months, several of them overflood their banks, and inundate whole miles of country; whilst, during the droughts of winter, they are scarcely seen to flow.

The shorter the river is, from its source to its mouth, the greater is always the fluctuation of its stream: whilst the larger and deeper ones, although less easily or frequently affected by thunderstorms, are, nevertheless, more devastating in their effects, and more tardy in resuming their original level, when once they have become swollen by heavy rains.

The effect of these floods is to clothe the whole landscape with the richest vegetation that can possibly be imagined; which, without them, would soon become parched and arid beneath the scorching sun of noonday. This effect, is not produced however, until some few days after the floods have subsided; while, at the time that they exist, a stranger, beholding the country, would suppose that nothing but devastation and destruction could accrue from such a cause.

The force with which these torrents flow, at such times, is certainly astonishing; sweeping before them enormous trees and portions of earth, torn from the overhanging banks of their beds; and the water frequently rising, during the flow, from six to eight feet.

As soon, however, as they have subsided, and the herbs and flowers begin to appear again on the surface of the ground, the cause is forgotten in the effect; and all nature rejoices in the refreshment of the atmosphere, and the beauty of the surrounding landscapes. The former is so truly bracing, that it at once exhilerates and excites the animal frame; while it also aids in vivifying and rapidly expanding the whole vegetable kingdom.

Within the latter are to be found, in these lovely lands, almost every species of plants and flowers, bestudding the surface of the earth, and, occasionally perfuming the air.

"To give some idea of the botanical riches of this country," writes Mr. Burchell, "I need only state, that, in the short distance of an English mile, though the most favourable season had passed, and many of the bulbous and herbaceous plants had disappeared under the influence of the drought, I collected, in four hours and a half, *one hundred and fifty distinct species;* and I believe that more than double that number may, by searching at different times, be found on the same ground."

It is no exaggeration to describe this portion of South Africa, as nature's botanic garden; for, at every footstep, some fresh novelty presents itself, delightful to the eye, and astonishing the beholder. If, indeed, the indigenous *tribes* of Africa—the Hottentots—be among the most degraded and mis-shapen of our fallen race; yet surely did the Almighty Disposer of the worlds grant to them the most perfect earthly habitation —the most enchanting and romantic landscape to dwell upon. And thus it is that we may learn, that he witholds from his creatures only what might be injurious, and gives to all an equal distribution of his bounties. It is of little import whether we ramble on the wild and rugged mountains of the Zwartebergen

and Snieuwberg, and behold the thundering
cataracts falling over their rugged sides, or
wander through the silent glades of the Knysna
Forests, or over the balmy and floriated plains
of Kaffirland; the same glory is manifested in
nature, whether viewed in the contour of her
general grandeur, or the individuality of her
minutest objects. All alike praise their great
God and Maker; yea, from the least even unto
the greatest.

To describe the floræ of Kaffraria, in a notice
of this kind, is hardly possible; the species and
varieties being so abundant. Above your head,
as well as beneath your feet, the orchidacæ,
clinging to the stems and branches, and uniting
with the jasmine, clematis, and ivy-geranium,
thus spread an unbroken sheet of blossoms,
from the moss and gloxinias at their roots, over
and around the loftiest branches of the forest
trees. And even when the cold of winter causes
these to wither, and, for a while, to droop away,
the trees themselves throw out their flowers,
and the dwarf and giant coralodendrum (called
the Kaffir boem) become enveloped in their gaudy scarlet colours; whilst the turf also throws
up its twelve varieties of everlasting flowers.

We here subjoin *a single page* from a botanical journal, kept by the author, during a week's
ride through the upper districts of Kaffraria.

It is inserted, as it was originally noted down, to explain, with more force than words, the extraordinary profusion and variety of the flowers of Kaffirland.

" Banks of the Kei River.

May 15th, 1853.   Found:

Petunia, blue, white, pale straw coloured.

Gloxinia, white, pink, lilac, blue.

Cyneraria, purple, blue, lilac.

Indigo-fera, in abundance.

Everlasting Flowers, (Helichrysum fætidum) white, small and large, yellow, large and small, pink and straw coloured.

Wild thyme, wormwood, balm, peppermint, tansey, camomile, sage, wood sorel.

Trifolium, white, pink, crimson, lilac, and blue.

Buttercups, white and yellow daisies, iris, white, blue, yellow.

Convolvolus major, lilac, scarlet, and white.

Crassula coccinea, blossoms white.

Gladiolus, white, lilac, pink, scarlet, pale blue.

Sandersonia aurantiaca.

Sebæa ambigua, geranium, scarlet, pink, ivy-leaved, and three small ground varieties.

Trachonanthus camphora, (aromatic shrub.)

Protea.   Coralodendrum (dwarf and giant.)

Brunsvigia multiflora, bulb. The bella donna, ditto.

Amaranthus tuber. The Palmiet, found on the bank of the Isixini river. The Todea Africana, or giant fern; the Zamia; the Schotia speciosa, or Boer-boontjes; Euphorbias; seventeen varieties—there are forty, in all, known.

Scarlet Antholyza. The Arum Lily; Lobelia pinafolia; Anemone Capensis; Metrosideros, or myrtle; Ixia; Scabious; Aloes; 7.

> Testudinaria elephantisses; Aristeas.
> Morea; Leonotis leonurus, purple and scarlet flowering shrubs on banks of the Gwaninza.
> Grasses.—1 Polypogon monspeliensis. 2 Cynodon Dactylon. 3 Andropogon hirtus. 4 Andropogon Allionii. 5 Cynosurus aureus. 6 Briza minor. 7 Briza maxima, &c., &c."

It is needless to multiply what could be found, in a sufficient number, to fill volumes. To the botanist, these regions are an interminable source of enjoyment, and present a field for research, the time required to investigate which would far exceed the limit of "three score years and ten." Nor is utility here excluded by beauty; for the herbal cures performed by the Kaffirs with ointments, poultices, and doses prepared from the roots, leaves, and flowers of these various plants, are as numerous as they are effective.

But not only do the trees and flowers, the the beasts, birds, and insects render this country picturesque and beautiful in the eyes of the traveller; but the landscape also is extremely interesting. Hundreds of miles are to be seen at one view, spreading out before the eye without the semblance of a fence, hedgerow, or enclosure, to intersect or divide the prospect into parallelograms, triangles, or squares, as in Europe. Nature, in this delightful region, is permitted to assume, at her will, the curved line of beauty, and only relinquishes it as she approaches the horizon; falling then, imperceptibly, into the horizontal plains of perspective distance.

Without the intense heat, or any of the other annoyances of *tropical* life, Kaffraria possesses all its charms. Insects and reptiles are certainly abundant, but, unless molested, they seldom approach the great lords of the creation. The climate is perfection; during the day the air being warm and genial, without oppression; at night, cool, balmy, and clear; and, in the morning, fresh and bracing.

The average range of the thermometer is from 58° to 78°. And if we connect with this, the enchantment of nature in her various grand, yet lovely forms; Flora, seen everywhere scattering blossoms around her; whilst the heavens, without a cloud to dim their clear azure face, are lit up by, and refract the light of, the sun in all his glory, we have then a true picture of the romantic earthly home of the Kaffirs.

We next turn our attention to the people themselves. These Ishmaelitish sons of Abraham now spread their habitations from the North-eastern boundary of the Cape Colony, to within a few miles of Delagoa Bay, on the North of the new Colony of Natal, in 26° South latitude. They are, without comparison, the most interesting of the South African tribes.

The traces of their early history in this continent are indistinct; and although tradition has merely taught them to point to the North-east, and say that their "*umkulumkula*" (God) came from there; yet the better confirmation of their origin is still existing in their continued and unwavering obedience to the usages of their forefathers. That origin, in common with many of the wandering tribes of Arabia, is, without doubt, derived from Ishmael the son of Abraham.

The twelve sons of Ishmael were the princes, or heads, of as many different families, and their descendants occupied a tract of country, extending from Havilah on the Euphrates, (which seems to have been a little below its junction with the Tigris,) to the wilderness of Shur, which forms a part of the isthmus of Suez.* In the progress of time, the several tribes of Ishmael's descendants would so increase, as to render an extension of country desirable, if not absolutely necessary. Accordingly, the more Eastern tribes would gradually pass down into Arabia; whilst the extreme Western ones descended to the Western shore of the Red Sea, whence they gradually spread themselves out

* Gen. xxv, 18.

to the West and South. Further, and successive emigrations would, doubtless, become necessary, for the same reason, as well as through the encroachments of other tribes; until, at length, they reached the several countries where they are now found, and where their migratory progress is finally stayed, by the advance, from the opposite direction, of another and more powerful emigration—the various European settlers.

Thus, at length, travelling in a different direction around the globe, the children of the freewoman have again met with those of the bondwoman. And, although the latter are found as they were left—cast out and forsaken, with "their hand against every man, and every man's hand against them"—yet they now have come together again as brethren, the younger holding out the promise to the elder! And so may it be, that, through the Kaffir Missions of the African Church, the two may become one—Jacob and Ishmael in their children may yet rise up, and worship together the God of Abraham.

In personal appearance the Kaffirs are handsome, stately, and imposing. Their height varies from five feet nine inches, to six feet two inches, the average being about five feet eleven. They are remarkable for symmetry of form, muscular development, and great strength. The lower limbs, however, are, from use, more developed than the arms, which, except in war, are left inactive and indolent. They enjoy robust health: sickness, disease, or deformity, being very rare amongst them. This is mainly attributable to the same cause which makes their teeth of such pearly whiteness, and perfect form and substance: viz, their use only of corn, vegetables, and milk in diet, and seldom masticating animal food; which is a luxury only indulged in on festal occasions, or during time of war. In bearing they are proud, haughty, and arrogant; they carry the head erect and thrown back; whilst their attitude is easy, graceful, and elegant. In form they are well proportioned; the head is large, but not disproportionate to the size of the body; the forehead is elevated and finely shaped. A phrenologist's opinion would, doubtless, be that the perceptive powers were good, although the reflective ones were not equally developed. Their hair, beard, and whiskers, are black and thick; and although not woolly and matted like the negro, yet not so flowing as the Arabs. Their eyes are keen, restless, and large, and they look you intently in the face, and appear to read your inmost thoughts. Their features are large and full, and vary throughout the different tribes; those in the Amampondo,

and many of the Amazulu tribes, being purely
Roman in profile; others, Grecian and handsome. Their teeth are their greatest beauty,
being white, regular, and large. They take great
care of these, always looking at them when
they obtain a mirror; and carefully washing
them after eating. Their chests and shoulders
are broad, square, and firmly set, and their
limbs are made in exact proportion.

The colour of their skin is of the darkest
brown, whilst its surface is rendered soft and
glossy by the frequent application of oil and
grease. They are very cleanly in their persons,
frequently bathing twice during the day, and
always once, and anointing after each bath.

The Kaffirs are certainly open to the accusa-
tion of vanity; being peculiarly sensitive to
flattery and praise, and even courting a compliment, by pretending to admire you first; and
then evidently feeling chagrined, when, in return, they are saluted (as is not unfrequently the
case with Europeans) by the polite rejoinder,
"Begone you ugly-looking Kaffir dog!" Such
joking, of a personal character, they neither understand nor tolerate, nor do they soon forget
an insult of this kind.

Their only article of clothing is the kaross.
This they wear around their bodies, in easy
and graceful folds, exactly similar, in the falls

of the drapery, to the ancient toga of the Romans.

They are fond of ornaments, and use them in great abundance; frequently wearing armlets composed of large brass rings, extending from the wrist to the elbow; as well as one large one of ivory, midway between that joint and the shoulder. They likewise use anklets of similar rings round the ankle joints, and another of their ingenious decorations consists of a girdle of brass rings. This they form from brass wire, which they buy from the traders by the yard; they cut it into half-inch lengths, beat it flat, and thus bend it into a multiplicity of minute rings, which they string on a piece of leather, or the sinew of an animal, and then tie them round their loins. To this girdle they append, over the left hip, their tobacco pouch, which is generally formed from the skin of some small animal, either a monkey, wild cat, or viverra.

These pouches, called by the Hottentots, "Dacgha-sacs," are the depositories for all their treasures; viz, money, tinder-box, knives, pipes and tobacco, kaross-needles, and the like. Their pipes are very handsome, and the manufacture of them does great credit to their ingenuity. They are formed of dark wood, cut into shape with the edge of their assegai or spear head. On the surface of the bowl, they then cut out several devices, either vandyke edging, animals, birds, or flowers; and, setting the pipe in sand, they run hot lead into the indentations, cutting and paring this with their knives, until the whole surface of the bowl is quite even; and by means of friction, against their hands and blanket, they succeed in giving it a brilliant polish. As articles of barbarous handicraft, these pipes (or as they are called, in Kaffir, "Inqunawa,") are very creditable to them. Having made them, they equally well understand the use of them: for they spend half the day lying, in indolent enjoyment, in front of their huts, smoking their tobacco, and watching their sleek and fat cattle grazing on the surrounding plains.

The narcotic weed is, as a necessary consequence, largely cultivated by them; but they now prefer it as manufactured in Europe. Cavendish tobacco is their favourite description, and this they solicit from every white man with whom they meet. So universal, indeed, has this custom of begging tobacco become, of late, amongst them, that the common salutation of every Kaffir now, through the Amakosa tribes, is, "Watoo Baas! Azali toobac" "Good day, master, give me a present of some tobacco!" and, amongst the Zulus, "Bona sacha inkose,

toobac!" "Good day, chief! give me tobacco!"

The habit of smoking, amongst these people,
is, however, by no means reprehensible; on the
contrary, during years of dearth and war, they,
doubtless, find it useful in alleviating hunger,
and soothing excitement. They are also very
fond of snuff, but this they use in a much more
cleanly manner than Europeans. Their snuff
boxes, which are ingeniously made, and are
of various forms and devices, have always
attached to them a picker, or long-pointed instrument, with which they stir the snuff, when
it becomes dry, or caked, and a spoon, made
of bone or ivory; called, in their phraseology,
"bodkins and lebakos." In the latter, they
raise the snuff to their nostrils, and, with the
edge of it, they also scrape away any particles
which may have adhered to the nose. A little
brush, which is also appended to the box,
then completes the operation, by being used to
follow the last office of the spoon.

One of their most ingenious methods of
making snuff boxes, is from blood. These they
call, in their language, "*Iquaka*." When preparing the skins of animals for karosses, the
process of tanning, or "*braeing*" them, as it
is called, being performed by stretching the skin,
or hide, tightly on the ground, and pegging it

around the edges, they afterwards, with the sharp edge of an assegai, go carefully over the surface, scraping away all the particles of skin, or meat, that may remain attached to it. These they mix with some of the blood of the animal, and pound into a thick paste, adding a little finely powdered red clay. Having worked this into a proper consistency, they next proceed to form, with their fingers, in clay, the model of some animal, generally an ox or a sheep; and, having moulded this to the size they wish their snuff box to be, and satisfied themselves as to the symmetry and resemblance of their quadruped to nature, they next place it in the sun, until it is baked perfectly hard. They then smear the paste which they have prepared, over the surface of this model; and, while it is soft, they go over it with the point of a needle, raising small portions of it, in imitation of the hair, or wool, of the animal, as the case may be. They then place it in the sun for two or three days, until it is again hard. When this has been attained, they cut a hole in the forehead of the mimic animal, about the size of a bullet; and, with the point of a long kaross-needle, or a pointed piece of bone, they pick out, through this cavity, the baked clay, on which the blood has been formed. This being finished and a grotesquely carved cork fitted

into the hole, their snuff box is completed.
They fasten their picker, spoon, and brush, together with a small chain, or thong of leather,
round the neck of the animal; and then sus-
pending it, by means of the latter, to their girdles, and keeping it well supplied with snuff,
they have frequent recourse to it, and by means
of the appendages already described, they supply, irritate, and finally cleanse their noses at
their pleasure.

In addition to their armlets, anklets, and girdle, they wear ear-rings and necklaces. The
former of these are usually made (except when
rings only) of quills, either from birds or porcu-
pines, with the tail-tuft of the Lepus-Capensis,
or Cape-hare, or that of the Jerboa, fastened as
a pendant from the points. Their necklaces are
varied: those usually worn amongst chiefs are
made from the teeth of the wolf or tiger; those
amongst the commoner people, from shells and
berries. They wear beads in great abundance,
strung round their necks, and hanging in long
bunches on their broad open chests; they also
append them to the "*nutche*," another of their
pendant ornaments.

Throughout the lower tribes they wear the
frontlet, which is a coronet formed of cowrie
shells, and worn round the head. Amongst
the Amazulus this is displaced by the coronal

or crown, into which they work their hair, standing erect on the head, to the height of about six inches.

These noble looking fellows do not require any appendages to shew off their fine muscular figures, although it cannot be said that they are not becoming to them. In their movements they are so graceful, agile, and easy that these ornaments do not appear as an encumbrance, but, as they are intended, an adornment.

In their hands they usually carry a bundle of seven assegais, and one or two thin herding rods : the former of these being their only warlike weapons, while the latter are used for driving their cattle. They also carry with them a "*knob-kerrie*," this is a stick about four feet in length, and an inch in diameter, terminated at one end by a knob or round ball. These are sometimes scooped out and the hole is filled with lead. They are usually formed from the young trees of the wild Kaffrarian olive, *(Olea berrucosa, or O. Ferruginea)* from the root of which they form the knob. They likewise use for this purpose the assegai wood, *(Curtisia Ferruginea)* and the Kaffrarian pear *(Pyrus Africana)*.

These weapons they employ for killing game or reptiles. Holding the thin end of the stick in their hand, and aiming at the object, they throw it, giving it, at the same time, a twirling motion, so as to make it revolve in the air, until the thin point strikes the ground first, a few feet short of the object, the knob thus being made to come in contact with it as it starts. They use this stick with great precision, seldom failing to strike what they aim at, and frequently killing a very small bird, snake, or animal, at an incredible distance. Unless, however, they have two "*kerries*" with them, they do not, generally, throw it at a snake, but reserve it in their hand till within reach of the reptile, and then, by one certain blow, they stun it.

They also use their "*kerries*" for a kind of manly exercise, similar to our old Saxon quarter-staff. For this purpose they employ two sticks; using one, held in their left hand, for parrying and guarding their adversary's blows; whilst, with another in their right, they vigorously attack and strike him. When well played, it is very graceful. Their principal offensive weapon, however, is the "*assegai*." This is a kind of thin light javelin, the blade of which is about half an inch wide, grooved similarly to the bayonet, the point very sharp, it also springs from a quadrangular iron shaft, which is barbed at the angles. These are set in a round wooden handle, of about half an inch in diameter, and are bound, at the junction, with the dried sinew or intestine of an animal. In length they are usually about five feet. One description, which they use for making their Karosses, baskets, bottles, pouches, &c., is quadrangular, and about the eight of an inch thick, coming to a very fine point. In another, the blade is broad, flat, and about fifteen inches long; being employed in hunting and killing game. A third has the blade smaller and narrower, but with a heavy barbed iron haft; this is used for stabbing, the latter portion of the weapon tearing and irritating the edge of the wound which the blade has made in passing into the body.

Such are the various forms and uses of these javelins, which form the exclusive Kaffrarian weapon in war, where fire-arms or gunpowder cannot be obtained.

In throwing the *assegai*, the Kaffirs display great dexterity. They take hold of it about the middle, between the thumb and the upper joints of the two first fingers of the right hand, the point being in front; they then raise the hand to the level of the shoulder, and, in drawing back the arm, they strike it against the wrist, thus causing it to vibrate. The effect of this is to give it a vibrating motion, whilst passing through the air, and by means of this to steady it in its course. Taking an exact aim at the object against which they wish to throw, they then impel it forward with the full force of their powerful arms; and seldom fail to strike surely. They do not poison them, and consequently their wounds are seldom fatal, except when they are inflicted by stabbing; and then, as their strokes are generally aimed at some vital part of the body, and repeated two or three times, they are certain messengers of death. They usually carry six or seven of these assegais in their hand, holding them at the end of their handles, over their left shoulders; they are thus very ornamental to their picturesque figures.

The Kaffirs dwell in tribes, over each of which an " *Ukumkani*," or king, presides; these being again sub-divided into petty-tribes, over each of which an " *Inkose Inkuli*," or petty chief, or, in the smaller ones, simply an " *Inkose*," or " captain of the kraal," bears sway.

Their tribal government is very complete, and their obedience, and attachment to their chiefs, praiseworthy and striking in the extreme. In the subdivisions, of the various branches, or tribes, of the Kaffir family; although often very numerous, they are always made in strict accordance with rule and order. And although, as a consequence of their number, the local laws for the domestic government of the various subdivisions become much diversified, yet they always own the sovereignty of the "*Ukumkani*" of their peculiar branch, and, with respect to war, in particular, are ever ready to obey his commands.

The great branches or tribes of the Kaffir family are as follows:—

Tribes.	*Ukumkani.*
The Amazulu	Panda
The Basutos	Moshesh
The Amampondo	} Faku
The Abatembu	
The Amaxosa	Kreli

Of these, the Amazulu dwell to the North of the New Colony of Natal; the Basutos reside in the interior of the South districts of the Continent, along the vicinity of the Dutch Free State; the Amampondo and Abatembu, under Faku, live along the Eastern coast, from the Southern boundaries of Natal to the Bashee river; whilst the Amaxosa tribes inhabit the whole of the frontier districts of the Old Colony, together with British Kaffraria.

These branches are subdivided again into smaller tribes: but, whilst each tribe owns the chieftainship of their own "*Inkose*" or leader, the leaders are all governed by the "*Ukumkani*" of the branch. Thus, for instance, amongst the Amaxosa Tribes, Kreli is the "*Ukumkani,*" and to him, therefore, the whole of the 90,000 Kaffirs of that tribe look as their king, and his war cry they obey. But yet, as regards the internal discipline, or interior economy of these, they are subdivided into *three* great sub-tribes; the Amagelika, the Amagaika, and the Ama T'Slambie; of which Kreli rules the Amagaika, Sandilli the Amagelika, and Umhalla the Ama T'Slambie. Each of these tribes numbers 25,000 or 30,000 souls; and amongst these portions, the power of their own "*Inkose Inkuli*" is paramount; whilst both the people and the "*Inkoses*" own the superior sway and sovereignty of Kreli, as the "*Ukumkani,*" or King. Thus, he is "*Ukumkani*" over 90,000, and "*Inkose Inkuli*" over 30,000.

Again, the tribes of the "*Inkuli*" are re-divided into smaller ones, over each of which a petty chief or "*Inkose*" rules. As, for instance, in Sandilli's Amagaika tribes, Tola, Anta, Boteman, Kama, and Swiani, respectively govern their "*kraals,*" or clans, each numbering, according to the importance of the "*Inkose,*" from a hundred to a thousand men. So, again, in Umhalla's Ama T'Slambie tribes, Pato, Cobus Congo, Tois, Delemma, and others, are captains of "*kraals,*" or petty chiefs; each ruling over from a hundred to two thousand Kaffirs.

THE KAFFIR CHIEF SWIANI, HIS TAMBOOKIE WIFE, COUNSELLOR, AND COUNSELLOR'S SON.

Page 212.

In enforcing their orders, and to aid them by their counsels in matters of difficulty, each chief is assisted and supported by ten counsellors, selected from the eldest, most experienced, and most acute of the tribe. These are called "*Pakati*," and always accompany the chief on expeditions of importance. They stand around and prompt him, by their counsel, at an interview with an embassy, and they usually spend most of their time in, or around, his hut. Some of these sages are very handsome, their hair and beards being quite grey, and figures bent with age; whilst the steady penetrating gaze, the piercing vivacity of their eyes, and the wonderful craft and practised cunning, with which they are ready, at any emergency, to help their "*Inkose*," shews how deservedly they occupy the positions of honor which they fill. In the counsels of the Kaffirs, ability and talent are quite as common, and are esteemed quite as important as power or wealth, as qualifications for their barbarous statesmen.

Their laws of tribal government are most remarkable, being purely monarchial and conservative in their code. And, wild and barbarous as these people are, their political arrangements, adopted from the expediency of barbarism, bear a most striking similarity to the more civilized polity; which, for so many years past, has governed our own land; and which, nevertheless, we seem to find so many willing to aid, at the present time, in undermining and deprecating as unsound.

Their habits of life are purely pastoral, they are also entirely a nomadic race, wandering from hill to hill, in quest of fresh pasturage for their vast herds of cattle.

Their principal riches consist in oxen; and the dignity of the chief, as well as the importance of the commoner, are both alike estimated by the number of cattle each possess. The dowry of the wife is also paid in cattle. The redemption of a pledge; the fine for a crime, or misdemeanour; and the principal transactions of barter and commerce are all in cattle.

The care of the cattle and dairy is the highest post of honor amongst them, and this is always allotted to the men. They milk the cows; herd the oxen; and keep the "*kraals*" or cattle yards. The women are never (under the pain of heavy chastisement) permitted to touch a beast: even the young calves and heifers are tended by the lads and boys, and should a woman or girl be found in or near the cattle, she is severely beaten.

A curious custom prevails amongst them in connection with this usage. If a woman has necessity to enter a cattle "*kraal*," she is obliged if married, to bring her husband with her, or nearest male relative, if not, to the gate of the enclosure. He then lays his assegai on the ground, the point being inside the entrance, and the woman walks in on the handle of the weapon. This is considered as a passport of entrance, and saves her from punishment: but, even in this case, strict inquiry is made as to the necessity for such an entrance, nor are the men very willing to grant, too frequently, such an indulgence to them.

Their breeds of cattle are varied but fine; being usually small and compact in shape, with wide branching horns. They are trained early, and answer to the names by which they are all designated. This usage of calling their oxen *by name*, is of universal occurrence throughout Africa. Thus the Dutch waggon drivers of the Colony, have a different name for each beast in their huge teams. They also take care to shew their nationality of disposition by naming the worst, and laziest, of them, "England," and " Englishmen;" and, by unexceptionable rule, the unhappy quadrupeds who receive these titles, receive an extra amount of flagellation; becoming the recipients of many a stray lash from their unmerciful two-handed whips.

The Kaffir mode of herding their cattle is peculiar; exemplifying the Eastern habits of the shepherds of Palestine.   In times of peace they always lead their herds—a trained ox following the Kaffir wherever he strays through the pastures, while the others are taught to follow him.   Beside the chief herd, there are usually one or two assistants, who carry long " herding rods," with which they keep the cattle together and stimulate the lazy.   In times of war, or danger, however, their mode of procedure is altogether changed; and then, whilst the chief herd changes his position from the front to the rear, driving instead of leading, the number of these assistant herds is materially augmented, their occupation now being to goad the outside beasts, and keep them compactly together.   In this manner they drive, with the greatest dexterity, vast herds, consisting of several thousand heads, many miles through the most difficult defiles of their mountain fastnesses.   Nor can this custom be witnessed by a student of Holy Scripture, without his being forcibly impressed with the remarkable coincidence it has with that description of the "Good Shepherd" which is given to us in St. John's Gospel, Chap. x, verses 1—16.

Besides using their cattle for food and draught, they also ride them; and are very dexterous in their management of them.   For this purpose, they select the strongest and fleetest cattle, and by boring a hole, when young, through the cartilage of the nostril, they insert a thong of leather or a "*reim*" as it is called, into their nose. This is drawn tight by the means of a noose, and then, holding the other end of this "*reim*" in their left hand, and aiding the progress of the beast with a thick stick, held in their right, they gallop at a furious pace over the hills.

This is a very favourite occupation amongst all their tribes; and *cattle races* form one of their most frequent and exhilirating pastimes. These they find beneficial both to train early their boys in riding, and their cattle in running: so that, in the case of any emergency of war, or otherwise, they may be able easily to remove themselves, and their herds, from one locality to another in a short space of time.

In connection with their cattle, their dairy arrangements may be mentioned as singular. Milk forming the principal article of food which they employ during times of peace, the care of it is amongst their daily avocations. Cows are esteemed very valuable by them, and are very carefully tended. One of their customs is to turn the cattle out at daylight, and allow them to graze until noon; they then drive them into the "*kraal*," and the hind legs of the cows being tightly tied with a "*reim*" of leather, the calves are brought to them and allowed to suck them for a minute or so, being then driven off amidst great clamour, the process of milking commences, which is always performed by men.

The milk is caught in baskets, made of plaited grass, ingeniously worked by the women so as to be quite waterproof. The milking being finished, the legs of the cows are loosened, and their teats become the contested property of the little Kaffir boys and the calves. It is very amusing to witness these contests, the little urchins holding the teats by one hand into their mouths, and striking the faces of the calves with the other; their resistance is generally useless, however, and the latter finally get undisturbed possession after a few moments.

The milk is brought by each Kaffir to the dairy hut of the village; and a man, specially appointed for the purpose, receives into the "*milk-sac*" (a large bottle made of leather, from the skin of a calf or sheep) the contents of the various baskets; whilst from a second bottle, which contains the milk of the preceeding day, he distributes to each Kaffir the same quantity of sour or curded milk as he brings in of sweet. On this curded milk, he and his family live, an equal share being given, in rotation, to every member of his family, to whom it is served, in large carved spoons, made of wood, the bowls of which contain a large tea-cupful.

When the baskets have been emptied, they are ranged in rows on the ground, and the half-starved dogs* of the *"kraal"* or village, then thrust their lean heads into them, and lick them dry. This process is considered amply sufficient for cleansing, so that they are then placed aside until next required.

Their use of curded, instead of sweet milk in their food, is founded on experience, the most violent internal inflamation being rapidly engendered, in that country, by the indiscriminate use of sweet milk.

In their domestic customs, the women merely perform the menial offices, and work in the fields at digging, hoeing, carrying water, &c., and other like occupations. They are kept in complete subjection, and are cruelly beaten for every supposed offence. Notwithstanding this harsh and rude treatment, they are apparently happy, joyous creatures, and make the village resound with their merry laughing and incessant gossiping. They are quite as fond of smoking and taking snuff as the men, and their hearts are as easily bought by a pipeful of tobacco, as by flattery; to which they are quite as sensitive as their fairer sisters of Europe.

* The Dutch Wilde-Honde.

They are extravagantly fond of ornaments, and cover their arms and necks with rings and beads; all wearing ear-rings as well as anklets.

In form, they are symmetrically made, although always tending to obesity; and the paucity of clothing employed by them, causes the breasts, in middle life, to become elongated to an extraordinary extent, reaching quite to the hips; the effect of witnessing this is, at first, rather unpleasing to Europeans; but, like many other things of a similar character, their eyes soon become as accustomed to it as those of the Kaffirs themselves.

In nursing their little ones, this extraordinary elongation of the breasts, is, however, brought into account; for as the "*picinini*" or infant is always carried on its mother's back, finding a seat at the extremity of the spine, of a less fictitious and more substantial character than would be the case with European mothers; so when the cravings of hunger render it troublesome to her, the mother immediately passes her personal "*milk-sac*" under her arm, and, giving it a gentle pressure between her side and elbow, thus alleviates the sufferings, supplies the wants, and calms the cries of her child. Or when the "*picinini*" becomes old enough to sit up erect, then, instead of passing it under her arm, the mother throws the "*milk-sac*" over her shoulder, and the child seizing it, with avidity, with both its hands, and tugging at it with all its might, is thus kept at rest, and its appetite amply appeased.

Several of the women have very handsome faces; their arms and lower limbs are perfect in mould and proportions. They usually wear a handkerchief, of some bright colour, bound round their heads. Around the neck they wear a string, from which is suspended a fringe of beadwork, which falls over the breasts, and hangs as low as the loins, called in the Kaffir tongue "*amecklāte.*" Around their waists they always have a "*kaross*" or skin fastened, and, under this, they wear the "*encyēes,*" answering to the "*nūtchie*" in the men; whilst out of their hut or village, they are never seen without a cloak of hide. This is usually adorned with stripes of leather, about four feet long and three inches wide, from which they append rows of brass buttons, usually attaching a button for each ox that their husband has in his "*kraal;*" and thus ostentatiously proclaiming their wealth and consequence.

Polygamy is universally practised among these people, each Kaffir generally possessing four or five wives. This, and the early mingling of the sexes, together with the little heed paid to external forms, tends much, it is to be feared, to make their morality of a very lax and debased description. The age of puberty with boys is fourteen, with girls, twelve. Still considering the great disadvantages under which these wild and untutored daughters of Eve labour, they even now possess an interesting, confiding manner, which induces one to believe, that if the influence of civilization and religion could but be brought to bear upon them, they would be one of the most peculiarly interesting races of barbarians to be met with, in the universe.

Their mode of life is quite as barbarous as their dwellings are unique. They dwell in " *kraals*" or villages, which consist of an enclosure for their cattle, usually surrounded by brambles and bushes, heaped together in a kind of circular hedge, and enclosing an area of several yards in circumference. Into this they drive their cattle at night, and, to protect them from the attacks of wild beasts, they build their huts in rows around the outside of this enclosure. Thus the word " *kraal*," in their language, is used, by general acceptance, to denote a " Kaffir village," but, strictly speaking, it means " an enclosure for cattle."

Their huts are like gigantic beehives. They are formed by sinking a number of long flexible rods or stakes, about fifteen or twenty feet long, into the ground in a circle, the diameter of which is usually about twenty feet. These having been firmly fixed into the earth, they are bent over at the top, and tied together. They next procure a number of thin thatching rods, and tie them round the frame-work, at intervals of about a foot apart; and on this skeleton they place bundles of grass, and sew it down with "*reims*" of leather. On the outside they fasten similar rods, so as to keep the grass firm; then smearing the floor with cowdung, and allowing it to dry thoroughly, their house is completed.

They enter by means of a small aperture which they leave in the side, about three feet high and two feet wide, and which serves the treble purpose of door, window, and chimney. They place a large earthen pan in the centre of the floor, and on this they burn their fire, spreading around it their mats and skins, on which they sit and smoke, by day, and sleep, by night, to the number of about twenty or thirty in each hut.

Their mats, baskets, earthenware pots, pans, "*milk-sacs*," or bottles, beadwork bracelets, anklets, &c., are all the work of the women. Whilst pipes, snuff-boxes, "assegais," "knob-kerries," "karosses," girdles, "nutchies," spoons, and other like articles, form the employment of the men; and in the manufacture of these articles they while away the hours, when they are confined within the doors of their huts by rain or cold winds.

In fine weather the men are engaged in the care of the cattle, and athletic sports and occupations, and the women in working in the fields, commingled with gossiping, singing, and merry-making.

They are, universally throughout both sexes, an indolent, cheerful, heedless people. They have few cares, and they do not allow sorrow to bend them. They live for the present, and beyond it they seldom look or think. The past they seem to think as little of as possible, and the future they banish altogether from their minds.

Cruel, revengeful, and savage, when their passions are excited, they are indolent, joyous, and merry, in their hours of recreation. Hospitable and generous to all, they expect the same from others, and if they do not receive it they are disappointed. Many of the vices of a vitiated nature they possess, but they are not altogether devoid of the few remaining sparks of virtue.

Everything connected with them encourages the hope, that if their hearts, as a nation, be opened and softened by God's grace, to receive, with acceptance, the ennobling truths of His religion, they may eventually shine as one of the most elegant and refined of the human races.

They are passionately fond of music, and possess considerable talent in acquiring tune, and appreciating harmony.

Their instrumental attempts are, of course, rude and untutored, although the strains are melodious and sweet. Their principal instrument, the "*gorrah*," is made of knotched reeds, the sinew of an animal being stretched tightly across them. The instrument being put in motion, and kept vibrating in the wind, makes a kind of humming sound; whilst the strings are struck with the hand, and kept in time to their voices. These are naturally sweet and deep, and their singing partakes more of the character of chanting than of singing. They are pleased, however, with listening to the performances of others, some being even moved to tears by the solemn strains of sacred melody.

Besides the refinements of life, they also cultivate the useful arts, manufacturing their "*assegais*" from native iron, and several of their ornaments from indigenous copper. Whilst in Natal we inspected a specimen of copper ore, smelted in a rude manner by the Kaffirs, near St. Lucia's Bay, in the Zulu country. The ore found in that neighbourhood was remarkably fine, and was reported as being in great abundance. Some jealousy was manifested by the Kaffirs, in concealing the lode ; but of its existence there could be no doubt. The ore must be very pure, considering the defective means of smelting ; for the specimen, with the exception of a speck or two, which had the appearance of lead or silver, and the particles of charcoal which had been embedded in it during the process, was a mass of pure copper.

From a similar specimen to this, they had manufactured some large rings for their arms and ankles. The heads of their "*assegais*" beaten out from iron, which abounds throughout the country, are smelted and worked, by themselves, in the interior districts, with great dexterity.

To illustrate their manufacture, we may here insert a brief account of a visit to a native blacksmith's forge, amongst the Amazula tribes of Kaffirs, by some officers of the 45th regiment, whilst at Natal.

The workmen were busily engaged in the formation of "*assegais;*" the work being carried on by the side of a little stream, so that the metal, when hot, might be plunged into the water as required.

The anvil was a large flat piece of stone, similar to those found everywhere through Kaf-

Kaffir Blacksmith at Work at his Forge.

Page 227.

firland, being composed of hard trap rock. The Kaffir smith heated the iron, and worked it with a small rude hammer, and a pair of pincers. When heavier blows were required, his assistant used a large stone, in lieu of a sledge hammer.

The fire was built against the side of a large ant-heap, at the end of a tunnel, which was bored through it. Into the other end of this little tube the noses of the native bellows were inserted; these latter articles consisting of two large bags made of ox-hide, a bullock's horn being fastened to the bottom corner of each bag, through which, the air caught in the bags was forced. The mode of inflating the bags was very ingenious. Along the top of each, which is left open, two sticks are attached, parallel to each other. The man working the bellows, having his fingers connected with one of these sticks, and his thumb with the other, by then opening and closing his hand, opens and shuts the mouth of the bag, which is on a similar principle to the clap-net of an entomologist. As the Kaffir raises the bags, he opens his hand to admit the air, and closing it as he presses the bag down again, he thus forces the current of air, through the bullock's horn at the bottom, into the tunnel, and from thence through the fire.

In this manner, by means of two bags, one of which the operator holds in each hand, and stands between, working them alternately, he is easily enabled to keep up a strong and regular current of air; which is quite equal in force to that produced by bellows of European manufacture; and thus he maintains an equable heat in the furnace. The fuel is composed of charcoal made from wood, baskets full of which are continually being brought up, by the women, from the neighbouring huts. The metal article when made, was immediately immersed in the water, which ran adjacent.

The surgery and medical knowledge of the Kaffirs is very effective and ingenious; though equally rude and untutored.

For instance, their mode of cupping is simple but very efficacious, and they very judiciously use it as a remedy. It may be described as follows :—

They first raise the skin with the point of a bodkin, or "*kaross needle*," at the spot where they wish to operate. They then, with a very sharp knife, make an incision in the flesh at each side of the needle, about half an inch long: between these they apply the end of a cow's horn, and by pressing it firmly against the part, and sucking through a little hole made in the point of the horn, they thus succeed in drawing in the flesh, and forcing out the blood more effectually and profusely, than a European surgeon does by his regular cupping glass and lancets.

Their knowledge of the medicinal properties of the various trees, plants, and roots, which grow in their country is very extensive.

The juice of the various species of the euphorbia they use as blisters, puncturing the skin with the point of an " *assegai*," and then rubbing in the juice; which, producing a kind of open running ulcer, answers the purpose of an English blister.

Aloes again they use largely, and the leaves and roots of several aromatic shrubs they employ as restoratives, in cases of exhaustion. Their wonderful effect we can vouch for, from personal experience. The author once fording the Great Kei river when swollen, in company with a Kaffir, was carried down the torrent, and with very great difficulty saved his own life and that of the horse, which rescue was mainly accomplished by the assistance of the Kaffir's presence of mind and activity. After the danger was past, and both man and beast lay on the opposite bank perfectly exhausted, his companion instantly disappeared in the bush, and, after searching for a few moments, returned with a quantity of leaves and bark in his arms. These he rubbed violently between his hands for a few seconds, and then applied them to the nose, and to that of the horse. The effect was instantaneous in reviving us, and, in a few minutes, we were both able to accompany him, and rode eleven miles on the same evening to the Kaffir *"kraal"* where we slept.

The poisons which they use, and thoroughly understand, are also extracted from various plants growing in Kaffirland, and which principally belong to the Daphne tribe. The effect of them upon the human frame is to cause violent thirst, swelling of the tongue, mouth, and throat; and, finally, congestion and death.

The umzumbeite wood is also highly prized amongst them, both as a superstitious charm against witchcraft, and as a cure for head-ache. They use it for the latter purpose ground into snuff. It is then aromatic in perfume, and acts as a powerful astringent. It grows a large spreading and handsome timber tree, and is principally found along the banks of the Umzumvubo river, between British Kaffraria and Natal.

In intellect, ingenuity, and acuteness of observation, the Kaffirs, both men and women, are surpassed by none; whilst many of the traits of their character and dispositions are ennobling and winning. They have a peculiar sense and appreciation of justice, which is very remarkable. They receive anger and abuse unmurmuringly, if they are in the wrong, or if they have justly given you cause to be angry with them On the other hand, if they are accused falsely, and fault is found with them, without sufficient reason, they then *never* forgive or forget what they consider an injury; but will resent and revenge it months and years afterwards.

In disposition they are very liberal, generous, and hospitable. As a proof of this assertion, we may simply enumerate an instance which came under the notice of the Author.

A Kaffir once came and begged some food, saying that he was "*Bania Lambelie*," i. e. "very hungry." He was given a sixpenny loaf of brown bread, a gift which he received with great thankfulness, and, putting it under his blanket, went away. Anxious to see what he would do with it, he was watched; when he was observed to go to a group of Kaffirs, who, close by, were awaiting his return, and, sitting down amongst them, he divided the loaf, with a knife, *into eight equal shares*, sharing it with them; the party consisting of four men, two women, a boy, and himself. On further enquiry it was satisfactorily ascertained that this poor fellow had partaken of no food himself for upwards of twenty-four hours.

"Blessed are the merciful, for they shall obtain mercy."

From a Kaffir, (if he has to give,) no one ever solicits aid in vain. Hospitable to a fault, they make the arrival of a stranger or guest the immediate excuse for feasting and dancing.

One of the most elegant and refined usages amongst them, is connected with their hospitality; this is their custom of immediately presenting the guest on his arrival, with an ox or goat, who, unable, of course, to use the whole himself, is obliged to solicit his hosts to share it with him, and thus the sentiment and compliment is elegantly implied that he, instead of being the recipient of hospitality, at once becomes the dispenser of the viands, and is transformed from guest to host. As during, war, these people are cruel, vindictive, and implacable foes; so, in times of peace, they are worthy objects of much admiration.

In many respects, indeed, their savage and barbarous virtues shame and put to blush the better knowledge of Christian nations. Let us not neglect them then, (for despise them we dare not) now that God has brought them into contact with us; but, while we admire their near

approach to perfection, even in their wild untutored state, let us see, in them, the most
interesting and promising objects for the reception and exemplification of that more exalted, and new, nature, which we have learnt
under the better dispensation of the Lord Jesus
Christ, "the Saviour of all men, and specially
of them that believe."

PORTRAIT OF THE KAFFIR NANA.*

* He belonged to Tois' tribe, and was the first Kaffir tried by
martial law: he was tried for murder, for killing his nephew, Swe-
leka, found gnilty, and sentenced to death. Sir H. Smith, however,
commuted the sentence to transportation for life.

CHAPTER IX.

THE KAFFIR LANGUAGE, LAWS, SUPERSTITIONS, TRADITIONS, TRACES OF RELIGION, SACRIFICE, PROPHETS, MOSAIC NAMES AND CUSTOMS, PATRIARCHAL HABITS, ISHMAELITISH USAGES, CIRCUMCISION, AND INFERENCES TO BE DRAWN FROM THE CONNECTION BETWEEN THEM AND SCRIPTURE INFORMATION.

AMONGST barbarous tribes no language is to be found superior to the Kaffir, in precision of expression, order, regularity, and system. It is beautifully soft and melodious in sound, and more resembles the modern Italian, in this respect, than any other known. It is usually spoken very slowly by the natives; their enunciation being distinct, and their musical and pleasing voices being modulated by the use of well-timed cadences and pauses.

It is also worthy of remark, that, as an invariable rule, this language is correctly spoken by *every* class of the community; which is perhaps not the case with *any* of our European tongues. As a general rule, a Kaffir will never be heard using an ungrammatical expression; and, not only so; but they always connect together their words and sentences in such a manner, as to preserve the proper system of alliteration, throughout the same proposition.

In the formation of the Kaffir dialect, much of its admired softness and melody is produced by the multiplicity of vowels that are used.

A universal rule, to which there are but *eighteen* known exceptions throughout the whole language, obliges *every syllable to end with a vowel;* this of course secures, to all its words, a peculiar harmony of sound. The only usage in it which tends to mar this softness, is the use of the "clicks." These, which are peculiar sounds given to the pronounciation of the three letters c, q, and x, seem to have been derived from the Hottentot dialects, throughout which they abound, more than as having any actual root or origin in the Kaffir language itself.

Even the harshness of these disagreeable sounds is somewhat modified by the melody of the Kaffirs' voices, and their mode of enunciation; whilst, in the Hottentot tongue, they are most repulsive.

The letter c forms the *dental* click, and is emitted by placing the point of the tongue against the front teeth, and then withdrawing it smartly.

Q is designated the *palatal* click, and is sounded by pressing the tongue against the roof of the mouth, and then quickly drawing it downwards.

The last or *lateral* click x, is articulated by

means of compressing the tongue and side teeth together.

The fluent use of these sounds, is most difficult of acquisition by Europeans, and at the best, they always give their speaking the impression of stammering.

In the orthographical construction, the formation of the words is worthy of note. They generally consist of *a root*, which contains the leading or fundamental idea, and of a *prefix* which is indicative of a *specific relation to the general principle of the euphonic concord*, and includes some accessory idea, more or less distinct, this modifying the radical one, according to the perfect idea intended to be represented.

The use of the prefix is a singular peculiarity in this language, influencing its whole grammatical construction. For while, in all European and Asiatic languages, a harmony of *gender* and *number*, and, in some, a harmony also of *case* is essential to the agreements of many of the parts of speech; in the Kaffir tongue, the whole construction is regulated by a totally different principle. This has been named by Mr. Boyce, *the euphonic concord;* the chief characteristic of which, is, "*that all the grammatical variations of form, are effected by means of prefixes*, which evolve a regular and uniform system of alliteration."

The *noun* here takes the lead, as upon the prefix of this, depends the particular form of most words which are subject to grammatical government. Each of these prefixes has its corresponding euphonic letter or letters, as also its own form of the adjective, pronoun, and verb.

Consequently, the alliteration of harmony between the nominal and other prefixes, is the essential thing in the construction of Kaffir propositions.

The ignorance of this peculiarity, which existed until lately, formed the main difficulty, to Europeans, in mastering the Kaffir language. And naturally so; for, when such total disregard appeared to be paid to *gender* and *number*, it was hard to understand its construction.

For instance, if one were speaking in English of *a man*, the pronoun *he* would be employed; if of *a girl, she;* and if of a house, *it;* while in the Kaffir, *Yona* would be used with all, that being the corresponding pronoun to the prefix *in*, which, by reason of their forms, would be used with each of the Kaffir words employed to express, man, girl, and house.*

* The prefix *Ama*, which takes also the forms of *Aba, Ba, Be*, &c., in the Kaffir language, marks the plural number; while the prefix *umu*, which appears also in the forms, *um, mu, mo*, &c., denotes the singular. Thus a single individual of the Be-chuana people is expressed by *Mo*-chuana, and their language is the Se-chuana; *Se*

The *modification* of some of these prefixes, especially the nominal ones, which frequently occur, thus merges this principle of *formation* into that of *composition*. Hence ideas considerably modified and extended, are often expressed in the united and compact form of a *single word*. Essentially, therefore, the Kaffir language is a *polysyllabic* one, the occurrence of monosyllables, either in words or roots, being comparatively rare.

Another most singular and unique idiom, in this language is, that the women have many words peculiar to themselves, arising from a national custom among them, called "*upuhlonipa.*"

This forbids a woman to pronounce any word in the expression of her ideas, which may happen to contain a sound similar to any in the names of their nearest male relatives. This usage, as may readily be supposed, occasions a very great difficulty in interpretation; for no

being the prefix used to denote *possession*. And this is the characteristic peculiarity of the Kaffir and its family of languages, that the dependency of words one upon the other, and their inflexions of number, case, and tense, are expressed not, as in the European languages, by changes of termination, but by means of certain *prefixes* which all depend upon that of the noun, or nominative of the sentence. Each noun takes its proper prefix, corresponding to its form and character, according to rule; and the other words, which depend upon it, take their prefixes with reference to *that*, and so as to produce a curious kind of *alliteration* with it.

E. G. Kose, is *Chief*, *in*-Kose *in*-Kulu, is *great Chief*.

definite rules can be given for the formation of these substituted words, nor is it possible to form a dictionary of them, their number being so great, and by reason of there being many women even in the same tribe, who would be no more at liberty to use the substitutes employed by some others conversing with them, than they are to use the original and forbidden words themselves.

The use of *metaphor* and *allegory* is very extensive, whilst the richness and expressive significance of the *types* and *figures* which they employ are striking. For instance, "to smell out," in Kaffir phraseology, means "to discover," "to eat up;" is "to kill." "*Dhlelana*," to eat together, is used invariably to denote "being on terms of intercourse." A few others we may subjoin:—

Kaffir Word.	*Literal Meaning.*	*Used For.*
Ihlati	a bush	a refugee
Ingcala	flying out	uncommon dexterity.
Umkonto	an assegai	anything valuable
Inja	a dog	a dependent
Jeka	to take	to marry
Hlala	to sit	to dwell, or continue

So "to sit still," is a Kaffir metaphor for being at peace. "To be your dog," denotes "I am ready to follow you, or obey you."

This language is wholly without a literature, being purely colloquial; but, as such, it is perfect and pure. Its origin is unknown; but several of the derivatives of the words are easily traceable to the Arabic and Hebrew tongues. The "*Awa*" Yes is used alike by Arabs and Kaffirs. So also "*Aie*" No.

Kafr itself is a word of Arabic root. "It is therefore very reasonable to expect," to use the words of Mr. Appleyard; "that a traveller, tolerably conversant with the language and customs of the Kaffirs, would be able to throw a considerable degree of light upon the origin of this language and people, as well as their past migratory movements, by a journey through the numerous tribes which lie between the river Nile and the Red Sea, and skirt the Southern parts of Abyssinia. On many accounts there are good grounds for believing that they were of Ishmaelitish descent; and, consequently, that they are of the same origin as many of the tribes of Arabia."

Ere concluding this notice of their language, it may not be wholly uninteresting to the curious, to insert here a few specimens of it. We consequently give a few common-place sentences of every-day occurrence, which will serve to exhibit its singular melody of sound, and the peculiarities of its construction.

"*Indoda i m yekile*," or "*I m lahlile umfazi wayo.*"   The man has abandoned his wife.

"*Imazi i yi bakule iknonyana yago.*"   The cow has abandoned her calf.

"*Asi nokuba u senga kade.*"   What a long while you are about milking.

"*U qondile je into u favele ukw' enza yona, uyakw' enjenjalo ke.*"   Now that you understand what you ought to do, will you act accordingly.

"*Yenge into ukuteta yenge into ukwenza.*"   It is one thing to talk, and another to do.

"*Maku be jingoko u fun ukuba ku be jalo.*"   Let it be as you like.

"*Aku fanele abakonzi ukuba ba kauyeze inkose zabo.*"   It becomes not servants to contradict their masters.

"*U katalelanina le' nto inga lungi kuwenje?*"   Why do you concern yourself with what does not belong to you?

"*Ingati ukuba ayinauga namhla ine gomso.*"   It will rain either to-day or to-morrow.

"*Kude Kunyakananina ukusuku erini ukuya Esinqenqeni?*"   How far is it from Graham's Town to Fort Beaufort.

"*Untsuku 'ngapina enjleleni?*"   How long have you been on the path?

"*Disi hlabile isaujla gesitshetshi.*"   I have run the knife into my hand.

"*Guye yedwa ouga yeuzayo.*" He only can do it.

"*Di swele ihashe.*" I am in need of a horse.

"*Doya aku buya yena. Nykauya ninima?*" I will go when he returns. When will you go?

"*Ilanga liya tshona.*" The sun is going down.

"*Inkliziyo yam izele hisizi.*" My heart is full of grief.

"*Uku bona.*" To see. "*Umtu wasema Xoseni.*" A man of Kaffirland.

"*Roda, wetu.*" Farewell, friend.

The laws of the Kaffirs next come before our notice. Of these, little is known, except as far as the general fundamental principles. As has already been observed, these are founded on a purely monarchial and conservative basis. The power of the "*ukumkani*" or king, is absolute; and, in the Amazula tribes, this amounts to a tyranical despotism.

Amongst the lower or frontier Kaffirs, the multiplicity of tribes is of comparatively modern date, and this has mainly arisen from the supposed importance given to certain petty chiefs by the Europeans, generally through ignorance. Amongst the Amazulus, no such distinctions are understood, and each petty chief is ranked, and employed simply as a general, under the one great paramount king Panda.

It was also a part of the policy adopted, some years ago, by Sir Benjamin D'Urban, when governor at the Cape, to try and subdivide the large tribes of Kaffirs into smaller ones, and then to endeavour to set these at variance amongst themselves; the supposition being that "a house divided against itself cannot stand." This further tended to increase the number of chiefs, whose tribes and divisions are now so puzzling and multitudinous to the comprehensions of Europeans.

The enforcement of law, however, and the unflinching obedience given, universally, throughout all the tribes, to the "*ukumkani*" is very remarkable; he alone having the power of life and death, and no "*inkose*" or petty captain being permitted to punish with death without his mandate so to do.

There is a singularly perfect chain of responsibility running throughout the tribes; the "*pakati*" or counsellors being answerable to their "*inkose*," and the "*inkose*" to the "*ukumkani*."

Disobedience is punished most severely, whether it be shown by the Kaffir to the orders of his chief, or by the child to its parent; whilst punishment for it is taken, by all amongst them, without a murmur.

Their laws respecting hospitality are very

strict, and the breach of them is summarily punished. If a demand made for hospitality be rejected by a Kaffir, and complaint of his refusal be made to the "*inkose inkulu*" of the tribes to which he belongs; a court of the "*amapakati*" is instantly assembled, the case is tried, and if found guilty, the captain of that "*kraal*" or village is at once fined in cattle. A portion of the mulct goes, as is generally the case, to the chief, and the remainder is given to the person who demanded the hospitality as the party aggrieved.

We here subjoin a sketch of the ethnology of the Amazulu tribes of Natal, as given by Mr. Fynn, the oldest English resident in Kaffirland, and the best informed with respect to Kaffir law and customs.

"As the native tribes are now very numerous —in explaining the government of a tribe, I shall confine myself chiefly to the mode in which affairs were conducted in the Zulu nation during the reign of Chaka—showing what was the practice of the most powerful tribe ever known to have existed; it will therefore be understood, that if the same customs do not now prevail among the smaller tribes, it is simply because their organization is less complete.

"The followers of a Chief, while in attendance upon him at his kraal, are generally designated "*amapakati*," or, as understood by Europeans, counsellors. This is an incorrect interpretation, though it is now so rendered by the frontier Kaffirs. "*Pakati*" simply means within, and "*amapakati*" is understood to signify those who are at the time within the chief's circle. To prove clearly that "*umpakati*" does not mean a counsellor or adviser, every man and boy who is in the chief's circle is called an "*umpakati.*"

"It has been shown, that the Chief is generally surrounded by an important portion of his tribe. He mostly occupies each day with his "*amapakati*," the topics of the times engage their attention, trials of criminal and civil cases, occupying also a portion of their time. These trials may correctly be said to be conducted in open court; for, as there are no professional lawyers, every "*umpakati*" may freely enter into the case under investigation. And, from the ridicule which would result from any interference of an "*umpakati*," incompetent to argue on the case, it seldom happens that any display of incompetency occurs. Thus the chief's residence may be appropriately termed the school where law is taught, and its rules transmitted from one generation to another.

"On examining, thoroughly, the nature of the penalties awarded to crimes by Kaffirs, in their purely native condition, it will be clearly seen that crimes are not encouraged by them, or regarded as virtues.

" As a general rule, Kaffir crimes are punished with fine or death, and confiscation.

" Death, and confiscation of property, follows commission of what, in their estimation, are the greater crimes, and, while it is most wantonly inflicted on the innocent, it still stands good, that what they regard as serious offences, are severely punished. Fines and confiscations are awarded to distinct kinds of offences :—

1. As damages claimable by private individuals, an evil doer is compelled to make restitution by payment of cattle, as in our civil cases.

2. Fines for public offences. This is the main source of the chief's revenue.

" Cupidity, which is a strongly developed feature of the Kaffir character, will not permit either the chief, or those who surround him, and between whom the fine is generally distributed, to forego the advantage to be derived from the infliction of heavy fines; so that offenders have but a small chance of escape.

" The crimes, common with Kaffirs, are peculiar to them as an uncivilized people; while there are many crimes, practised among civilized nations, which do not occur among them.

" The enlightened, and the unenlightened, regard crimes with very different feelings, and from a combination of causes, punish them in different ways.

"When a chief, or a parent, is murdered, death is usually the punishment; but, in other cases, a fine is only levied, which is so light a punishment for such a grave offence, that I cannot approve of it. I am, however, of opinion that murders are not oftener committed, because the punishment is light.

"Death was the penalty attached to the crime of a follower deserting his own chief, to join a neighbouring one. This apparent severity was necessary for the safety of the state.

"No chief could maintain his rank and power, by resting solely on his hereditary claim. He could be secure, and great, only in proportion to the number of his men, or his ability to maintain his position, and protect the cattle of his tribe, from the inroads of his neighbours. The desertion of one or more of his followers endangered, in a greater or less degree, the safety of the whole tribe; not merely by adding so much to the strength of his neighbour, but from the amount also of valuable information he could communicate to him.

"The circumstances of the native tribes living in this district, having been so materially altered, by living in a state of peaceful prosperity, under British protection, the punishment for such an offence no longer remains among them, as the necessity for inflicting it has passed away.

"I attach a list of the principal Kaffir crimes, with their respective punishments :—

> Murder—death, or fine, according to circumstances.
> Treason, as contriving the death of the chief, or conveying information to the enemy—death and confiscation.
> Desertion from the tribe—death and confiscation.
> Poisoning—death and confiscation.
> Practices with an evil intent, termed "witchcraft"—death and confiscation.
> Adultery—fine, sometimes death.
> Rape—fine, sometimes death.
> Using love philters—death or fine, according to circumstances.
> Arson—fine.
> Theft—restitution and fine.
> Maiming—fine.
> Injuring cattle—death or fine, according to circumstances.*
> Causing cattle to abort—heavy fine.
> False witness—heavy fine.

* The following curious Kaffir law-case, in Kreli's tribe, came under the personal notice of the author, and will serve to elucidate the shrewdness of the "*amapakati*" or Kaffir lawyers.

A verdict was required in the case of a Kaffir, who, as plaintiff, brought on the trial, asserting that an ox of his had been stabbed, and a portion eaten by six Kaffirs, who were placed before the bar as prisoners. They pleaded "not guilty," on the ground that the ox had been gored by another ox, and having died from the wound, they had eaten it, thinking it no harm. The case caused great excitement in the tribe, and the shrewdest "*amapakati*" were employed by the chief in the trial. After a careful hearing, the senior

" In all tribes governed solely by their own laws, it is a matter of surprise to Europeans, that those offences which they consider very small indeed, are regarded by the natives as of considerable magnitude. The severe punishments inflicted for these, which civilised men even ridicule as unworthy of notice, are, however, the foundation of that order in which they are kept; and, by a strict observance of those customs, greater crimes are prevented.

"Thus, when natives enter the service of Europeans, and begin to understand that these very customs, which hold them in check among their own people, are ridiculed, the restraints are broken down, and they soon commit offences which cannot be overlooked.

prisoner made a very eloquent defence, and urged therein, that from *the length of the wound*, it was quite impossible that *a man* could have inflicted it. He was heard throughout patiently, but when he finished, an old "*umpukati*" cross-examined him, thus :—

Q. Where did the goring ox's tail grow ?   A. On its rump.

Q. How did it grow there ? Up or down, or at the side ? A. Down.

Q. Where did its horns grow ? A. On the head.

Q. How did they grow there ? Up or down, or at the side ?
    A. Up.

Q. If then that ox gored the other, to do so, he would have to
    put his head down, and tear up, would he not ? A. Yes.

Q. He could not tear down, could he ? A. No.

Now examine the wound, and see where the first incision was made, at the top, or at the bottom ? He answered, with reluctance, The wound is largest at the bottom.

Finding, The ox was stabbed, not gored, the prisoners are guilty. *Sentence*, Each to be fined two cows. This judgment was received with great applause.

" As an instance—there is no greater crime, in the estimation of a Kaffir, than speaking disrespectfully of authorities. It is, however, a common failing among the European population, and this is not confined to the lower classes, that, upon a native declaring his intention of appealing to the authorities, he is given to understand, very frequently, that, in the estimation of the white man, the authorities are held in contempt. This leads the Kaffir to cherish the same feeling, which is productive of evil to himself, and nothing but evil, present and prospective, to the European population.

" It should be borne in mind that the authorities are the only medium by which the white man can obtain redress for the wrong which may be done him by the native; but, whatever amount of authority or influence he who administers the law, may or should, possess over the native, the contemptuous manner in which he has been spoken of by the European, cannot fail to break down the only means of securing that respect for the laws, so necessary to be maintained in the mind of the native, and which is so essential in securing that justice sought by the European. Connected with this I may mention another circumstance which I have noticed as operating upon the native population regarding the labour question. When Kaffirs are governed entirely by their own laws and customs the chief is the centre of their thoughts and actions; with him rests their prospects, and even their lives; but, from the period when the young men of a tribe begin to enter into the service of colonists, those ties, which heretofore bound them to their chief, are weakened. Formerly they were entirely dependent on him, and on their parents, for counsel and aid, not only in marrying, but also in every emergency. By their connection with Europeans they have lost much of that respect which they were accustomed to pay to their chiefs and to their parents, and have even learned to contemn the English authorities; and thus, in their new position, they have become greatly unwilling to submit to government of any kind.

"The state in which I found the natives of the Colony, particularly those in the service of colonists, or living in their vicinity, was one very difficult to control.

"Those in the division of Pietermaritzburg are under better control than those in the division of Durban; which difference I attribute to the circumstance that there has not yet been any competent authority appointed to the latter division.

"Two of the most prominent offences, committed by Kaffirs in the service of colonists, are absconding from service, and impertinent conduct on leaving their masters. There are many other offences, gradually increasing among them, which are caused mainly by that freedom forced upon them by their European masters; the consequences of which, to themselves, the Kaffirs cannot foresee.

"I am of opinion, that if competent European authorities were placed over the natives in this district; having, for their object, the mutual benefit of every class in the community, the Kaffirs might be brought into a proper state of order. For it is a fact, that there are many native tribes in the district, and I may mention also the entire division of Durban, which is above eighty miles in length, and nearly fifty in breadth, viz, from the Umlazi station to the Umzimkulu, which embraces a very large amount of native population, dwelling in their tribal state, who have never yet had a magistrate appointed over them; independently of those in the service of Europeans.

"The only authorities they have ever yet seen, in the greater portion of that division, have been those who have collected the native tax.

"From the imperfect and ungoverned state of the natives at the present period, more particularly those in the vicinity of Europeans, an extensive, but very natural, distrust prevails between the two races, and it becomes a matter of importance to consider what measures are requisite in order to its removal.

"I am also of opinion that the great numerical superiority of the native population, located as they are in the midst of the Europeans, is the cause of such uneasiness as to urge the necessity of their being removed. On the other hand, the natives are also distrustful of the whites.

"I must here state, however, that I cannot concur in the opinion given by several of the witnesses in their plans for removing them. I believe that war would be the inevitable result of such a proceeding, therefore I could only fall in with any plan of which the Government approve, subject to the opinion of the diplomatic agent as to how far such plan would be acceptable to those tribes proposed to be removed, and that thus safety might be ensured.

"There appears to me no other mode of avoiding a collision with the natives, than that to which I have alluded; and also *the introduction of emigrants in sufficient numbers to act as a counterpoise to the numerical superiority of the natives, and, at the same time, dispossess them of the belief that they are able to contend with us.*

"From time immemorial, hunting and war have been regarded as the chief pursuits of the native tribes of Africa.

"As a general rule, manual labour has never been practised by the male population.

"It has been stated by some individuals in the Colony, that the male population of the Kaffir tribes, according to their own laws, are required to perform works of manual labour at the will of their chiefs. This is correct so far as regards building their chief's *"kraal,"* cultivating fields, and any work of a public nature which may demand their services; but it must be borne in mind, that, while there are two distinct modes by which Kaffirs are governed in different parts of the country—the one being patriarchal in its nature, and the other pure despotism—both systems agree in this, that the chief, in all his acts, is obliged to consider what effect his commands will have on the minds of his followers. Even Chaka, one of the greatest despots who ever governed any nation, constantly kept this consideration in view, being perfectly aware that his reign would soon terminate if he opposed the will of his people.

"Hence the manual labour which, at any time, has been required by the chiefs from their followers, has been of very brief duration.

"It is generally believed that, throughout the whole of the Kaffir tribes, the women alone labour in the fields. This is not strictly true. Many of these tribes, dispersed, as they are, over a wide extent of country, have, during the last three centuries, more or less diverged from their original character.

"The frontier Kaffirs have become a materially different people, owing to their proximity to the Cape Colony. Those tribes, also, to the Northward, and under Chaka and Sotyangan, by whom wars of a more extensive and decided character have been prosecuted, than were known prior to their reign, have also experienced a considerable alteration.

"Leaving these tribes to the North, and the frontier tribes to the South, we find a somewhat central tribe in the Amapondo, under Faku, which has been less affected by the violent commotions in the above directions than most of the others.

"This chief was not originally greater, nor had he a force superior to many of his neighbours, until the remnants of tribes despoiled and scattered by Chaka, sought refuge with him. Other tribes also, dreading the great Zulu chief, although unmolested by him, attached themselves to Faku.

"The country occupied by the Amapondo nation, is particularly well adapted for defence; hence, in two attacks made upon it by the Zulu army, although Faku lost many thousand of cattle, he held his territory.

"I also find that among the Amapondo and several neighbouring tribes, including the Amaswasi, the fields are cultivated by men as well as women."

As regards their law of marriage, there are some peculiarities worthy of note. They purchase the wife by dowry; that is to say, the Kaffir about to marry is obliged to pay to the father of his intended wife a dowry of cattle. To decide what the value of this fine is to be, or, in plainer terms, how many oxen and cows the girl is worth, she is brought before the "*amapakati*" of the tribe, and whatever judgment they pass, is considered final. Hence, if the Kaffir does not possess the number stated, he is obliged to defer his marriage with the girl, until he has acquired a sufficient number to enable him to purchase her. This he has to accomplish, either by working for, and buying them, or, as is more frequently the case, by warfare, pillage, and theft.

As polygamy is largely practiced amongst them, this necessity for the acquisition of cattle, forms one of their main incitements to war, and their untiring love and prosecution of thefts in cattle.

A singular usage amongst them is, that the "*amapayati*," in passing judgment in cases of this kind, or in any legal proceedings, always assemble their court *at the entrance of the kraal or village*; which custom seems to bear an unconscious resemblance, in their habits, to the usages of the Jews and Israelites of old.*

Their marriage festivities are always carried on with feasting, dancing, and singing; the wife being the principal actor in the dance, and performing her evolutions before her intended husband, who sits by sedately watching her, rolled up to the chin in the ample folds of his "*kaross*," or blanket.

So soon as her exertions to please him, have succeeded in arousing the swarthy amourante from his dreamy lethargy, he arises, takes her by the arm, and leads her to his hut, amidst the resounding shouts of the women of the tribe; and thus he proclaims her as his wife, and soon after impresses her with the fact, by giving her a good flagellation the first time she may chance to offend him.

Dancing is a favourite occupation, and seems to be mingled with all their observances. The full moon is their favourite season for practising this, their nocturnal orgeries being usually kept up until the day begins to dawn. Their movements in the dance are graceful and stately.

Like all barbarous races, the Kaffirs are very superstitious. They have a distinct and con-

* See Genesis xxxi, 37; Ruth iv, 1—13; 1 Kings, xxi, 8.

firmed belief in the immortality of the soul, and upon this they graft a superstitious dread of evil spirits, witches, witchcraft, and the transmigration of the spirits of the dead to the bodies of the living. Every tribe is supplied with its "witch-doctor," and its "rain-maker." These miscreants are used by the chiefs as their instruments for every kind of barbarity and cruelty; whilst the dread of the *"ama-ikoboka,"* or commoners, is thereby much increased.

All diseases, sickness, and death, are supposed to be the effect of invisible agency or witchcraft; and whether it be amongst the human race, their cattle, or crops, if they should fail or die, it is certain that they are *"bewitched."*

Their tradition of life and death, is that they were brought in amongst them by means of two reptiles, a chameleon and a lizard, the last of which out-running the other, came and bewitched the first Kaffir *"ukumkani,"* and so death entered. This is a singular coincidence; but, like all their other traditions, it is given and held in an ambiguous manner, and only preserved by oral-agency. They are fearless of death, which shows clearly that they have no belief in future punishment. Nor do they appear to apprehend any satanic agency, or anything worse than the incarnated evil spirits amongst themselves, the witch-doctors.

The Bishop of Natal, in his recent researches amongst these most interesting tribes, has ascertained that they have a distinct traditionary belief in the Supreme Being, whom they acknowledge under the two-fold titles of " *Umkulumkulu*," the great essence, and " *Umvelinquange*," the first comer-out. Of him or his attributes they understand nothing, neither do they worship or invoke him.

The only approach to reverence or veneration amongst them, is shown to their chiefs, both *living* and *dead*. The power of the former is, in all cases, indisputable, absolute, and supreme; that of the latter is superstitious and traditionary. They say that they believe that the spirits of their " *inkoses inkulu*" come back amongst them, go out with them to battle, and bewitch their enemies for them. They consequently sacrifice to these before they go to battle, and invoke their interference in their behalf. The sacrifices are made of the hoofs, horns, and skulls of the oxen, which are invariably slain, immediately before going to war; "slay and eat the ox," being an order (synonymous with "prepare for war,") which is issued by the chief, whenever his " *amapakati*" have advised war.

The evident utility of this order is, to stimulate and excite their passions, whilst strengthening their muscular and corporeal energies.

For as, in times of peace, except at marriage and other festivities, hunting scenes, or in hospitality, they never kill their cattle, or eat flesh, but subsist mainly on milk, corn, and roots; so, in times of war, this sudden transition from vegetable to animal food, inflames their appetites, and excites their passions. This is also doubly effected, by the brutal and revolting manner in which they slaughter the cattle, and by their devouring the flesh and blood half raw and quivering.

These scenes of savage butchery are transacted in the following cruel way. When about to slay a beast, several Kaffirs assemble around it, and, dividing their number into two bands, range themselves at either side of their victim. Twenty or thirty of them then throw the weight of their bodies against the ribs and shoulders of the ox, and thus succeed in holding it, wedged in between them, while a strong, powerful man comes forward, and, with the point of a large sharp "*assegai*," makes a deep incision in its chest about a foot long. Then, baring his sinewy arm to the shoulder, he thrusts it into the centre of the poor beast's body, and seizing the heart, liver, and lights, he drags them out by main force; thus tearing asunder the life-strings, while the blood spirts out, in all directions, from the ruptured arteries and vessels. The bystanders then close in, throw down the unfortunate animal, rip it open with their knives and *"assegais,"* and stifle its dreadful cries by cutting its throat, and effectually extracting those vital parts which the first operator has seldom sufficient strength to drag out at once. Thus a lingering death of cruel torture is inflicted upon the poor beast, whose deep and piteous bellowing resounds through the surrounding valley. During this revolting scene, the men and women, and even little children, cluster round the spot, skipping and leaping in the wildest joy; while shouting, dancing, and throwing themselves down, they even lap up, with their tongues, the hot and reeking blood in which the carcase of the ox is weltering.

Such are their training schools for war, and the modes that they employ to excite their tastes and appetites for blood. It is at these orgies that they reserve the horns, hoofs, and skulls of all animals slain, and burn them as a sacrifice of propitiation to the spirits and shades of their great departed chiefs. Round the fire and heap, or *altar*, on which they burn them, they form in a circle, dancing slowly, and chanting a solemn invocation. Debased, and degraded, as is this observance, enshrouded with cruelty and superstition, and a hideous mockery of that

which is good; still it cannot but be acknowledged, that it clearly demonstrates that, in
the breast of the wild untutored Kaffir now, as
was the case with the polished, and more refined,
heathens of olden time, there is an inherent
feeling of the *necessity of a sacrifice to propitiate.*
It also tacitly acknowledges, on their part, the
admission of the great axiom of Christianity
and philosophy, viz, that they *need* some supernatural aid to assist them in the hours of their
emergencies.

Their acknowledgement of the Supreme Being
in a twofold character, together with their belief
in spiritual influence for good as well as evil,
give very strong presumptive evidence that, at
some past period of their history, they have had
the knowledge of a "more excellent way of
religion," than those faint and indistinct superstitions which they now alone possess.

This assumption is very materially strength-
ened also by a further knowledge of their
usages and traditionary observances. Their
belief in, and reverence for, prophets is remarkable. They imagine that these are beings
into whose bodies the spirits of their great
departed chiefs have gone; and that then they
return to foretell great coming events. Amongst
them, in latter days, was "*Links,*" whose wonderful power over the Kaffirs, during the war

of 1835, induced the government to offer a large fine for his apprehension. He was arrested and confined, for several years, at Robben Island prison, Cape-Town; but he escaped from thence and redoubled his former influence, confirming the Kaffirs' belief in "the school of the prophets," by re-appearing to them, and recounting strange sights and doings. During the last war of 1850, "*Umlumgenie*" also arose, and foretold all kinds of wonders which were to come to pass—that the white man's bullets would melt to air, and those of the Kaffirs turn to fire, and drive the white men into the sea. He outlived the war, but died shortly after its close, in Kreli's country; as some report, from poison secretly administered, but this we believe, to be incorrect.

Many of the prophets of Scripture were of the same character and calling as these Kaffirs. Zechariah, we read, (Zec. xiii, 5) was a husbandman and keeper of cattle, and Amos was a herdsman of Tekoa, and a gatherer of the sycamore-fruit; (Amos i, 1; vii, 14, 15.) Elisha, also, was an agriculturist at Abel-meholah, (1 Kings, xix, 16.) Whilst many of the Kaffir customs also are of the purest patriarchial character; as well as their names being Ishmaelitish and Eastern.

Their reverence for the chief; their riches in

cattle; their pastoral habits of life; the purchase of the wife by dowry; the character of their ornaments, armlets, anklets, frontlets and the girdle (which latter they always tighten when preparing to run,); the faint traces of religion already named; and, added to these, their strict observance, to the present day, of the "feast of first fruits;" their use of a "heap of stones" piled in front of the door of their hut, when they are about to leave home for a time, and which is thus placed, as a "pillar of witness" to their "*inkose*" that they do not intend to desert him, but are only absenting themselves on an errand (resembling the Mizpah or Ebenezer of Genesis xxvii, 16—22; xxxi, 43—55; xxxv, 7—14.); all these combine to give them a place in patriarchial days, amidst the Eastern nations of Scripture. The great chief of the Tambookies is "*Moshesh*," (Moses) a name reverenced among them as very great. "*Dushani*" the red chief, seems to have the Hebrew root שני shani, scarlet or crimson; (Isaiah i, 18.) and again the name of "*ikoboka*" or slave, will bear a Scriptural root and derivation. And when we find them still, from tradition, not only reverencing, but *actually observing* many of the rites of the Mosaic law, then this presumptive evidence strengthens into almost certainty, as to their origin being from Ishmael.

For instance, all the animals pronounced unclean, in the Mosaic law, are *unclean* to the
Kaffirs. They turn with absolute disgust and
loathing from swine's flesh, under every form,
and will not even *touch* a pig. If urged to do
so, or to partake of its flesh, they instantly
conceive that you are intending to insult them,
and will always resent it. The hare, the bat, the
owl, all kinds of fish, and several other animals
and birds they never think of touching, although the Hottentots, Bushmen, and other
tribes dwelling in the midst of, and around
them, eat all these indiscriminately.

So again with respect to their observance of
uncleanness. The woman at, and for several
days after childbirth is unclean, and is separated in a hut by herself. Those touching a
dead body are also unclean, and are separated,
and made to shave their heads and beards. So
in grief, as also when they have made a vow,
and until they perform it, they are obliged to
shave their heads and their beards.

And lastly, we mention their strict observance of the rite of *circumcision*, throughout
all the Kaffir tribes, on every male child at
the age of fourteen.* This is a conclusive

* Another most conclusive evidence of their Abrahamic origin,
seems to be the fact that whilst, as an *invariable rule*, "all barbarous
tribes pass away before civilization;" the Kaffirs form the solitary

evidence; for, although the Mahomedans are known to practice this rite, yet their observance of it appears to be from expediency, and is in no way accompanied with these many Israelitish and Jewish traditionary observances still existing, and practised, amongst the Kaffir tribes.

The performance of this rite on the male children at the age of fourteen, and of a similar one on the young females at the age of twelve years, is always conducted with great solemnity, and afterwards is concluded with dancing and festivities. The attendant usages are singular and grotesque, and anything but becoming to their personal appearance.

Whilst undergoing the operation, and for several days before and after it, all the persons on whom it is performed, are brought inside the cattle " *kraal.*" There large quantities of white clay, blood, and water are mixed together, and, with this, they are painted from head to feet. They are then set to dance, in a state of nudity, until it becomes perfectly dry. Another coat is then applied, and the same process is repeated. In this manner they proceed, laying coat over coat, until their bodies are perfectly

exception within our knowledge, for instead of decreasing in number or strength, they are known to be annually *increasing*, and that very extensively and rapidly.

white. A number of dresses are then provided, painted of the same colour, snow-white. These dresses are composed of reeds, strung side by side through one end, on a piece of sinew or leather, and similar thongs are passed through them at intervals, so as to make them to resemble flat stiff mats. By drawing the strings at the extremities tight, they form these into bell-shaped garments, and fasten them on their bodies; one round the middle reaching to the knees; one round the neck reaching to the elbows; and one round each arm and leg, fastened on, respectively, at the elbows and knees, and reaching to the extremities of the figure. A large cap, formed of rushes, is placed on the head, tied into a point at the top, (which is about two feet above the head) and this also is painted white. Long sticks are then given to them to carry in their hands, and dressed in these costumes, they go about until the next moon; these solemnities being always commenced at one, and concluded at the following full moon.

When the latter comes round, they assemble again in the cattle *"kraal;"* oxen are killed; and there is a great display of feasting and dancing. Each person is then taken out in rotation, the white paint is washed from their bodies, their white-washed clothes are taken off, and they are brought in their nude condition before the "*inkose inkulu*." He then anoints their bodies with grease, and handing to each boy a "*kaross*" and a bundle of "*assegais*," confirms him as a warrior, capable and competent to bear arms. Dancing, music, and singing, then ensue, whilst large vessels, filled with Kaffir beer, and pipes and tobacco are handed round.

In the war-songs of the tribe are then recounted, before the young warriors, the deeds of fame performed by their chiefs and forefathers, and they are invited to follow their good examples; to be obedient to their chief; and to enrich and enoble him and themselves, by the acquisition of cattle and plunder. When all are supposed to be sufficiently aware of the dignity of their position, the "*ukumkani*" rises, and, in a moment, silence prevails throughout the village, and he commences an eloquent harangue to the young around him.

He declares them henceforth Kaffir warriors *in his army*; he pronounces them eligible *for marriage*, and he urges them to *practise war*, in order that they may acquire cattle thereby, wherewith to purchase wives. He extols the girls, as useful and pleasing, and exhorts them to choose well their husbands, and serve well those they choose. He promises them plenty

of cattle and cows, meat, milk, and "*scoff*,"
(food) if only they remain faithful to him and
obey his orders; and he generally concludes
his address by some terrific picture of a chief
in anger, and the certain ruin of those who
oppose his sway.

All around loudly applaud the oratorical
effusions of their king, and the ceremony closes
with the slaughter of more oxen presented by
the chiefs, together with feasting, dancing,
drinking, smoking, singing, and merry-making.

As may be supposed, these seasons of tribal
festivities, are, amongst the Kaffirs, what wakes
and fairs are with us—periods in the history of
the young, from which many can date their first
and early demoralization, and where scenes of
wanton immorality, vice, and sin are perpetrated
and pursued. These feasts of circumcision are,
consequently, as they at present exist in their
abuse, most detrimental to morality and virtue
amongst the Kaffirs; for not only are the incitements to vice then more profuse around
them, but further, by a singular enactment of
law, an indiscriminate intercourse and mingling
together of the sexes is permitted, during the
time of the circumcision ceremonial, i. e., thirty
days, and at that time only.

Their pertinacious tenacity to the observance
of this, and other like rites, is, however, very

remarkable. Nor is it, perhaps, so great a matter of wonder, that they should be found so over-clothed with the inseparable concomitants of barbarity and heathenism, vice, immorality, and cruelty; rather is it more singular, that though cast out and forsaken, forgotten, neglected, and despised, a race of beings should yet be found, (after so many years spent in barbarism,) so exclusively national, and so distinguished through their traceable traditionary observances, as these Kaffirs are. They excite admiration in the mind of every traveller who visits them and their country, and a still more lively interest in the breast of every Missionary who investigates their origin, usages, and customs, or seeks their civilization and conversion to Christianity.

But ere turning to say a few words on the brighter picture of Missionary work amongst them, we must give a short outline of those hideous orgies of superstition and cruelty, which the advent of this Better Testament is calculated to remove, and we shall close this chapter with a few remarks on the superstitions which they believe in and practice, in connection with the " witch-doctor " and the " rain-maker."

These two miscreants, who are always to be found attached to every tribe, are intimately connected in their use, occupation, and pursuits, and they are alike made the instruments of oppression and tyranny by the chiefs, whenever the dictates of their perverse and evil hearts lead them, through jealousy, cupidity, or revenge, to the commission of crimes of the darkest character.

The visitation of sickness and disease, whether from natural causes, or through the instrumentality of drugs and poison administered, are all regarded, amongst the Kaffirs, as the effect of witchcraft. Hence the witch-doctor is looked upon as a necessary appendage in every tribe, to ward off these calamities, to "smell out" or discover wizards and witches, and to "eat up," (i. e., to destroy) them when they are found. At these deceptions the chiefs gladly wink, because they always tend to increase his stock, besides giving him an easily accessible medium through which to satiate his revenge or jealousy on those obnoxious to him.

The witch-doctors are generally chosen for their personal ugliness, combined with inherent cunning and deception; and they live secluded in a hut, by themselves, near to that of the chief. The influence that they exercise is very extensive, for not only do they keep all the "*ikoboka*," or commoners, in awe of

them, but, if shrewd, which they generally
are, they soon succeed in getting the chief so to
commit himself in their atrocities, that he is
held, henceforth, quite in their power. Sometimes, however, in their anxiety to effect this,
they overreach themselves, as was the case
about a year ago, in Umhalla's tribe, where the
"amapakati" discovered a witch-doctor trying
to implicate the chief; which fact, the instant
it was made known to Umhalla, he at once condemned, and, notwithstanding the awe and
dread in which the hoary old wretch was held
by all around, he burnt him to death before
the assembled tribe.

The various modes in which these creatures
practise their craft, are, of course, multitudinous; but the most effective and favourite,
though most revolting, of their avocations, is
that of "smelling out" the witch, which is thus
described. If, at any time, a Kaffir should become the object of envy or jealousy to his
chief, in consequence of his cattle increasing
too rapidly; or from fear of his opposition and
influence, should he be permitted to grow too
rich; or, from cupidity, the chief then sends for
the witch-doctor, and tells him privately that he
wishes to "eat up," i. e., to kill this man, and
to possess himself of his cattle. He promises a
proportionable reward and fee to the doctor

for his participation; and he again, on his part, promises "to smell him out."

Having arranged these preliminaries, the chief generally sends the Kaffir out on some errand, and enticing his wives and children away from his hut, under some frivolous pretence, the doctor then enters it, and steals from it some two articles, both alike, and of the same kind; as for instance, two pipes or two spoons. One of these he buries under the floor of the hut, covering the spot over with the matting, so as to prevent its being observed by the inmates on their return; the other like article he takes away, and buries it in the same spot or part, within the chief's hut. Having done this, on the return of the Kaffir and his family, he administers a quantity of diluted vegetable poison to the chief's cattle, in the water which they drink; he also mixes it with the milk and food of the chief, his wives and children, and awaits the result. Very frequently, having done thus much, he disappears from the "*kraal*," and goes off in the night to some neighbouring tribe—for the twofold purpose of disarming suspicion as to *his* having had anything to say to the matter, as well as to increase his own importance in the eyes of his tribe, by the confusion which he knows will be created by searching and sending for him.

The effect of the poison is, of course, soon made manifest by the chief and his household, and his cattle also become violently sick, perhaps one or two of the weakest among them dying; or, what is regarded as equally unimportant, a " *picanini* " or two from his young nursery being added to the number.

Search is immediately made for the "witch-doctor," as of course it is at once conclusively seen that "somebody has bewitched the chief." This is a crime of high treason, and one always visited by capital punishment; the greatest excitement then prevails to see who is to be "smelt out" as the delinquent.

On the arrival of the "*Æsculapius*," his first care is to alleviate the sufferings of the bewitched; and, with every expression of concern and outward demonstrations of alarm, lest the life of his chief should be sacrificed through the malignity of the dose of witchery which he has unfortunately swallowed, he hurries about, officiously preparing medicines, and administering remedies to man, women, children, and cattle alike. His consummate skill seldom fails in effecting a speedy cure, and then, all apprehension as to the mischief spreading further, being allayed, he next appoints a day for the ceremonial of "smelling out the witch." Great preparations are made for this solemn ordeal.

An extensive gathering of the tribe is convened, and oxen are slaughtered, and devoured in the revolting manner (before described) in which this is always performed.

The cattle are all removed from the interior of their "*kraal*" or enclosure, in the centre of which an immense fire is lighted. Around this the tribes assemble, and sit in rings in mute silence and expectancy; whilst large baskets, full of bullocks' blood hot from the animals' veins, are passed round and drank off in silence.

As night approaches (for their deeds of darkness are always, by choice as well as by instinct, performed "in the night-season") the "doctor" appears in the ring, quite naked, except a few tigers tails as a fringe round his loins. A low solemn chant is then raised by the women; whilst several old crones, placed in the rear with sticks, and ox hides stretched upon frames, beat time to the singing. The cadences of this are first very slow, but gradually increase, whilst the "doctor" leaps and dances, and shouts in the wildest, and most demoniacal manner. The lurid glare of the fire; the pitchy darkness of the surrounding night; (the time chosen usually being at the new moon, and in the darkest weather,) together with the glaring eyes, inflamed countenances, and excited frames of the swarthy community, and dusky "doctor" in the centre; these all combine to make the scene one of the wildest and most awful that can well be imagined upon earth.

A few hours of such employment and fare as this suffices to bring the assembled tribe into a state of absolute frenzy, and fit them for being engaged in any scenes, or amount of barbarity and cruelty. This the "witch-doctor" anticipates, and so soon as he deems their feelings and evil passions to be sufficiently inflamed, he then ceases dancing, as gradually subsiding in time to the music, as he before rose and increased to that degree of rapidity which kept him in a motion so excessive, that he not unfrequently falls upon the ground, during his evolutions, quite exhausted.

A solemn silence then ensues, during which the "doctor" rests himself, and then proceeds with a bundle of divining rods in his hand, to walk round throughout the assembly. As he approaches the chief, he watches the rods in his hand, and dexterously makes one of them move, or leap out, from amongst the rest. He then singles out this rod, and throws the others into the fire, and being rubbed with a kind of inflamable matter, they there crackle and blaze brightly, thus demonstrating to the Kaffirs that they are charged with supernatural powers; with the remaining one he then proceeds through the assembly again, and this time, he makes it vibrate, not only when opposite the chief, but also when in front of the victim whom he is about to single out. When this is perceived, he stands several minutes confronting this man, and gazing intently at him, whilst the silence of death ensues. This process he repeats three times, and then he leaves the *"kraal,"* and proceeds to the chief's hut. Here he walks about, always making the rod leap from his hand, whenever he comes over the place where he buried the article which he had stolen from his victim's hut. He then marks this spot by driving an *"assegai"* into it, and proceeds to the suspected man's hut. Here also he goes through the same mummeries, and pretends to discover the corresponding spot, in this hut, to that in the other, and marks it in a similar manner.

The next part of the proceeding is to commence excavations at these spots, which is done by numbers of the surrounding Kaffirs; when, as a necessary consequence, the articles deposited there are brought to light. This is deemed conclusive evidence, and on it the supposed culprit is seized, tried, condemned to death, and all his cattle are forfeited to the chief. From these the "witch-doctor's" promised fee is paid, and too great honour cannot be heaped upon him, by the tribe, for having so ably delivered the chief from the influence of the wizard.

The most terrible part of the picture then appears—the death of the victim. The usual manner of this is by causing him to be stung to death by ants and reptiles, or by burning.

The former of these they effect by stripping him naked, and rubbing his body over with honey, and then pegging him down on his back, (through the hands and feet) on the top of an ant-hill, where he is quickly covered with insects, which settling in his eyes, ears, and nostrils, soon sting him to madness, and thus bring him to a cruel and agonizing death.

If the other process is selected, they generally preface it by first pegging him up against a tree, and setting the young lads to practice the *"assegai,"* throwing at his body as a target, thus torturing him whilst the fire is preparing to consume him. When this is sufficiently large, they roll huge stones into the centre of it, and leave them there until they become red hot. Having a supply of these in sufficient number, they then transfer the body of their victim from the tree where he has been placed, to the side of the fire, and there peg him with *"assegais"* upon the ground on his back, and proceed to roll out the stones, one by one, from the fire; and, placing them upon different parts of his body, they thus burn, or rather roast, him to death.

There are other modes of torture and death practiced amongst them, on these and other occasions, too lingering and horrible even to be here recounted. The selection of these, and the degree of previous torture to which they subject their unfortunate victims, always depend upon the extent of excitement into which they have been inflamed; the supposed or imputed enormity of the offence; and the extent of love or dislike that is felt for the wretched victim personally.

The "*rain-maker*" is another offshoot of barbarism amongst these people, who is closely allied to the "witch-doctor," and who plays into his hands, for the purpose of increasing his own importance, and enriching his own cattle "kraal." His office, is to make or bring rain, during seasons of drought and distress; and the necessity for such an appointment is, as may be easily imagined, often felt amongst them.

These charmers exercise their fictitious profession with similar mummeries and incantations to the "witch-doctor;" and, if by chance, a shower of rain, or a thunder storm, falls within twenty-four hours after their orgies have been held, they are, in consequence, extolled above the clouds, loaded with gifts and presents, and become the objects of peculiar honors. If, however, they fail, in bringing a visit from the element; then they feign sickness, and internal pain, they swallow reptiles, such as frogs, lizards, chameleons, and taking an emetic, they disgorge them before the tribe, and then, asserting that some one has bewitched the clouds, and him as their chief or "*ukumkani*," he has recourse to the "witch-doctor," whose services then come into requisition, in "smelling out" who is the transgressor in this instance.

On these occasions, they generally fix on some person, whom they either dislike themselves personally, or one who is known by them to be obnoxious to the chief; and as confiscation of cattle only, and not death, is the punishment in these cases, they thus succeed in effectually averting popular indignation from themselves, and in turning its tide upon their enemies, or the substitutes for them. Beside this, before the ceremonial of the "witch-doctor" is brought to a close, and another renewed attempt of his own has been performed, very possibly a sufficient period of time may have elapsed, to bring round another thunder-storm, or shower of rain, and so to provide materials for the re-establishment of his professional celebrity.

The existence of these cruel, degrading, and disgusting rites, practised, in all their barbarity, by a race of people with intellects so superior, and dispositions so generous, confiding, and noble, as these Kaffirs are, only serves to demonstrate the true condition and tendency of our nature, in its unregenerated state, together with the responsible duty, as well as high privilege, that is laid upon us, of bringing to them the Gospel of Christ; and of endeavouring to remove from amongst them, through its mission, these sounds and sights of depravity and sin; seeking also to replace them with those fruits of righteousness and holiness of life, which are sure to spring everywhere from the right reception of its truths.

GENESIS xvi, 12.

CHAPTER X.

THE MISSION FIELDS OF SOUTH AFRICA REVIEWED IN A COMPARATIVE LIGHT, AS TO THEIR PAST HISTORY, PRESENT CONDITIONS AND EXTENT; TOGETHER WITH THE APPARENT PROBABILITIES FOR FUTURE AND ULTIMATE SUCCESS.

THE first preacher of the Gospel of Jesus Christ, in Southern Africa, amongst the Hottentot tribes, was George Schmidt, a member of the United Brethren *(Moravians)* at Herrnhuth, who landed at the Cape July 9th, A.D. 1737. This was about eighty years subsequent to the foundation of the Dutch Colony there.

During the whole period of the Portuguese settlements, no effort at Missionary work was attempted; and thus it would seem that their occupation of this vast territorial possession not having ever been fructified by any attempt being made by them to ameliorate the natives, the stewardship was, under Divine Providence, taken from them, and handed to the Dutch.

The history of their Missionary labour is little better or more cheering than is that of their Portuguese predecessors. Several efforts indeed were made to evangelize the Hottentots, but these sprang, not from the Dutch rulers or

Church, but from George Schmidt and his followers in the field. Indeed the state of wilful ignorance, in which the first Dutch settlers at the Cape tried to retain their Hottentot neighbours and slaves, is most lamentable to contemplate. They appear to have regarded these miserable people as no better than beasts—as having no souls; no capabilities for receiving religious instruction; no hopes nor fears for eternity.

A few families, here and there, of the better disposed of the Boers, made the effort of teaching their slaves to sing psalms, and, it may be hoped, somewhat more; but these, alas, appear only as the exceptions, not the rule itself. According to the then existing law, so soon as any of these slaves were *baptized*, they at once obtained their freedom : and hence it was the policy of the early colonists to discourage all attempts for the conversion of their servants; this being very plainly exemplified by the violent opposition which the Moravian Missionaries met with from them, when at length their merciful efforts began, through God's blessing, to be crowned with success.

At this period of the colonial history of the Cape, some of the very worst evils of slavery were there, alas! as elsewhere, to be found. And not only were these poor slaves debarred wilfully from the knowledge of that truth which makes wise the simple, and makes glad the humble of heart; but their very heathen notions of the Divine Being, shadowy and indistinct though these were, were even yet further darkened by their intercourse with these faithless professors of Christianity.

To illustrate this, we have but to quote the words of a Hottentot woman. "Before we came to the land of the Christians, we knew that there was a God. We called him *Sita*, which means the "God and Father above." If we were in distress, we always called upon him. Only those Hottentots, who have been born and bred among the Christians, know little or nothing of Him."

Whatever be the amount of veracity that is to be attached to such statements as this, it nevertheless shews that the contact of heathenism with civilization, wherever they came together without the healing balm of Christianity and religion, was invariably to degrade further the savage, as well as to demoralize the professing Christian.

Neglected as were these native tribes, however, by the Dutch, they became the objects of the most prayerful solicitation with George Schmidt and his pious followers; whilst God crowned their self-denying labours with success.

For many years Schmidt remained alone in his work, with no other white man near him. He built himself a little cottage, and laid out a little garden in the wilderness, many miles away from Cape Town, and here the free Hottentots gradually gathered around him. At the end of *five* years, he had from thirty to fifty in his school, and at the end of that time, A.D., 1742, he also had the privilege of baptizing the first Hottentot convert. In the following year 1743, he found it necessary to return to Europe, comforting himself, however, and his people with the hope of a speedy return to the scene of his labours. But he returned no more. The enemies of the brethren prevailed to thwart his plans, and, for fifty years, the little flock was left, as sheep without a shepherd.

At length, in 1792, the affairs of the Company came, in the course of God's Providence, to be presided over by men, who took a warm interest in the affairs of the Brethren, and to their request, to be allowed to send a second Mission to the natives of South Africa, a favourable answer was at once returned. The three Missionaries then sent, were helped upon their way with every kind attention from the authorities, and reached their future place of residence, *Bavian's Kloof*, (Baboon's Glen) on the eve of Christmas day, 1792. This spot lies about 170 miles to the East of Cape Town, and is still one of the principal scenes of labour for the Moravian Missionaries, though its name has since been changed to *Genadendal* (Valley of Grace.)

This was the very spot where Schmidt once laboured. They found part of the wall of his house standing, and fragments of others which pointed out the situation of the huts of his little flock. Amidst briars and thorns, which had grown up over his garden—meet emblem of the moral wilderness o'erspreading the spiritual soil which he had cultivated—there were yet to be seen some fruit-trees planted by his hands. And one old pear-tree, in particular, remarkable for size and luxuriance, afforded, for many years, a shelter to the patient Missionaries and their hearers, while they sat and spake together of the things of God.

Nor was this all. There were actual proofs of the abiding effects of those by-gone labours. The new teachers were soon surrounded by a number of Hottentots, whose parents, or grand-parents, had personally known Schmidt, and had long and anxiously wished for his return. They had died, indeed, without that consolation: but they had taught their children, as best they could, the knowledge they had themselves received, and they had charged them to seek out the first Missionaries who should be sent to instruct them.

And, beyond this, there was one aged woman, bending under the weight of four-score years, who had been herself baptized by the hands of George Schmidt. She remembered him well, and produced her Dutch New Testament, which he had given her, and which she had safely preserved in a leathern bag, wrapped up in two sheepskins; and, shewing it to the Missionaries, she then opened one of the Gospels, and read the history of our Saviour's birth. By frequent teaching, her recollection revived to the truths she had learnt so many years before. She spent the rest of her days with the Brethren, at Bavian's Kloof, and, amidst much weakness and many bodily sufferings, she exhibited the character of a true child of GOD. She was well known, and much respected, throughout the Colony, and was frequently visited by the English officers, who went, from time to time, to see the settlement. At last, she gently fell asleep in Jesus, on the 2nd of January, 1800, in her hundredth year.

From this period, the Mission flourished, although the measure of prosperity, which attended the Missionaries, was of a fluctuating character. Many and great were the difficulties that they had to contend with. The malice

and menaces of the Dutch often not only terrified, but actually endangered, their meek and
unoffending lives; and finally, on the 3rd of
August, 1795—a few days before the Colony
passed into the hands of the British—they succeeded in breaking up the station, and the
Missionaries were obliged to return to Cape
Town. This, however, was but a temporary
interruption; for, by the British authorities,
and, subsequently, by the Dutch during the few
years of their second occupation, they were
again kindly encouraged.

Nor was this the only, though but temporary,
interruption they had to meet with. On the
7th January, 1808, the British again landed in
the midst of a violent cannonade, which, beginning at eight in the morning, lasted until night,
and, for a time, again impeded their labours. On
this occasion that eminently holy man and Missionary, Henry Martyn, was present in Southern
Africa, being, at that time, with the fleet on
his way to India. After describing, at some
length, in his journal the landing of the soldiers,
and the horrors which he witnessed upon visiting the field of battle, he says, " At length I
lay down on the border of a clump of bushes,
with the battle field in view, and there lifted
up my soul to God. May the remembrance of
this day ever excite me to pray and labour

more, for the propagation of the Gospel of peace. The blue mountains to the Eastward were a cheering contrast to what was immediately before me. For there I conceived my beloved and honoured fellow servants—the Moravian Missionaries, companions in the kingdom and patience of Jesus Christ, to be passing the days of their pilgrimage far from the world, imparting the blessed Gospel to benighted souls. May I receive grace to be a follower of their faith and patience."

From the commencement of the British occupation of the Cape, the rays of Missionary light have spread through this vast continent; and now, instead of this one isolated station, there are many dotted out over the hills and plains of Southern Africa.

The only regret to the pious mind in viewing these multiplying seed beds of Divine grace, is that so few of them were attempted by the established Church of England. Teachers of twenty-two different denominations of Christians are now, side by side, endeavouring to carry out the Gospel amongst the native tribes. Only within the last few years, however, has any effort been made by our National Church towards Missionary work. The London Missionary Society, and the Wesleyans were amongst the earliest followers of the Moravians in the

field; and whilst the former of these have pushed their Missionaries furthest into the interior
deserts of Africa, the work of the latter, more
particularly in Kaffirland, has received the most
manifest blessing, and has yielded the most
satisfactory and abundant fruits.

In confirmation of this it may be mentioned,
that, besides *eleven* Missionaries and *sixty-eight*
lay-teachers in the Cape districts, together with
five Missionaries and *thirty-two* lay-teachers in
the Natal and Amazulu districts, the Wesleyans have *twenty-four* Missionaries, and *one hundred and twenty-three* lay-teachers in Albany,
Kaffirland, and the Bechuana country. Whilst,
in these latter localities, the number of full and
accredited church members, according to their
last returns, is 2869, with 3884 attending
schools.

If no more positive good was accomplished
by these self-denying pioneers of Christianity
in Africa, than that which their printing press
has effected, it of itself is a mighty boon to all
Missionary labours. This establishment, which
is now located at Mount Coke, near King
William's Town, has been kept in constant
work, and, within the last year, has issued a
new and revised edition of 2000 copies of the
Kaffir New Testament. In addition to this
it has also completed 6050 copies of the first,

and 2000 of the second Kaffir spelling book; 2000 Bible stories from the German of Dr. Barth; 1500 Dutch catechisms and spelling books; and 450 sets of periodicals; thus aiding greatly the dissemination of knowledge throughout the land.

A single extract from the last report received (1855) from the venerable Mr. Shepstone, of 'Kamastone Station, will suffice to shew that God is no respecter of persons, but that, in every nation, those that work for and honor him, he will honor.

He says, "The circumstances of this circuit throughout the year past, have been of a very satisfactory nature. The services of God's house have been well and regularly attended. A marked attention has been paid to the preaching of the Gospel; and while there has been a powerful influence checking moral depravity, as also counteracting heathen customs, in consequence of the voluntary interposition of some of the subordinate chiefs, there has been, at the same time, a stronger influence operating within narrower limits, which gives us much satisfaction. The members of the Society have been steady in their profession, and, we hope, have grown in grace. We have added to the Church by baptism during the year, *twenty-one* adults; *several* children belonging to the members of the Society have also been baptized, and thus we hope they are being prepared ultimately to take the place of their parents, when the latter shall have passed into the eternal world. By our present arrangements, we have from *six to seven hundred* attendants on Divine service weekly —the average attendance amounting to 200."

In other parts of these districts, and on other stations besides that of 'Kamastone, we can bear testimony, from *personal* inspection and experience, as to the valid work that these devoted pioneers have been, and are engaged in carrying out amongst the Kaffirs; and if, amidst other bodies and Societies of Christians labouring there, the same amount of good be not equally manifested, it is nevertheless a matter of deep and earnest thankfulness to every reflecting mind to know, that, whilst some slept, others were awake, watching and working.

Many, however, besides the Wesleyans, are in the field, and have been also labouring long and successfully. Robert Moffat, Dr. Livingstone, and Messrs. Brownlee, Archbell, Alison, and Lindley, are men well known amongst the now aged, and most untiring of these; while their contributions as travellers, geographers, and botanists, are too well known and appreciated to need mention as adding, in any way, to the lustre of their usefulness as Missionaries.

The Berlin and Paris, as well as the American Societies, and various other dissenting bodies from England and Scotland, are represented by their respective teachers in Kaffirland; and all have, more or less, fruits springing up from their labours of love.

Whilst, however, giving due credit to the zeal and laborious energy of the various bands of *supplementary* corps, who from the first, may have been engaged; it must, nevertheless, not be forgotten, that the *regular* troops, whenever they become engaged, are looked upon as those who are expected to bear the heat and brunt of the battle. They are those who, wherever they are, represent the efforts and honor of that nation to which they belong. And this applies as much to the Missionary soldiers of the Anglican Church, as to the services of Britain's brave naval and military defenders.

Hence it is, that the extensive and promising Missions of the South African Branch of Christ's Church, as now maintained and fostered there, by the venerable and incorporated Society for the Propagation of the Gospel in Foreign Parts, are occupying the attention of all those who feel interested in Missionary work.

This offshoot branch of the Anglican Church of Christ, was founded and established on St. Peter's day, in the year 1847; when, through the munificence of a Christian lady (Miss Burdett Coutts) in England, the first South African bishoprick of Cape Town was established, and the Right Rev. Robert Gray, D. D., Vicar of Stockton-upon-Tees, was consecrated to that see. At that period, the South African Diocese included the Cape Colony, British Kaffraria, Kaffirland, Natal, the Sovereignty, and the Island of St. Helena ; whilst the Bishop, situated at Cape Town, was, on the one side, upwards of 1000 miles from Natal, and, on the other, 1000 more from St. Helena.

The population of the Diocese, was 790,000 souls, of which, 652,000 were of the coloured tribes ; but at this period there were, beside the Bishop, only thirteen clergymen, and one catechist of the Church of England, scattered throughout the whole of this territory, and *not one single Church Missionary amongst the heathen*; whilst the Mahomedans were actually proselytizing *from among the ranks of Christians*. A cheering revival has, however, taken place within the last few years, and the South African Church has now " taken root downwards, and is bearing fruit upward " in a degree which far outstrips the sanguine expectation even of its most hopeful well-wishers.

In 1848, Dr. Gray made his primary visitation tour of his extensive Diocese, travelling over a large portion of it. His Lordship also undertook a second tour of inspection in 1850, and completed the circuit of the whole. The first of these visitations was performed in *four months*, and in it he travelled upwards of 3000 miles; whilst, in the second, 4000 miles was traversed amidst great difficulties, privations, and hardships, occupying a period of nearly *nine months*.

The spiritual destitution which his Lordship everywhere witnessed, together with the lively and growing feeling of piety existing amidst the exiled members of the Church, whom he found amidst all classes scattered out over the Continent, induced the determination in the Bishop of returning to England, and endeavouring to effect the subdivision of this Diocese, thus securing also that multiplication of inferior Clergy, which always accompanies the extension of the Episcopate.

This stupendous work his Lordship accomplished in the year 1853; wherein, on St. Andrew's Day, two other suffragan Bishops were consecrated for South Africa, the Right Rev. John Armstrong, D. D., Vicar of Tiddenham, Gloucestershire, to the See of Graham's Town; and the Right Rev. John William Colenso, D. D., Rector of Forncett St. Mary, Norfolk, to that of Natal. Dr. Gray, the Bishop

of Cape Town, was, at the same time, consti-
tuted Metropolitan of South Africa. This has
had the desired effect of increasing the Clergy,
who now number, scattered through the three
Dioceses, upwards of *seventy*; to these are also
to be added about *forty* Catechists, who are as-
sisting in the work.

Through every part of these Colonies the English population are now provided with the de-
cent and orderly ministrations of their Church;
whilst extensive Missions amongst the heathen
are already not only contemplated and established, but at work.

These are supported, jointly and equally, between the British Government and the incorporated Society for the Propagation of the Gospel in Foreign Parts. A large head Station
has been established at, or near the *"kraal"*
of each Kaffir chief; whilst out-stations, under
the superintendence of catechists, are scattered
over the whole of Kaffirland: and thus, at
length, the English Church has awakened to
her national duty of making known, to the
heathen of South Africa, not merely the knowledge of her power and sway, but also of her
God and His Church.

"It is impossible to overrate," to use the
words of Dr. Armstrong, the Bishop of Graham's
Town, "the importance of this present crisis, as

regards the Church of England.   I feel that I am not pleading for my own Diocese only, but for the Church of England at home, when I ask her, through the venerable Propagation Society, to offer noble gifts both of men—earnest, self-devoted men—and of money, at such a time as this.   We must make a great stride in Missionary efforts.   It is just that one opportunity upon which our whole character and career, as a Missionary church loving and seeking the souls of the heathen, may in all likelihood rest."

The present governor of the Colony is labouring zealously to advance this great effort; whilst the parliaments of England and the Colony are supporting him in those noble efforts, the former with a grant of £40,000, and the latter with one of £5000, towards defraying the expenses of teachers and institutions for civilization and Christianity.   "The Church has now an opportunity of retrieving her character, and of recovering lost ground.   *She* will greatly embarrass my Government, if she does not rise up to her duty."   Such are the words of that governor, Sir George Grey.   Most cordially then is it to be hoped that the Church will *hear* and *obey* this call, and will cheerfully and readily come forward with the necessary supplies of both *men* and *money*, and so enable her Missionary handmaiden, the incorporated

Society for the extension of her borders, to meet the emergencies in this part of the Mission field, by supporting and strengthening the hands of these self-devoted Missionary Bishops who are now endeavouring to unfurl the banner of the cross over the benighted shores of Southern Africa.

Four hundred thousand unconverted heathen souls are now spread before us there, and are placed, in God's providence, *within the hearing* of our Church's voice, and those glad tidings of salvation, through "Jesus Christ and Him crucified," which that voice is ordered to preach and proclaim not only in Africa, but "to every creature."

In occupying her position, and retrieving here her lost ground, the Church has also a field, of sufficient extent, whereon to expend her best energy against the heathen strongholds of sin and Satan, without in any way interfering with the labours of those more zealous soldiers, who are already up and doing the work. This is a consideration of some satisfaction to many. May *all* therefore unite to aid forward the Missionary march of our English Church's soldiers; and, whilst it may long be the boast of our country, in her hours of need, that many sons are found to obey her call in danger, and to go out in her armies, and man her navies; so may it likewise be the boast and glory of our Church, that *her* calls for aid ever receive as ready and ample a supply both of men and sinews, for waging her spiritual wars against the enemies of " the great captain of our salvation."

The probabilities of success, are also sufficiently strong and numerous, to induce the most apathetic to believe, that those efforts, if now put forth with zeal and energy, will be crowned with fruit and success. The dispositions of the Kaffirs are naturally good and easily impressed, and appear only to be vitiated through heathenism. Their early training and national forms of government, all tend to induce them to prefer, and to reverence, everything presented in a system, above that which is unmindful of external forms and discipline. And hence, the superior Episcopal order of the Church of England, together with the fact of her presenting all the purity of truth in her doctrines, with these yet enshrined within the external discipline, forms and regularity of that Church, peculiarly adapt her for teaching the Kaffirs with acceptance, and receiving their respect and attention.

The religion presented to them by those already in the field, appears, as it were, of too spiritual a kind (if we may be allowed the expression) for the unregenerated and unenlightened minds of the Kaffirs to understand it, if wholly unaided by those external forms, habits, and observances, which past experiences have taught our Anglican branch of the Church to use, not only with advantage and acceptance, but also with permission and without evil. The body may and must go with the spirit, and where both these are kept in their proper places, and used rightly, there is, humanly speaking, the greatest success attained. Such we have in the system of the English Church, and this is the peculiar qualification she possesses for obtaining the attention, and receiving the consideration, of the Kaffir mind. The story of the Bible, if grafted on the traces of their Ismaelitish origin, may also be presented thus to their consideration with peculiar charms; whilst the use of music and chanting, in the services of the Church, are in exact unison with their own tastes and habits.

The intellectual powers of the Kaffirs are of such a calibre as will fully enable them to appreciate the exercise of talent and ability, when these are manifested to them. Nor are they undeserving of the exercise of these, nor of the flow of eloquence in exhortation. The well educated, carefully trained, disciplined, and, at the same time, *earnest* and *spiritual* style of the ministers and system of the English Church is therefore to be considered as of considerable weight in the balance of their fitness, and adaptation to be the established teachers of the Kaffirs.

In the same order, regularity, and decency then with which we have received the Gospel in Britain, in the same may we not hope and believe it will be received in Southern Africa. If its evangelical truth has lost none of its lustre or brightness by being established amongst us, in the true apostolic order; if its catholic love was strong enough to keep alive the zeal of those who first planted that banner on Britain's shores, and was able, in their hands, to expel and extirpate the barbarous rites of Pagan Druidism; shall it be said, or even supposed, that it has lost any of that power now, or that the same is not to be found as all-sufficient in uprooting heathenism from Africa, and uprearing there, in its stead, the kingdom of Christ and His sceptre of righteousness? No, let England's Church not doubt the power which belongs, not indeed to her own inherent excellency, or her superior worth, but to HIM, who is her Head, her Sovereign, and her God, and through Him to her, and who has said that the conflict is won, by his servants, not "by might, nor by power, but by my Spirit saith the Lord." In that name and Spirit let us then now go out, as it was in the days of the apostles, "Paul planting, Apollos watering, but GOD giving the increase." If we work in faith, so it shall be found that He who gave the command to His Church, "Go ye into all the world and preach the Gospel to *every creature*," has not forgotten the promise which he added thereto, but the result will assuredly be as he has said, "And lo! *I* am with you always even unto the end of the world." Amen.

JEREMIAH viii, 22.

CHAPTER XI.

ALTHOUGH incidental notices of the Amazulu tribes of Kaffirs residing in Natal, as well as other points of connection between the two Colonies, have induced mention to be already made of these parts of the African continent; it may not, at the same time, be inapt here to introduce an epitome of those connecting links in the past colonial history of Africa, which led to the establishment and subdivisions of these various parts and states. A brief sketch of the localities themselves, together with their present inhabitants and products, may likewise be acceptable in a work of this character.

The New Colony of Natal is so intimately connected with the Orange-river free state, in its origin and rise, that these two divisions of Southern Africa must be included in one general notice.

The first special mention of this part of the Continent was at the same period, when the other portions of the promontory were discovered; at which time, namely, in the year 1497, it is mentioned that Vasco de Gama, the Portuguese navigator, touched here, discovered it, and, on Christmas day of that year, gave to it the name of *Terra Natalis*. The extent of surface, in the portion of the Eastern coast of Southern Africa, that now bears this title, is about 18,000 square miles, situated in latitude 29 to 31 S. degrees. Like the rest of the Continent, it rises from the shores of the Indian Ocean in distinct steps or terraces. They are here four in number. Along the coast the heat is greatest, and towards the interior more equable. The prevailing character of the scenery is woodland and park-like, but this diminishes as the traveller advances inland, rising in elevation as well as attaining more moderate temperature in the interior. The atmosphere is clear and refreshing, except at the time of the hot winds, when it becomes oppressive.

The two principal towns are D'Urban, the sea-port, containing a population of 1100, and that of Pieter Maritzburg, fifty miles in the interior, containing 1800 souls, including the military stationed there. Situated inland, beyond the latter of these towns, are the Drakenberg or Quathlamba mountains; while, scattered through the various districts of the Colony are the rising villages of Richmond, Ladismith,

View of the Bay of Natal and Town of D'Urban, from the Berea.   *Page* 301.

York, Verulam, Weenen, Byrne, and Pine-town, &c. The soil is rich and well adapted for the combined cultivation of wheat, potatoes, coffee, indigo, sugar, and arrowroot; all of which flourish in this genial climate.

The present population of this colony may be numbered at about 6000 Europeans, of whom perhaps 1000 are Dutch; and from 100,000 to 120,000 Kaffirs. It is abundantly watered, a stream flowing through every four or five miles of country. These are never dry, except a few of the smaller ones in the winter months of May, June, and July. During this season, there is scarcely any rain, the temperature is delightfully cool and pleasant, but not, like the districts of Kaffirland, frosty, except on the hills and mountain tops beyond Maritz-burg, where not only frost, but snow lies for several days together.

To present a brief, but true and most in-telligent, account of the more modern circum-stances which led to the first establishment of this colony and the neighbouring districts, we condense our information mainly from the au-thority of the Recorder of Natal, whose intimate and accurate acquaintance with all the circum-stances well qualify him to afford it.

The first combination of causes which induced the Dutch farmers of the Old Cape Colony to emigrate beyond the Orange-river, found the new colony of Natal, and finally to settle in and establish the Trans Vaal republic, are traceable to many different sources, which appear to date back as far as the begining of the present century.

The Dutch governor, Van Plettenberg, in the year 1778, formally defined the boundary of the Cape Colony by the great Fish river to the Eastward, and by an ideal line, running through (what are now called) the districts of Somerset, Graaf-Reinet, Beaufort, and Clanwilliam, up to a little rivulet, "the Koussie" which flows into the Southern Atlantic, to the North West. These boundaries, though existing in name, appear to have been disregarded by the border Kaffir tribes (the Amakosa) who constantly crossed over and pillaged the farmers of their cattle, along the frontier line of Graaff-Reinet and Utenhage; until, in 1812, they were finally expelled from the colony. For many years the Cape farmers also, kept within their own bounds, and were not desirous of wandering. At length, about the commencement of the present century, small parties of a half cast breed derived from European and Hottentot origin, joining themselves to the Mantatee tribes, gradually occupied the lands lying beyond the Orange river, at the N. E. boundary of the Old Colony, and from them the race denominated "the Griquas," formed themselves. With these, the colonists opened a regular intercourse, as they soon found that in seasons of excessive drought within the colony, (where their herds and flocks were dying for want of pasturage,) the lands to the Northward of the Orange river, were generally favoured with more frequent and regular thunder-storms, thus ensuring a better supply of grass, during the summer months, than the colony itself afforded. From that time all the grazing farmers in that neighbourhood began to form establishments in the country between the Orange and the Vaal rivers, (the Kye and the Knu Gariep) and took possession of such tracts as they found unoccupied, or otherwise entering into regular leases with the prior occupants of those lands. They still, however, continued to consider their domicile to be within the colony, to which they returned whenever the seasons of drought had passed away, or whenever called upon to pay their "*opgaaf*," or annual assessed taxes, not even then considering themselves absolved from the duties and ties which bound them to the old colony.

This erratic life conduced, however, to deaden their attachment to any particular locality, and gradually weaned them from all desire to cultivate their land; and thus these boers were gradually and imperceptibly, even to themselves, prepared for the reception of discontented, and easily excited trains of mind.

The minor and primary causes for their discontent, first sprang up about the year 1813, when the vast and reckless expenditure of the colonial revenues seemed to have laid the foundation for that distress throughout the country, which, when retrenchment began in 1815, was at once engendered.

The administration of justice in the country districts of the Colony also tended to excite strife.   There was at that time hardly any regular communication with the interior, and although the boards of landdrost and hemraaden* in each district could take cognizance of minor offences and civil suits of a limited amount, yet access even to these two tribunals was (from the then vast extent of the districts) exceedingly difficult and precarious. To remedy this evil, Lord Caledon, then governor, very wisely instituted the " commission of circuit," which consisted of two members of the supreme

* The boards of "landdrost and hemraaden," was a judicial court formed under the old Dutch law of the colony, and consisted of a landdrost or chief magistrate, with six hemraaden or burghers under him, who acted throughout the country districts of the colony in the same capacity as our country magistrates and their courts do in England.

court, who were annually to travel through the districts, and hold court in each.

The accumulation of crimes brought forward, "en masse," on the first circuit thus held, amounted to between seventy and eighty cases for murder, aggravated assaults, and such like. Two Missionaries, Dr. Vander Kemp and Mr. Read, also came forward as protectors of the Hottentot race, and transmitted to the local government, charges of cruelty against members of almost every respectable family on the frontier. These were referred by the Government to the "commission of circuit," and it was occupied for a protracted period in investigating them. It was not, in fact, until the third sitting, that they were brought to a conclusion; of all these, no single case of murder was proved, and a very few of personal assault brought home and punished. These ill-judged prosecutions, however (in which nearly one hundred of the most respectable Dutch families on the frontier were implicated, and more that one thousand witnesses summoned and examined,) engendered a very bitter feeling of hostility, amongst the Dutch, towards the administration of justice in general, and more particularly against the Missionaries who brought forward these charges.

The next "commission of circuit," in 1815,

held its session at Graaf-Reinet, when one of those untoward events took place, which set the whole Eastern province in a blaze, drove a great mass of the population into open rebellion against their Sovereign, and brought many heads of families to an ignominious death; thus causing an alienation from, and bitterness of feeling towards, the local Government, which has never since been eradicated.

This was the case of a Dutch Boer, named Fredrick Bezuidenhout, who lived in Bavian's River district.   He refused to appear before the court of landdrost and hemraaden, on a charge of illtreatment of a Hottentot preferred against him, threatening to shoot the messenger or sheriff if he ventured again to approach his farm.   Being known to be a very daring character, a warrant of "personal summons" was issued against him, in serving which, resistance having been made by him, and the military being called out, he was unhappily shot in the affray. His brother then raised a conspiracy against the Government, and with several other boers proceeded to make an attack on the nearest military post and thus to be revenged.   To suppress this, the military had again to be called out, and several collisions took place.   Thirty of the boers at the first surrendered, the remainder retreated and resisted.   At length having been pursued into, and surrounded in, a deep kloof in Kaffirland, whither they fled, the second Bezuidenhout was killed, two others were wounded, and the remainder captured. Of the latter, six of the leaders were sentenced to suffer capital punishment in sight of their companions, on the spot where they had first assembled in rebellion—a place still alas! too well remembered amongst the boers, called "Slachters Neck."—The others after witnessing the execution, were to undergo various degrees of punishment, such as transportation, banishment, and fines. Five of these unfortunate men were put to death, their sufferings being much lengthened in consequence of the scaffold giving way with the weight of their bodies, and obliging them to be hanged a second time.

This ended the Dutch rebellion of 1815, which mistaken and unhappy event sowed the indelible impressions of distrust, and a rankling dislike which gradually ripened into that utter alienation of feeling, between the Dutch and English, and finally led the former to leave the Colony, and "*trek*" beyond the Orange river.

Another minor cause of dissatisfaction arose from the change in the currency of the colony, which took place in June, 1825. The ordinance effecting this, which was sent out by the

Home Government, was then first promulgated. It introduced British silver money as a legal tender, and directed it to be taken in exchange for the Cape *paper rix-dollar*, at *one-shilling and sixpence* sterling, although it had been originally issued, and recognized at the value of *four shillings* for every rix-dollar.

The three great grievances, however, under which the Dutch considered themselves to be mainly the sufferers, were the three questions of, first *the Hottentots*, second *the slaves*, and third *the Kaffirs*—and these combined, finally induced them, during the period between 1815 and 1835, to "*trek*"—and attempt to establish their own republic.

We shall endeavour to give a brief digest of the circumstances connected with each of these points, taking first, the "*Hottentot question.*" This appears to have had its rise in that animosity which sprang up between the boers and the early Missionaries, who were connected with Dr. Vander-Kemp, and Mr. Read, and which has already been mentioned. From these disagreements the worthy Moravian Missionaries appear very justly to have been exempted, and, amidst them all, to have grown in the estimation of the whole community, and become deservedly entitled to their respect and admiration, through their unostentations and persevering labours amongst the natives. Such, however, was, unhappily, not the case in the other Missionary stations which then sprang up along the border districts of the old colony.

The very independent ideas which, in conjunction with religious teaching, were there inculcated amongst the Hottentots, conduced, it is to be feared, to confirm them in habits of idleness and indolence; and it was soon manifest, that they found an undisciplined and unmolested life spent in and around these stations, far preferable to those of work and industry which they had been accustomed to, on the various farms of the boers.

No government interference or controul of any kind, was claimed or exercised upon these stations, and even disclosures were made which tended to shew that, occasionally, a magisterial authority was assumed, to punish offenders by juries, and modes of punishment also devised by the Missionaries within these schools. These being left unnoticed by the Government, were jealously viewed by the Dutch, as unjustifiable interferences, all tending to widen the breach between them and the Missionaries and their Hottentot protegées.

These were some of the causes which induced the farmers to become dissatisfied on this point, mainly because they believed, to use the words of Mr. Cloete, "that the numerous Missionary schools, and last of all, the extensive establishment at Kat river, took from the service of the farmers every Hottentot or servant of Hottentot descent; who were not only induced to retire to these schools, as the abode of ease and indolence, but were moreover taught to consider themselves as a distinct race, who "ought" not to owe any service to the Saxon farmer."

The want of labour thus arising from the gradual withdrawal of the whole Hottentot race from agricultural and pastoral service, together with the spirit of hostility which was manifested by them towards the frontier colonists, first induced the latter to think of seeking for a location elsewhere, where their herds and flocks might be safe, and they could obtain labourers on more easy terms.

But great and serious as this cause was considered by them, it was secondary in the intensity of their feelings, when put in comparison with their second grievance, *"the slave question."* This arose from the circumstances connected with the carrying out of the Emancipation Act, in the year 1833, and the year following, throughout the Cape Colony. At that period, and previous to it, the value of an individual slave not unfrequently rose there, to from £400 to £600, and although, doubtless, the stern necessity for the emancipation of slaves was past all denial, still it cannot but be believed, that where the value of individual slaves was so high as this, their well-being was more likely to be attended to, than their ill-treatment allowed, and the instances of the latter were the exceptions, not the rule. The principle of slavery, however, so repugnant both to religion and civilization, demanded and justified its abolition, although it is ever much to be lamented that the manner in which that was carried out was so hasty. Few who have visited our colonies, or who there may have carefully and impartially investigated the interests of all parts of their communities, will not allow, that both slaves and slave-owners, the colonies and England herself, would have been saved many present evils, had that emancipation been effected *gradually*, not *instantaneously*—had slavery been permitted to wear away, and not to be, as it was, *at once* abolished.

In theory, the latter doubtless sounds better, but, like many other things, the practice has not borne out the superiority of mere theory over an exercise of judgment and prudence. The consequence of the valuation of the slaves, being estimated, moreover, far lower by the Government appraisers, than was their actual value in *the colonial markets*, was, of course, to reduce the nominal income of all the slave owners. The establishment of the "*record book*" also, (wherein owners were obliged to enter their own misdemeanors, and such punishments as they inflicted on their slaves,) which was instituted about this time to try and find out how slaves were treated, was stoutly resisted by the Dutch. They assembled for this purpose in Cape Town, to the number of nearly 4000 persons, and, marching up to the government-house, they stated to Sir Lowry Cole their determination to resist it; the governor promised to intercede for them, and thus this was finally withdrawn.

Again, when the abolition actually took place, and the government valuation appeared, (depreciating as it was supposed to be in value, but which value had been accepted by the boers) it stated that 35,745 slaves were found in the Cape Colony, and that a sum of £3,000,000 would be required to compensate their owners for them, thus yielding their average value at £85 a head. The whole parliamentary grant made by England, as a compensation for the slave owners throughout the colonies, was, however, but £20,000,000, and when this was divided amongst them all, it was found that it could only be done *proportionably, not by the valuation.* Hence, instead of £3,000,000 as estimated, but

£1,200,000 came to the share of the Cape, thus again reducing the average value to £48 each slave. Several of the owners having effected mortgages on their slaves, this second sudden reduction in the amount to be received, tended to ruin many families. Added to this, several of the boers being bad men of business, fell into the hands of persons representing themselves as alone acquainted with the requisite forms, &c., who bought up their certificates at various sums, varying from eighteen to thirty per cent. discount, thus reducing their compensation again another fifth, so that, by the time they received their several amounts, it was, of course, a renewed source of discontent, and in no way tended to obliterate the rancourous feelings which were festering in the breasts of many of these boers.

The third and last matter mentioned as leading to the Dutch emigration, was the "*Kaffir question.*" This was the last and paramount cause. It was, of course, intimatoly connected with the various incidents which occurred in the different Kaffir wars of the period, all of which tended to render their property more insecure, and themselves, consequently, discontented with their farms, for which their affections had long been wavering. The continual vacillation of policy that marked the constant changes of

Government, which, from time to time, were occuring, disheartened and displeased every one, and it may be readily believed it was not received in the most favourable light by the discontented Dutch boers. During the fourteen years which intervened between 1820 and 1834, the whole of the inhabitants of the Eastern frontier of the old colony were kept in a perpetual state of "*unrest*," arising from a series of petty thefts and robberies committed by the Kaffirs. These were sufficiently palpable to make the owners of the plunder feel its loss, though not sufficiently extensive or manifest to induce the then concilliatory government to declare hostility, or provoke disturbance, in trying to suppress them. The several wars, moreover, as they sprang up one after another, were so destructive to property and cattle, that the boers had certainly ample cause for feeling the miseries of a frontier life.

About this time a party of them collected some twelve or fourteen wagons, and numbering in all about twenty persons, headed by some Dutchmen, named Piet Nys, Cobus Nys, Haus de Lange, Stephanus Maritz, and Gert Rudolph, they started to explore Natal, and, taking the lower route along the Eastern slopes of the Quathlamba or Drakensberg range, they followed nearly the same track by which Dr.

Smith and his party had shortly before explored that district. They were much pleased with what they saw, and effected a settlement at the bay of Natal, where Messrs. Ogle, King, and Tooley, had previously located themselves. They loitered about shooting in this locality for some time, and visiting the neighbourhood, until alarmed by the intelligence of the breaking forth of the third Kaffir war of 1835. They then speedily retreated through Kaffirland, and finally reached the colony again in safety—reporting, of course, to their friends what they had seen.

This war again ended by the refusal of compensation to the farmers for their losses, which had been very numerous and severe, together with the censure on the then governor, Sir Benjamin D'Urban, the reversal of his—the best, the only feasible, and now again resumed —policy, and the appointment of Sir Andreas Stockenstrom to the lieut. governorship of the frontier. He was commissioned to attempt the policy of *concession* to the Kaffirs. This not only failed in attaining the desired effect, but also (as was foretold by every intelligent observer), in preserving peace. This brought to a crowning point the incipient determination of the discontented boers who, in the year 1836, to the number of 200 persons, headed by Hendrick Potgeiter, crossed the Orange river, and bidding farewell for ever to the Cape Colony, they "*treeked*" or travelled, to Thaba 'Nchu, where the Baralong chief Moroka gave them a most friendly reception, and where they also obtained every facility for grazing their cattle.

These were soon followed by a more numerous and wealthy party from Graaf Reinet, headed by Gert Maritz, and these were again succeeded by other large parties from the Uitenhage and Albany districts, headed by the aged Jacobus Nys, together with Carl Landman, Gert Rudolph, and others. Their numbers thus fast increasing in the Baralong territory, soon gave rise to divisions amongst themselves, and the older emigrants, making way for the latter arrivals, advanced gradually along the banks of the Vaal river, (or Ky Gariep) in a Northerly direction, until they came into contact with the numerous and powerful tribe of the Matabilii, under Mazulekatze.

It is supposed, that this sanguinary chieftain having been frequently attacked by the Zulu and Griqua forces in that direction, was always particularly jealous of any approach from that quarter; whilst the farmers unaware, of course, of this, gradually kept moving onwards, quite unsuspicious of danger. Suddenly their advanced posts were attacked, and twenty-eight of their numbers were murdered. Elated by this partial success, the Matabilii again attacked another party of boers, and killed twenty-five more of them, massacring their wives, and destroying and plundering their property. A few of this last party, however, escaping gave notice of danger to their neighbours, who had barely time to collect into a " *laager* " or camp, when they were attacked by the whole army of the Matabilii.   A most desperate struggle then ensued. The boers manfully maintained their stand, and their enemies unable to force entance to their camp, captured and drove away 40,000 of their sheep and 6000 oxen.

These disasters were, of course, communicated by the Dutch, to their friends at Thaba N'chu, who at once sent to their assistance and relief; and, mustering a party of 200 men headed by Gerrit Maritz, they crossed the Vaal, making a flank movement across the western boundary. Here they attacked one of Matzule-Katzes' chief military towns, named Mosega, and, in revenge, killed several hundreds of his principal warriors, recovering about 7000 head of cattle, together with the wagons which the Matabilii had taken there in triumph.

Immediately on their return from this victorious foray, disunion amongst themselves again broke out, but, at this period, Pieter Retief having appeared amongst them, he was at once chosen as their "commandant general."

This man was descended from one of the French Protestant families, which found refuge at the Cape, on the revocation of the Edict of Nantes. His family lived in the Paarl district, and there cultivated vines and oranges. Pieter was there born, and brought up, but being possessed of an active, restless spirit, he disdained the quiet life of a vine-dresser, and passed to the frontier; there he first became a trader to the interior, and afterwards, in 1820, a large contractor for supplying the "Albany settlers" with provisions. He next undertook contracts for erecting the Government buildings on the frontier, and thus obtained a large fortune. Through failures, losses, and other untoward circumstances he lost all his property, and became much embarrassed in pecuniary circumstances. He however, was so much respected, that he was appointed, in 1834, one of the "commandants of the frontier." In this capacity he served for several months, until Sir A. Stockenstrom refused to recognise and enforce his stringent measures, against the vagrant Kaffirs, for the frontier defence. On this, a very angry discussion ensued between them, which ended by Pieter Retief selling off all his property in the colony, and joining his emigrant brethren over the Vaal, just at the period when Gert Maritz* had returned from his successful attack upon Matzule-Katze and the Matabilii.

Having been elected commandant general of the emigrant boers, Retief immediately set about forming regular treaties of friendship and alliance with the native chiefs by whom he was surrounded, except Matzule-Katze. Moroko, Mosesh, Tonana, and Sikonyela, entered apparently with cordiality into all his arrangements, and, upon this footing, all the emigrants then spread themselves over the land situated between and along the Modder, the Vet, and the Sand rivers, and gradually formed themselves into a more settled form of government. Their numbers were, about this time, also increased by another large clan, headed by the venerable Jacobus Uys, then about seventy years of age, and his eldest son Pieter Uys; who, having visited this district before, cherished the idea of settling down here in preference to going further into the interior of Africa. This party issued a manifesto, declaratory of their intention to shape their course towards Natal, and to secede from all those parties who seemed more intent on occupying the banks

---

* The principal town of Natal, Pieter Maritzburg is named after these two Boers, viz, Pieter Retief, and Gert Maritz, being two of their most distinguished leaders, "*burg*" being, in Dutch, a town.

fo the Vaal river, or what *was* called "the Sovereignty," and even to proceed Eastward to Delagoa Bay.

This determination of the clans of Uys, Moolman, and Potgieter, appears to have induced Retief to follow their track, and he at once sent exploring parties from the Sand river, who at length succeeded in finding two or three paths across the Quathlamba or Drakensberg, which might be made passable for wagons; for, up to that time, every attempt to cross that range of mountains by wagons, from the Zuurberg to the West, as far as the Oliviers Pass, at the extreme North East extremity of the district, had failed.

We now adopt the words of the Honorable Henry Cloete, in detailing the remainder of the early history of the Natal settlement, as incomparably the best and truest account ever presented.

" Retief," he says, " succeeded with his party in crossing at one spot, and reached Port Natal in safety, where he met with a hearty reception from the British emigrants; who, strange to say, had also formed themselves into a little independent community. For, upon Capt. Gardiner, of the navy, arriving among them, and asserting a magisterial authority, under the provisions of an extraordinary law passed by the British legislature, and entitled "the Cape of Good Hope Punishment Bill," which he proceeded to promulgate there, they at once repudiated his interference, and maintained their independence from all authority except from such as would emanate from themselves, in consequence of the then Secretary for the colonies, Lord Glenelg, having expressly "disclaimed in the most distinct terms, any intention on the part of His Majesty's Government to assert any authority over any part of this territory." This mutual feeling of independence, seemed to serve as a bond of union between them, and there can be no doubt that, if a person like Retief had continued to be the acknowledged head of the Dutch emigrants, a more firm and lasting tie would have bound them together.

"Pieter Retief, however, in the conscientious view which he had always taken of these matters, felt that as both Chaka and Dingaan had nominally given away this territory to various other persons before his arrival, the occupation of this country by him and his followers, might hereafter subject them to disputes, either with the Zoolah chiefs, or with such English emigrants as had received such ill-defined grants from the Zoolah Sovereigns, he therefore determined to proceed in person to Dingaan's capital, and to negociate with him a treaty of peace, and obtain a formal cession of such extent of territory as the latter might feel inclined to cede to him and the emigrant farmers. Upon reaching the Zoolah chief's capital, Umkongloof, he accidentally found there a Missionary of the Church of England, (the Rev. F. Owen) who materially assisted in apparently disposing the chief to give him a kind reception, and, upon being made acquainted with the special object of Retief's mission, he at once promised him a formal cession of this territory, upon his first recovering back for him a quantity of cattle which Sikonyella, a Mantatee chief residing on the sources of the Caledon river, had recently taken from him. Retief accepted these terms, and, returning to this district, at once called together several of the parties who were preparing to settle down in this territory. They determined upon an attack on Sikonyelly, but, before doing so, sent messengers to him demanding restitution, with a significant notice, that it would be enforced. This communication had the desired effect, for Sikonyella immediately gave up seven hundred head of cattle, together with sixty horses and some guns, which he and his tribe had, at various times, captured from small immigrating parties of farmers.

"During these proceedings, which took place during the last months of the year 1837, nearly one thousand wagons had already descended and passed down the slopes of the Draaksberg into this district; and the emigrant farmers, finding the country entirely denuded of all population (with the single exception of one small party under the chief Matuan, who now still occupies nearly the same ground), spread themselves over the whole of the Klip river division, down to the Bushman's river, where the remains of thousands of stone kraals clearly indicated that a very dense population must have once been established there; thus giving a promise of the great fertility of the soil, as it could not otherwise have maintained so large a population.

"Upon Retief's return to that part of this district, on his way to Dingaan, with the cattle surrendered by Sikonyella, to be delivered to the former, a sad presentiment seems to have come over many of the leaders of the parties, who, however, then still acknowledged Retief as their commander. Gert Maritz proposed that he should proceed to Dingaan, with the cattle recovered, taking only three or four men with him, arguing, very justly, that the insignificance of such a force would be its best safeguard; but Retief appeared to have desired to show Dingaan something like a respectable force, and insisted upon taking some forty or fifty of

his best horsemen with him, leaving it, however, optional to any person to accompany him
or to remain behind; this only induced an
additional number of spirited young men to
join, and during the last week in January,
1838, Pieter Retief, accompanied by seventy
of the most respectable and picked men from
among the emigrants, with about thirty young
Hottentots and servants riding or leading their
spare horses, formed an imposing cavalcade,
with which he crossed the Umzinjaate, or Buffalo
river, and on the 2nd February arrived at Umkongloof, Dingaan's capital, and delivered over
the cattle recovered from Sikonyella, with the
receipt of which Dingaan expressed himself
highly satisfied; and having collected several
of his regiments from the neighbouring kraals,
he entertained them for two days with their
favourite sham fights, which give a fearful re-
presentation of their mode of warfare. On the
4th of February, Dingaan had fixed for signing
a formal cession of the whole of this district to
Pieter Retief, for himself and the emigrant
farmers for ever; and the Rev. Mr. Owen,
still then residing with Dingaan, was requested
to draw out, and witness the instrument, which
he accordingly did in English, and to this document, Dingaan, and some of his principal councillors, affixed their marks, after the tenor

thereof had been fully interpreted to them by the Rev. Mr. Owen. Retief's business being thus satisfactorily ended, he made his arrangements to depart the next morning, when Dingaan desired him to enter his *"kraal"* once more to take leave of him, requesting, however, that his party should not enter armed, as this was contrary to their usage; and this Retief unguardedly did, leaving all their arms piled up outside of the *"kraal,"* while they sent their *"achter ryders"* to fetch and saddle their horses. Upon approaching Dingaan in his *"kraal,"* they found him surrounded (as usual) by two or three of his favorite regiments, when, after conversing with Retief, and some of his leading men, in the most friendly manner, he pressed them to sit down a little longer, offering them their *"stirrup cup,"* in some *"chullah"* or maize beer, which the Kaffirs enjoy as a favorite beverage. This was handed round to the whole party, who partook freely thereof, and, while a number of them were thus sitting down with the bowls in their hands, Dingaan suddenly exclaimed *"bulala matagati,"* or, *"kill the wizards,"* and, in an instant, three or four thousand Zoolahs assailed them with their *"knob kerries,"* and although many of the farmers instantly drawing their clasp knives (which they usually carry by them and use in cutting up the game they kill, or the viands they eat) made a determined resistance, and took the lives of several of their assailants, yet they soon fell, one after the other, under the overwhelming pressure of the thousands by whom they were charged and beaten down; and, after a desperate struggle of half an hour's duration, their expiring and mangled corpses were dragged out of the kraal, to an adjoining hillock, marked, and infamous as the "aceldama," or rather the "golgotha," where the bones of all victims to the fury of this despot were hoarded up, and became a prey to the wolves and vultures.

"Dingaan, following the precept of Cæsar, who deemed nothing done so long as anything remained undone, ordered instantly ten of his regiments to march into this territory, to attack all the emigrant farmers, (who, in perfect security, were spread all over the district, awaiting the return of their friends,) and exterminate them root and branch. It certainly is remarkable that the doubts which the majority had entertained as to the good faith of Dingaan, vanished so soon after the departure of Retief and his party. The young men were enjoying the pleasures of the chase, and supplying their friends with the game that abounded, and the women, seemingly also unsuspicious, were only awaiting the return of their husbands, sons, and relatives; when the Zoolah army, having divided itself into several small detachments, fell at break of day, on the foremost parties of emigrants near the Blue Krantz river, and close to the present township of Weenen, which has obtained its name (meaning wailing or weeping) from the sad events of that day. Men, women, and children, were at once surrounded, and barbarously murdered, with horrors, which I should be sorry to dwell upon and detail; other detachments of Zoolahs surprised, in other places, similar small parties who were likewise scattered all over the Klip river division, and who all fell under the Zoolah "*assegai*." From one or two wagons, however, a solitary young man escaped, who, hastening to the parties whom he knew to be in the rear, at length succeeded in spreading the alarm among them, so that, as the Zoolahs advanced further into the district, two or three parties of farmers had been able hastily to collect a few wagons, and arrange them into a "*laager*," or encampment, where they made their preparations to secure their families just in time, before they were also attacked, and they thus succeeded in repelling the most daring attacks made upon them; not one of these "*laagers*" having been forced or penetrated by the Zoolahs. The latter, however, advanced still further Southward, until they met a still stronger party of emigrants on the farm, now called "Vecht Laager," (at present the property of Mr. Ogle,) on the Bushman's river, where they sustained a very serious engagement, which lasted throughout the whole day, but where, when the farmers' ammunition was nearly exhausted, luckily their last shots, from a three pounder which had been rigged to the back of one of their wagons, struck down some of the leading Zoolah Chiefs and forced them to a precipitate retreat.

"The moment these attacks were thus repulsed, the emigrant farmers sallied out from their "*laagers*" to rescue, if possible, any of their friends who had been in advance, and to ascertain the havoc which had been caused among them ; when, upon reaching the stations which those had occupied, a scene of horror and misery was unfolded, which no pen can describe. All the wagons had been demolished, the iron parts wrenched from them, and by their ruins lay the mangled corpses of men, women, and children, thrown on heaps and abandoned to the beasts of prey. Amongst these heaps, at the Blue Krantz river, they found lying amongst the dead corpses, the bodies of two young females, about ten or twelve years of age, which still appeared to show some signs of vitality.

The one was found pierced with nineteen, and the other twenty-one stabs of the "*assegai,*" leaving every part of their little frames completely perforated, and every muscle or fibre lacerated. The one was named Johanna van der Merwe, and the other Catharina Margaretha Prinslo. They were taken up and tended with the utmost care, and, strange to say, live to this day, the sole survivors of the immediate branches of those families. They are, however, perfect cripples, although one of them has, which is still more remarkable, married, and is the mother of one or two children; but with these solitary exceptions, all these small parties which had not been able to combine and concentrate themselves in "*laagers,*" were utterly destroyed, and, in one week after the murder of Retief and his party, six hundred more victims were thus immolated by the fury and treachery of Dingaan and his army.

"The survivors in this fearful catastrophe, after recovering from the panic in which they had been thrown, resolved to avenge themselves for this dreadful loss.

"The whole clan of Uys, which from some little feeling of jealousy of Retief, had lagged behind on the Draaksberg, and had thus escaped this onslaught, on hearing of this destruction, came down into the Klip river, with many other smaller parties of farmers who were advancing towards this district, and their precarious situation was soon made known to the English party resident at the bay, when the latter determined upon a movement on Dingaan, to support the cause of the emigrant farmers, but they being few in numbers, took with them a body of seven hundred Zulus, four hundred of whom were armed with guns, having learnt to use them in their hunts of the elephant and buffalo. This party, which placed itself under the command of Mr. R. Biggar, crossed the Tugela at its mouth, and advanced a few miles across that river, when they attacked and destroyed the town of Tatabasooke, while the Zulu forces hid themselves in the Matikoola and Imsimdoosa rivers; but advancing a little further they were suddenly surrounded, and attacked at break of day by three divisions of the Zoolah army. After a desperate and murderous engagement almost every European or man of colour belonging to the party here lost his life; a fearful number of the Zoolahs were also killed, but of the English population of the bay, R. Biggar, Blankenberg, Cane, Stubbs, Richard Wood, William Wood, Henry Batt, John Campbell, Thomas Cambell, and Thomas Carden successively fell, and only one or two Europeans succeeded in fighting their way through these masses, to convey to the small party who had remained at the bay, the sad result of this engagement. That portion of Dingaan's army followed up (as usual) their success, and advanced as far as the bay, but the few English who had survived, took refuge on board of the *Comet*, Captain Hadden, then luckily lying at anchor in the bay, when after sweeping away all the cattle, this detachment of Dingaan's army retired again into the Zulu country.

" Dingaan himself, with his principal forces, was, however, at this time still watching the Dutch emigrant farmers, who, having now collected about 400 fighting men in the Klip River Division, placed themselves under the command of Piet Uys, and of Hendrik Potgieter, and advanced about the same time (in April, 1838,) towards Umkongloof, Dingaan's capital, intent upon destroying it, and expelling Dingaan from the country.

" This wily chieftain allowed the emigrant farmers to advance to within a few miles of his capital, where the approach to the town is closed in between two hills, and there the Zoolah forces first showed themselves, but gradually retiring, drew the emigrant farmers still further into this hollow way; when another division of the Zoolah forces, emerging from behind one of these hills, and cutting off all retreat, a desperate hand to hand fight ensued, the farmers being so hemmed in, that they could not fire, or fall back rapidly on horseback, and again load and charge, as was their usual and efficient mode of warfare. They accordingly, as by one consent, directed all their fire on one mass of the Zoolahs, where their fatal aim having cleared a path by bringing down hundreds in this volley, they rushed through and thus escaped; but their chief, and unquestionably most gallant commander, Piet Uys, having taken a somewhat different course, in a country but little known to them, found himself surrounded with a small party of about twenty faithful followers, and his favourite son, a young lad of twelve years of age, before a ravine, which their horses could not get over or clear.

"Finding himself wounded, he called to his followers "to fight their way out," as he could not follow. All obeyed his command, except his son, who remained by his father until both fell, pierced with wounds. The remainder of their party, and the great majority of the emigrant farmers, having ultimately succeeded in thus fighting their way out of this trap, which had so ably been laid for them, effected a retreat out of the country, without any further great loss of life, leaving, however, the "prestige" of victory with the Zoolah chieftain, to whom the loss of several hundreds of his best warriors, was always considered but of little moment, imparting only an exciting interest to his fiendish propensities and habits.

"The emigrant farmers were, however, so disheartened by the result of their attack, and that of the English settlers from the bay, upon Dingaan's forces, that they gave up all hope of resuming hostilities for the present. They had been taught a lesson of prudence by the talent and daring displayed by the Zoolah armies, and they accordingly kept a watchful eye upon their Northern frontier, and sent messengers out in various directions, imploring further accession to their numbers, both from the Cape and the present Sovereignty. Many parties upon hearing of their distressed state, came to join them, but this, at the moment, only increased their misery and wants, as their cattle and herds having been swept away, (these being still in the hands of the Zoolahs) and, having been prevented from cultivating any lands, they were exposed, not only to the greatest want, but were actually in a state of famine, when some liberal minded countrymen of theirs at the Cape, hearing of their distressed condition, sent them supplies of food, medicine, and other necessaries of life, which helped them through the miseries of the winter of 1838, during which season, want, disease, and famine stalked over the land, making fearful ravages among them.

"Dingaan, ever watchful when to attack his foe with advantage, being fully informed of their wretched condition, made another attack upon them in August, 1838; but, on this occasion, the emigrant farmers (having their scouts always out to give them timely intimation of his advance), were everywhere prepared to give him a warm reception, and at every "*laager*" the Zoolah forces were driven back and defeated with great loss, only two or three lives having been lost among the emigrants during several successive engagements. But although Dingaan was thus defeated, the emigrant farmers were still contending, up to the close of that year, with the greatest difficulties. Small parties were pouring in to join them, but bringing little effectual support; until in the beginning of December, the season appearing propitious, and a number of young men having come in by the Sovereignty, 460 fighting and mounted men put themselves under the command of Andries Pretorius, who had also recently joined the emigrants, among whom (having formerly been a Field-cornet in the Graaf-Reinet district,) he had made himself extremely popular.

"They were powerfully aided by the brave

Carel Landman, who joined them with all those emigrants who had already commenced settling themselves down near the bay; and these combined forces, profiting from the experience of the past, advanced with great caution, securing their position every evening, so that when they had nearly reached the Umslatoos river they were fully prepared, as, at the earliest dawn of day, on Sunday the 16th December, 1838, the whole of Dingaan's forces, about 10 or 12,000 strong, attacked their position with a fury far exceeding all their former attacks; for three hours they continued rushing upon them, endeavouring to tear open all their defences and force the emigrant camp, until Pretorius, finding the Zoolah forces concentrating all their efforts upon one side of the camp, and their own ammunition nearly failing, ordered 200 mounted men to sally forth out of one of the gates at the rear of the line which the Zulus were attacking, and these mounted warriors charging both flanks, and pouring their deadly vollies upon the immense masses which were gathered together within a small space, at length beat them off with a fearful loss. The emigrants assert that nearly 3000 Zoolahs licked the dust before they retreated; and their defeat must have been complete, as Dingaan fled quite panic stricken, set fire to the whole of his town of

Umkongloof, and hid himself with the remnant of his forces, for a considerable time, in the woods skirting the Umvaloos river.

"The emigrants having had only three or four men killed, and as many wounded, in this decisive engagement (among the latter of whom was Pretorius himself), advanced upon the town of Umkongloof, which they still found partially burning, and, on the awful hillock out of the town, they beheld, on one vast pile, the bones and remains of Retief, and their one hundred companions in arms, who, ten months before, had fallen victims to Dingaan's treachery, but whose deaths they were then in fact avenging. Many of the straps or "*rheims*" by which they had been dragged to this place of slaughter, were still found adhering to the bones of the legs and arms by which they had been drawn thither. The skulls were frightfully broken, exhibiting marks of the "*knob-kerries*" and stones with which they had been fractured, and, singular to relate, the skeleton of their ill-fated leader, Reticf, was recognized by a leathern pouch or Bandalier, which he had suspended from his shoulders, and in which he had deposited the deed or writing, formerly ceding this territory to the emigrant farmers, as written out by the Rev. Mr. Owen, on the day previous to his massacre, and signed with the mark of Dingaan, by which he declared, " to resign to Retief and his countrymen, the place called Port Natal, together with all the land annexed: that is to say—from the Tugela to the Umzimvooboo river, and from the sea, to the North, as far as the land may be useful and in my possession."

These are the words of the original document, which was found still perfectly legible, and was delivered over by the Volksraad in the year 1843, and is now (or ought to be) among the archives of the Colonial Office of Natal.

"After decently interring the remains of their unfortunate countrymen, the emigrant farmers found that their horses and ammunition were ill-calculated to continue a harrassing warfare upon Dingaan in his fastnesses, and they, therefore, resolved gradually to fall back, which they did with little loss, taking with them some 5000 head of cattle, which they distributed among themselves, as the lawful and hard-earned trophies of this campaign.

"On their return from this successful inroad, they were not a little surprised to find that Sir George Napier (who had succeeded Sir Benjamin D'Urban in the government of the Cape Colony,) had sent a small detachment of Highlanders, under the command of Major Charters, to take possession of the Bay of Natal. This measure had been evidently taken, and in fact was acknowledged, in a proclamation of the 14th November, 1838, to have emanated from a desire to "put an end to the unwarranted occupation of parts of the territories belonging to the natives, by certain emigrants from the Cape Colony, being subjects of His Majesty;" and that proclamation, gave the officer commanding these forces, the further power to "search for, seize, and retain in military possession, all arms and munitions of war, which, at the time of the seizure of Port Natal, shall be found in the possession of any of the inhabitants."

" Major Charters returned immediately to the Cape, when the command of the detachment devolved on Captain Jarvis, of the 72nd Regiment, and from the vague and ill-defined nature of his instructions, some serious differences, if not conflicts, might have arisen between him and the emigrant farmers, in regard to the authority and orders he had received to seize upon their gunpowder and ammunition. But the good sense and good feeling of that officer soon smoothed away every difficulty between them, and he delivered them up their gunpowder, which he had provisionally seized, upon their engaging not to use it in aggressive hostilities against the natives. The necessity of keeping and maintaining the detachment, led to some regular demand for supplies, which kept up a mutual interchange

of wants, and the most friendly interourse was
ever afterwards maintained between them. In
the meanwhile, the emigrant farmers laid out
the township of Pietermaritzburg and what is
now called the town of D'Urban. Landdrosts
were appointed to both townships; they established a more regular system of government,
and, with the the able assistance of Mr. Boshof,
(the present Registrar of the Court,) who, about
that time, arrived in the district with his entire
clan, various laws and regulations were framed,
which gradually redeemed them from the state
of anarchy, into which they were fast falling.
While the winter of 1839 was thus taken up
by these duties and labours, Dingaan, somewhat
recovering from the effects of his late defeat,
commenced sending in some special messengers,
first delivering up 316 horses, which he, at various times, had captured, and thereafter professing every disposition to enter into amicable
arrangements with the emigrants; their answer
was plain and manly, that they would not enter
into any treaty of peace with him, unless ample
restitution had been made of all their cattle,
and sheep, and until the value of their property,
taken or destroyed by him and the Zulus, had
been paid for. This led to frequent embassies,
promises of restitution, and fixing places where
some at least of the cattle, and some guns, were

promised to be delivered; but the farmers soon discovered that these messages and promises were mere pretexts to keep up a constant and regular espionage upon them, as one of these pretended messengers or spies being caught, he admitted that he had been sent to report to Dingaan whether the farmers were gradually returning to their farms, or whether they still kept near to their "*laagers*," thus clearly showing that he only waited the opportunity to attempt another "*razia*" upon them. This naturally paralyzed all their agricultural pursuits, and prevented them from spreading themselves about, to carry on their farming pursuits, being thus kept constantly on the alert. However, in the inscrutable decrees of Providence, one of those events was brought about for which they were quite unprepared, in which they were not even the chief agents, but which led to their undisputed possession of the whole territory of Natal.

"There were only, at that time, two brothers remaining alive of Chaka and Dingaan; the elder Panda, or Umpanda, (as he is called by his subjects,) and a young lad "Clu Clu."* Umpanda had just reached manhood, but brought

* "Clu Clu was murdered by Panda, in the year 1843, on which occasion their "Aunt" Maria, with a great number of Chaka's and Dingaan's followers, fled into this country; and these are at present still settled in this District, chiefly in the Umvooti and Inanda Locations."

up in the midst of debauchery and sensuality, he was only known for his unwarlike habits, and became the object of derision with the warriors, and of contempt with Dingaan, who seemed for a time to give full scope for the indulgence of his passions, as most conducive to his own personal safety; while Dingaan's appetite for war, was so insatiable, that notwithstanding his signal defeat by the emigrant farmers in December last, he had again mustered a strong army, with which he attacked Sapusa, but in which he was defeated with fearful loss.

"It was therefore not unnatural, that even among the Zulus, a party was forming, deprecating these murderous wars, and apparently inclined to support Panda, with a view to bring about peace with the emigrants and the surrounding nations. From that moment, Dingaan determined to watch the opportunity of murdering his brother; but it appears, that a hint of of his intentions to this effect, having transpired, Panda at once fled with a number of followers, and, crossing the Tuguela near its mouth, took possession of some lands near the Umvotee, and sent messengers requesting the support and protection of the emigrants. Some suspicion was at first entertained, that this was but a deep laid plot between him and Dingaan, to inveigle them into the Zulu country; but, after repeated conferences, which were managed with great tact and ability by the Landdrost "Roos" of D'Urban, by G. Kemp, Moolman, Morewood, Breda, and several others, a formal treaty of alliance, offensive and defensive, was concluded with him; by the terms of which, the emigrant farmers pledged themselves to support and defend Panda, while he, on the other hand, promised to support *them* in any attack upon Dingaan.

"The beginning of the year 1840, being considered the best season for commencing offensive operations, the emigrant farmers again mustered a force of 400 mounted warriors, who, under the chief command of Andries Pretorius, joined Panda's army, about 4000 strong; and this combined force, in January, again entered the Zulu country, by the Sunday's River and Biggar's Mountain, but, with proper caution, the emigrants kept themselves at some distance from Panda's army, which, under the able guidance of "Nonklaas," (still Panda's chief counsellor and captain) seemed quite intent upon coming into action.

"While this commando were preparing and mustering their forces in this town, one of Dingaan's principal messengers, Tamboosa, arrived here, with one of those specious messages and offers of peace. He was however, seized, with his attendant Combizana, and upon being rigidly questioned, frankly admitted, that he had also been sent with a view of reporting to Dingaan, the state of the combined army of emigrants and Zulus under Panda. The latter, evidently embittered against this person, (one of Dingaan's principal counsellors,) charged him with having been the chief cause of the murder of Retief and his party; that he had plotted and advised his (Panda's) death; and in short, brought such a series of charges against him, that (contrary to every usage of civilized life,) he was taken along with the army as a prisoner, until they reached the banks of the Buffalo or Umzimjaatee river, where a court martial was formed, which, under the excited feelings of the occasion, soon passed a sentence of death upon the unfortunate prisoners, and it was carried into execution within a few hours after; Tamboosa, not only upbraiding his executioners, with the violation of all usage towards messengers, even amongst savages, but expressing his perfect readiness to die, he implored, (but in vain,) mercy on behalf of his young attendant, who was only a camp follower, and had thus been but doing his duty, in following his master.

"This may be said to have been the only blot, which seriously reflected upon the conduct of

the emigrant farmers, in their several engagements with the Zulus, for they otherwise constantly endeavoured to spare the women and
children from massacre, and have uniformly
conducted their wars, with as much discretion
and prudence, as bravery.

"A few days after this sad execution, the Zulu
army, under Panda, encountered that commanded by Dingaan, whereupon a desperate engagement ensued, in the course of which, one or two
of Dingaan's regiments, went over in a body to
Panda : after which two of Dingaan's best regiments, who fought bravely for him, were totally destroyed, the battle ending in his total
defeat and flight. The emigrant farmers not
having been engaged in this action, followed up
this success, (as soon as they heard of it,) with
great vigour; they drove Dingaan over the
Black Umvoloos, and from thence still further
to the Banks of the Pongola; where, deserted
by almost all his followers, he endeavoured
with about a hundred warriors, to find shelter
amongst a small tribe, living near Delogoa
Bay, named the " Asmasuree," but who, (it is
supposed, for I believe there is no actually
authentic account of his death,) murdered him,
to ensure their own safety, from his constant
and fearful forays upon them and the adjacent
tribes.

"There existing, however, no doubt as to his death, and the dispersion of all his army, the emigrant farmers assembled in great state on the banks of the Umvoloos, on the 14th February, 1840 ; and there, under the discharge of their guns, Andries Pretorius proclaimed Umpanda the sole and acknowledged King of the Zulus ; and by a proclamation issued by him, and attested by the other commandants, they declared their sovereignty to extend from the Umvoloos Umfana, or the Black Umvoloos, and the St. Lucia Bay, to the Umzimvooboo, or St. John's river : and in fact, by their proceedings of that day, assumed a certain authority, or sovereignty, over Umpanda himself, from whom they received, as their indemnity, 36,000 head of cattle, 14,000 of which, were delivered to those farmers who, residing beyond the Draaksberg, had only come in as allies to their friends, and the remaining 22,000 (or rather, the sad remains of them, for very many were lost or stolen on the way) were brought to the foot of the Zwart Kop, near this town, where, at a spot still named the Deel Laager,* they were distributed among such farmers as belonged to this district, and had claims for losses sustained in the previous wars and engagements.

"A few days before the emigrant farmers

* "Anglice ;" camp for distributing or dividing.

started on their last and crowning victory over Dingaan and his forces, Sir George Napier, having been ordered to send the 72nd regiment home, and finding that the Secretary of State for the Colonies, still continued little inclined to support his policy of occupying this district, sent a vessel to the Bay, with orders to Capt. Jarvis to embark with his whole detachment; on which occasion, he addressed a letter to the Landdrost, "Roos," at D'Urban; which, after referring to some complaints of natives as to encroachments on their gardens, contained the following farewell address and peroration. "It now only remains for me on taking my departure, to wish you one and all as a community, every happiness, sincerely hoping, that aware of your strength, peace may be the object of your counsels; justice, prudence, and moderation, be the law of your actions; that your proceedings may be actuated by motives, worthy of you as men and Christians, that hereafter your arrival may be hailed as a benefit; having enlightened ignorance, dispelled superstition, and caused crime, bloodshed, and oppression to cease, and that you may cultivate these beautiful regions in quiet and prosperity, ever regardful of the rights of the inhabitants, whose country you have adopted, and whose home you have made your own."

The Dutch were then left in possession of Natal, for some two or three years.   At the end of this time, some interference with the Kaffir tribes, considered by the Cape government, to be injurious to the alliance made with them, led to a remonstrance, on their part, being sent to the Dutch. This, meeting with no attention, a small military force, which was despatched from the Cape to enforce it, was further overpowered by the Dutch, and very straitly beseiged in a small fort at D'Urban. Reinforcements arriving, the English were, however, more successful; and at length, the Dutch were induced to surrender the Colony into the hands of the English, who claimed it by virtue of the original cession of the Cape of Good Hope settlements, among which Natal was reckoned from very early times.

Some of the Boers then determined to remain under British rule. Others took titles for farms from the British governments, but some of these have only very lately been taken possession of. The great body of them, however, determined to "*trek*" once more, over the Drakensberg, and to set up again their independence. In doing this, however, they made an effort to induce their old friend Panda, to join them, and to attack the English in Natal; and in consequence, Sir Harry Smith went against them, and, after a stubborn resistance, he defeated them at the battle of Boem Plaats, in the year 1848. Those who then submitted to his arms, were allowed to remain upon their new possessions, and to govern themselves, very much by their own laws, on condition that they would recognize "the Sovereignty" of the Crown of England. Hence it was, that the whole central district of Southern Africa, between the two branches of the Orange river, the "*Nu Gariep*," and the "*Ky Gariep*," (of which the former is called the Orange, and the latter branch, the Vaal river,) acquired the name of the "Sovereignty," beyond the Orange river.

A large portion, however, of the defeated Boers, under their leader Pretorius, migrated still further to the North, beyond the Vaal river, and at length succeeded in forming a republic there for themselves, called the "*Trans-Vaal Republic*," beyond the reach of British interference. Some 25,000 Dutch Boers now reside there, scattered over that rich and picturesque tract of country. The chief town of Poschefstrom, which stands at the confluence of the Mooi and the Vaal rivers, contains some 400 or 500 inhabitants. There is another smaller village named Rustenberg, at the foot of the Magaliesberg range of mountains, where about 150 more dwell. Eight days journey to the North-east from this, there are again about fifty families more, settled under the Zontspans-berg mountains. Beyond this, however, the country becomes unhealthy, and, consequently, is uninhabited.

The Sovereignty, as established in 1848, be-came the conjoined residence of some 20,000 English and Dutch, who were induced to set-tle there, together with about 80,000 Kaffirs, mainly Basutoes, owning the chieftainship of Moshesh. With these Kaffirs, the battle of the Berea was fought by our troops, in 1853, under the late Sir George Cathcart. Since then, the whole of this territory has been abandoned by the English government, and the Dutch have now established their new " Orange River Free State ;" by which title, at the present time, that part of Africa is styled and known.

The Colony of Natal has been in the posses-sion of the English since 1845, and still con-tinues to remain so. It is inhabited by a mixed population of Dutch, English, German, and Zulu Kaffirs. The latter are not only there as servants to the Europeans, but are also settled as refugees, having fled from the despotism of Panda and claimed the English protection. For this, they pay a tax to Government of 7s. for each hut they erect within the colony. They are governed by Magistrates, and amongst them, as also to the paramount Chief, Panda, and his tribes, the Bishop of Natal, and his Missionaries of the Church of England, have now gone. The capabilities of the colony are being daily developed by the settlers. Sugar mills are rising on the various estates, and the extended cultivation of it, together with coffee, indigo, arrowroot, and pine-apples, is increasing : thus it bids fair to be ere long, a prosperous and very productive colony. The bay and harbour are admirably situated for the shelter of shipping, and, as the local revenues of the place become more permanent and extensive, the rise of more commodious piers and stores, and the establishment of other public buildings and institutions, will tend to advance the stability of the place, and the security of its inhabitants and their property.

The permanent establishment of two such states, as Natal and the Dutch Trans-Vaal Free State, cannot but be regarded as of vast importance, towards aiding in the exploration of the vast interior of the continent, as well as tending to extend a wider commercial intercourse with the native tribes. Let us hope that they may be, not only thus the pioneers of commerce, civilization, and research in Southern Africa, but also the precursors of the rays of that brighter light of Christianity, which ever shines over and around the flaunting folds of our British flag and ensign.

A ZULU UMPAZI, OR NATAL-KAFFIR MARRIED WOMAN.

CHAPTER XII.

HAVING thus travelled from Cape-point to the Trans-Vaal territory, giving, as we progressed, an outline sketch of the country, its tribes and products, we now turn to notice cursorily, the natural history of the lower animals, which are found scattered over this portion of the African continent.

A voluminous catalogue of so extensive and varied a subject as this, does not, of course, come within the compass of the present volume. It will therefore suffice merely to insert here a few of the more striking notes, taken on the spot, on the various heads of this branch of its natural history. In the appendix annexed, a classified catalogue of the South African Animal Kingdom, so far as it has yet been ascertained is given; for the minute and detailed individual accounts of which, we must refer the more curious reader to larger works than the present, an abundance of which, on every branch of this science, are now happily extant. As regards the larger quadrupeds, little can be added to the notices of Dr. Andrew Smith, and Captain Harris, although accumulated and various accounts all tend, of course, to develop the subject.

More or less, every African traveller is, of necessity, a Nimrod, and, consequently, the author must claim exemption from professional censure, if he here insert a few adventures amidst these objects of the lower kingdoms of creation, which, in Europe, might be considered by some to be rather unclerical.

In those portions of the country personally visited by him, the more gigantic mammalia have now wholly disappeared. The lion, the elephant, the giraffe, and the rhinoceros, having fled from the haunts of man, are now seldom met with lower down in Africa, than along the line which stretches from the Quathlamba mountain range on the Eastward, to the Southern border of Namaqualand on the Western coast. The districts lying along the banks of the Orange, Vaal, and Mooi rivers, in the in-

terior, are still, however, peopled with countless herds of the larger varieties of deer and
antelope, zebras, quaggas, and leopards; but,
it is not until the hunter crosses over the Magaliesberg, and Zoutspansberg ranges, that he
falls in with the more gigantic species of the
elephant, giraffe, or rhinoceros. The rivers,
throughout the lower districts of Kaffirland,
are still the haunts of the hippopotami; several
also, in Natal, of the crocodile, the alligator,
and the cayman; whilst the hyæna, jaager,
ounce baboon, jackall, wild boar, and buffalo,
are still numerous throughout the kloofs, glens,
and bush country, of the divisions lying in the
latitudes between 30°. 45°., and 33°. 50°.

We here introduce the notes of some of these,
interspersed through the recountal of a less
formal sketch of

"A DAY WITH THE BUFFALOS."

We started from Graham's Town, on our expedition against these, into the Cowie bush in
Lower Albany, about 4 P. M. on a lovely day,
in March, 1853. The rays of the setting sun
painted the surrounding foliage with tints of
gold, as we rode through the picturesque vale
of Belmont, and wound our way towards the
wooded banks of the Blue Krantz river.

Our purpose was to encamp for the night on
the highlands of Langholme; and then, starting

from thence a little before sunrise, to be on our
hunting ground as the first streaks of the light
dawned on the horizon the next morning.
This is the only chance there is of obtaining a
glimpse of these wary creatures, which always
feed on the rich pasturage of the valleys by
night—drink in the rivers at dawn—and then,
passing into the densest parts of the bush, lie
sleeping in obscurity during the hours of mid-
day, light, and heat.

We completed our afternoon ride just at sunset, and pitching our tent and lighting a large
fire, we proceeded to cook our supper in gypsy
fashion, and enjoyed ourselves, for the remainder of the evening, in that manner which is
only known to those who have had the peculiar
delights of a life in the bush.   The surrounding
landscape was truly beautiful, although its face
was sadly marred by the burnt houses and
devastated farms, which lay scattered on every
hand—the monuments of the brand and "*assegai*" of the late Kaffir war.   Few districts of
the Colony, have suffered more severely or frequently from this cause, than this one of Albany.   Lying along the frontier line, it naturally is the first scene of each renewed inroad
from the savage.   And certainly we felt little
inclined to answer· the reply of one of these
frontier farmers, to our enquiry put to him,

whether he intended to rebuild his house. "What," was his rejoinder, "for the *third* time?—No Sir, I'll keep this as it now is, and if I do build again, it shall be a new house. But I'll keep this one as it is, to look at, in order that it may remind me of what I once was—where we all once lived—how happy we then were—and what I now am; where we all now are, and *what all human happiness comes to*." Well, indeed we thought, would it be for those, who live at home in comfort, if their experience taught them, by unmolested ease, as good a lesson, as adversity has done to many of these colonist farmers of Africa.

Our supper being over, we settled ourselves to sleep, but not before our guns and gear were first put in order for the morrow's work; then, pulling our large woollen caps over our ears, and rolling ourselves in our blankets, we soon forgot all else save sleep. An hour before daylight saw us, however, awake, and on the move. Our horses saddled, and the Hottentots and dogs ready, we started for the bush, and, after a sharp ride of about an hour, gallopping at full speed, up hill and dale, through ravines over "*vlaats*," and through "*vleys*" of water. We were thus proceeding at a furious pace, when suddenly my companion drew in his rein, exclaiming, "Hah! here they have been."

With the eye of an experienced hunter, he had descried their "*spoor*" or footmarks on the ground. In an instant he was out of his saddle, and, with the greatest attention, he proceeded to examine and observe the little minutiæ in connection with them, such as blades of grass bent down, the dew as it lay upon them, and other matters wholly insignificant to all save the eyes of the Cape hunter. After a careful scrutiny he again mounted, saying, "This herd was here the night before last; but they are not far away." This, as he afterwards explained to me, he had discovered by seeing the dew of that night lying undisturbed upon them all, although the footprints themselves had been but recently formed.

Finding ourselves now in the vicinity of the buffalos, we deemed it necessary to use the greatest caution, lest, heading them, they might get scent of us, (as they always move up the wind,) and then we might search in vain. Beside this, expedition was also necessary, as the dawn was fast approaching, and the starlight, by which we had hitherto alone been travelling, was growing dim. Our party now, therefore, separated; the Hottentots, or servants, were sent round along the ridge of an extensive hill, (on the summit of a spur of which we were then standing,) whilst we were to proceed down the hill into the bed of the Blue Krantz river, in which it was thought the buffalos might be found drinking. It was further agreed that, if the Hottentots on the hill saw where the beasts were, one was to remain and mark them, whilst the other was to come to a spot appointed, near the river where we were going, and there to wave his cap aloft three times, as a signal for us to join them.

Having settled these preliminaries, we resumed our headlong course, each in their own direction, ours of course being down the hillside. And downhill it assuredly was, never shall we forget that ride; as to attempt to stop the horses, it was madness to expect it, and had the buffalos been feeding in our path, they and we must, inevitably, have rolled headlong together to the bottom, had we accidently come in contact. As it was, however, no more serious obstacle impeded our course than a few " *Vyacht-um-bige* " thorns, which, coming in contact with our clothes and flesh, carried considerable portions of both away.

On arriving at the banks and bed of the river which flowed through the valley, (and which we reached in an incredibly short space of time,) we again found the "*spoor*" of the buffalos. Here, however, they had also been the night before the last. Consequently, whilst demurring how we should next proceed in " *trekking* " this new " *spoor*," we descried our Hottentot riding towards us, as for his life, and waving his cap, not three times, as directed, but thirty times, in the most grotesque attitudes of excitement.

"They have seen them ! now then, up, after them, and away !" With these exclamations, uttered in an under tone, my companion turned his horse's head ; and, ere we could see how or where to ride, he was far up the hill side, his horse panting and blowing as he fled. We soon followed in his wake, but had not proceeded twenty yards, when, in turning a corner, charge went horse and rider into the centre of a "*witte-doern*" thorn bush. The spines on this were like lancets, but, bleeding though the horse was, he seemed to care as little for them as if they were of no account. He soon tore himself and his burden through it; but, in doing so, he left my cap and part of my coat behind. This was a serious matter, for, as the heat of the day promised to be great, to go through it without any covering on the head was not to be thought of. This, therefore, obliged a halt, and, consequently, I had to dismount. Regaining and replacing, at length, the tattered remnants of the cap, I was trying to remount the excited and restive steed, when my companion was seen far up the hill, urging me on by vehement signs of impatience. Off therefore in an instant I went again, and soon was by his side, when, galloping on together, we shortly reached the summit of the hill.

The scene there awaiting us is not easily to be forgotten. We were upon the farthest point of a long ridge of mountain land, which ran out into the valley beneath. Both sides of this were clothed in dense bush. The point on which we stood was the extreme edge of a huge precipice, which dropped perpendicularly into the bed of the Blue Krantz river, to be seen flowing at its foot, as it meandered through the valley. On the opposite side of the hill from that by which we had ascended, the slope was more gradual and ended in a ravine, which, formed by the side of another range of mingled bush and "*krantz*," ran down to the banks of the river, at a point where it took a broad and graceful sweep. The slanting banks of the river were here low and gentle, and clothed in long reeds, sedge, and grass; while, on the opposite shoulder of the bend, a broad valley, covered with rich pasturage, and dotted with "*mimosa*" bushes, stretched out over several acres, but having a gradual descent to the water.

Herd of Buffalos in the Valley of the Blue Krantz.

Page 365.

On this piece of land, a long string of buffalos were leisurely wending their way toward the water at the bend of the river, where, in the centre of the stream, a huge bull stood snuffing the air. The herd consisted of sixteen large sleek cows, while two more gigantic bulls brought up the rear, lagging some thirty or forty yards behind the others, and acting as a rear guard, thrown out to prevent the possibility of the herd being taken by surprise whilst drinking. In crossing the water, they all appeared to exercise the greatest caution. The pioneer bull was several yards in advance of the others, and each step he took forward, he seemed to measure, whilst his nose was constantly kept snuffing the wind, as he went along. The cows, also, as they neared the water, halted, and then cautiously advanced, one by one, smelling the footsteps of the bull, and of the others preceding them, on both banks of the river, before they attempted to follow them.

Whilst we remained stationed on the hill, thus watching and observing the beasts, my companion had proceeded to stalk them in the bush, into which they were leisurely passing. Some twenty minutes were occupied in the process of drinking and bathing, ere the last two bulls had finished, the whole nineteen beasts drinking singly; when, just as these two were emerging from the reeds on the opposite banks of the river, we heard the sharp crack of a rifle, then a pause, and then a second shot. In an instant the whole herd took the alarm, and were in the bush, whilst the air resounded with the crashing and breaking branches, as they forced their huge horns, heads, and carcases through it, into its densest glades.

After an anxious hour of suspense, our companion joined us, and we were informed, that he had succeeded in reaching a hanging ledge of rock, covered with bush, overlooking the path by which the herd were advancing through the valley. He had hardly espied the first of them, when the bull seemed to smell him, and giving the alarm, started off at a rapid pace, in a sidelong direction. Observing this, he measured his distance to another point in their new course, where he saw they must appear, and taking a steady aim, waited the result; when, at length, they did emerge, singling out one large cow, he lodged the contents of both barrels of his rifle behind her shoulder. He then proceeded by the "*blood spoor*," (that is, the drops of blood, which fell from her wounds,) to trace her to her lair, and, after a few moments, he came upon her, lying wounded in the bush, and having satisfied himself that she was severely hurt, he there left her, and returned to us, to tell of his success.

The Hottentots were now despatched back to the farm from which we had started in the morning, to bring up more dogs, and an increase to our numbers for the " hunt," whilst we returned slowly to a point of rendezvous, where they were to meet us. Having arrived at this spot, we off-saddled our jaded horses, partook of some refreshment which we had carried, and then proceeded to settle ourselves to rest and sleep. From this we were aroused about nine o'clock, by the arrival of the servants and dogs: and then, resuming our guns, we commenced our day's sport. We entered the bush at the spot where the buffalo had been wounded, and again following the track by the " *blood-spoor*," we advanced to where she lay. The extraordinary acuteness displayed by my companions in " *trekking* " the " *spoor*," was to me most marvellous. Here a small drop of blood lying on a leaf—there, another one on a stone—then, some ten feet further on, a branch broken down, and *slightly* smeared with gore—or a single drop of blood lying on a leaf—each was quite sufficient to indicate the path that had been pursued by the wounded beast. We also noticed, that in many parts through which she appeared to have passed, the thorny boughs, although they were tinged with blood, yet seemed so matted together, that it was apparently quite impossible that any living creature could have passed through them. So dense, indeed, were these parts of the bush, that we were delayed several minutes at each, in forcing *our* way through. This difficulty was explained, however, by reflecting that, as the wounded animal forced her huge horns through the bush, the elastic branches, first giving way, then flew back behind her with greater force, as she crashed along, and thus, meeting together they matted again more closely than before. In one of the densest of these deep labyrinths of the forest, we suddenly came upon the skull and skeleton of a very large elephant; thus shewing that, at no very distant period, these creatures had found shelter there.

After about an hour's search and "*spooring*," we at length came upon its object, lying near to where she had been left a few hours before. Our approach to her was timely indicated to us by the furious barking of our dogs, together with the discordant voices of the Hottentots, shouting and yelling at them, joined with the violent crashing of boughs and bushes. We now proceeded to take up our position, and prepare for the bloody onslaught. We placed ourselves behind the stumps and stems of the largest neighbouring trees, whilst the dogs were encouraged to attack and bait the Buffalo. Thus pressed, she came rushing through the glades, and made directly for where we were posted. When she appeared within sight of us, she halted; and, glaring at us for a moment, pressed on to the charge. When, however, within our reach, and just as we anticipated the *finale*, she seemed suddenly to change her mind; for, turning upon one of our finest hounds, which was following close upon her heels, with a single gore from her enormous horns she rent him into pieces: and then, turning round and fiercely trampling over his mangled body, she fled in an opposite direction, down the side of the glen, not, however, before one or two more bullets were dispatched after her, to add to her sufferings.

The chase now fairly began, and continued from that time, until relinquished at seven o'clock in the evening. At several points it was most exciting, at others harrassing and wearisome, but still never sufficiently so to induce a wish to abandon it. At one point, as we reached a knoll on the side of the hill, the buffalo broke cover immediately below us, and fled full speed up the centre of the valley, pursued by the hounds and hunters at full cry.

It was a glorious sight, and could not have been better witnessed than from the spot where we then stood. At the end of the valley, she swam the river, and on the other bank the dogs came to fault; this gave us time to get up again, and join in the tedious "*blood-spooring*," to which we had again to have recourse, to make her out. This never-failing alternative once more betrayed her to us, lying wallowing in the mud at the bottom of a half dry "*vley*" of water, some mile and a half away, her wound bleeding copiously. From this the dogs soon aroused her, when she again charged us, and we here got a full and close view of her. She was a noble beast, about six feet in length, and four in height: her huge horns spread out, on either side of her frontal, to nearly two feet; whilst her limbs were formed with the most perfect symmetry, and appeared slight and fragile in comparison with the size of her enormous carcase. A second time wounded, she still eluded us, and crashed once more into the middle of the bush. She gave us chase throughout the remainder of the day, without our again seeing her; although we often heard her close beside us, trampling down the bushes, and tearing away the surrounding branches.

Twice again, we tracked her into this "*vley*," and once, so exhausted and weary were we all, from thirst and excitement, that men and dogs were fain to lay down, side by side, and drink from the mud, in which she had been bathing her wounds. In doing this, we had to hold our teeth together, and suck the filthy slimy water through them. And though we thus prevented the tadpoles and animalculæ, (which floated in it in myriads,) from going down our throats ; we yet felt them wriggling about inside our mouths, and against our gums and teeth, as we drank of this refreshing beverage. Thus, truly, we were here made practically to *feel*, that " necessity has no law."

Once, in the mid-day chase, we were sadly dissappointed in our expectations. The dogs had been much mutilated and wounded by their frequent attacks, and those that were remaining appeared so scared, by the ferocity of the buffalo, that they would not follow her closely. We consequently were obliged to track her by the " *spoor*." This was, of course, very wearisome and tedious, though, in the end, more sure. Three times she had joined the herd in the bush, but they had at once fled from her. At length, at one of these junctures, we ran in close upon her. The dogs came to bay — crash ! crash ! went the branches — and the hallo ! of the Hottentots, told us of her return once more to the charge. For this we prepared again, ensconcing ourselves behind the trees. A violent barking followed, then the dreadful death shreaks of two of the dogs, next two rifle shots, and then a rush. On she came, (as we thought,) the tree in front gave way with the falling weight—another shot—another—and a huge wild boar rolled at our feet—dead! Bitter indeed was our disappointment, for the buffalo, killing two more of our best dogs, had escaped; whilst our two remaining dogs had preferred the encounter of the boar, which had accidentally crossed the path, to their other more formidable enemy.

It was now about four o'clock, and worn out, we lay down on our backs to sleep, while the Hottentots proceeded to cut up the pig, and stow it away in hiding places, to which they could return, and fetch it away at their leisure. After an hour's rest, we were again on the chase, and then pursued it steadily until half-past seven in the evening. The setting sun then warned us to desist, and we were fain to leave our prey still at large, although pretty sure of finding her next morning, nor far from where we had last left her. Two days afterwards, her mangled remains were found close to her favourite retreat, the muddy "*vley*." She had returned and breathed her last there, "dying game," in the fullest sense of the words. The wild dogs and hyænas had, however, found her out before we did, and had mangled and mutilated her body, though her head and horns were left, the trophy of the huntsmen. These "*vilde-hondes*," as they are called by the Dutch, are most destructive to the game in the bush country, and hunt them in regular packs for miles together: they are the *hyæna crocuta*, one of which was lately brought to England.

Our day among the buffalos ended with an enjoyable night supper, and bivouac in the bush—our huntsman-like appetites doing justice to the former, in a manner that would have astonished an English Nimrod. As we, at length, rode, by moonlight, towards our home, we could hear the bellowing of the wounded beast echoing through the valley. Nor were we sorry, after our day's work of fifteen hours, in which we had walked over thirty miles of country, to reach our tents, and rest our weary limbs in our blankets, and sleep.

Whilst passing through the bush, in this day's hunt, we found, here and there, the traces of the haunts of a small and rare animal, which we had previously seen in the upper parts of Kaffirland, and as we can find no account given elsewhere of this variety, we claim its discovery. It is a small "*Viverra*," but instead of being as they all are, "*tetradactyli*," this one is "*pentadactyli*."   Its colour is also darker than any of those kinds hitherto described, and it is of very rare occurrence. Two dead specimens of it have been brought by us to England, which were killed on the banks of the T'Zilie river, in Kaffraria. When pursued by dogs, they took to the water, and endeavoured by both rapid swimming, and diving, to elude their pursuers : they were eventually speared. In formation it resembles the weasel, to which class it belongs. It appears to be, in fact, the South African "*Ichnumeon*," which had been supposed not to be in that part of the continent. In colour, it is dark brown, the hair long and glossy, and towards the points runs to dingy white; the tail is about nine inches long, and bushy near the body, but running to a point; the snout is long and sharp; the ears round; the eyes black, bright, and active; the dental formation carnivorous; and the feet are "*pentadactyli*." It measures twenty-one inches from the tip of the tail to the snout. By the Dutch, it is called the "*Comitjehout*," from the singular posterior formation, which is like a small bowl; from this, when attacked, it emits a powerful and disagreeable odour. It appears to be an entirely new variety, and I therefore here introduce it as the "*Viverra pentadactyli Caffer*."

Another little subterranean animal we would here mention, as not often brought to light; it is the " *Chrysocheoris Caffer*." It is similar to, but is not a mole. The muzzle is broad and recurved; its fore feet have but three nails, of which, the external is very large, (half an inch in length) arcuated and sharp, the others decreasing inwards; the hind feet have five nails, as usual to the mole; it has no tail; the eyes and ears are not perceptible. Its length of body is five inches, rounded in shape, and one and three quarter inches in diameter. The colour of this little animal is light brown, shaded with light red under the belly, and with a metallic green tint over the body. Beside it, there are three other species of moles in South Africa—a large brown one; a smaller one of the same colour; and a large white one, about thirteen inches long: but this latter kind is very rare.

We next turn to the ornithology, which is here so rich and multitudinous in its varieties. In this the most interesting are the *"Raptores,"* or Birds of Prey, which are more numerous, and varied here, than in any other part of our globe. We, consequently, insert a short classified list of such varieties of these, as have come under immediate notice, during a five years' residence and minute observation among them;

deeming this the more acceptable, as in no other published work has such been yet presented. We divide them into the following classes:—1. Vultures; 2. Eagles; 3. Falcons; 4. Kites; 5. Hawks; 6. Buzzards; 7. Owls, Ravens, and Crows, &c.

Of the first of these there are four varieties. The "*Astvogel*," or Common Gregarious Vulture of Kaffraria; the "*Condor*" or Black Vulture; the "*Ixalanga*" of the Kaffirs, which is the Sociable Vulture; and the "Egyptian Vulture."

1.—The "*Astvogel*," is the commonest kind, and flocks by thousands through every district of Southern Africa. It appears to be the "*Vultur Fulvos*," or Griffon Vulture. The head and neck are quite bald, the beak is massive and strong, the plumage is of a dirty white: it devours its food ravenously, and vomits it again to feed its young, or if wounded. It is a gregarious bird, and feeds only on carrion. Across the wings it frequently measures seven and eight feet. It discovers its prey by sight, and not, as was supposed, by scent. This fact was ascertained by an experiment tried in Kaffirland. A dead sheep was cut in two, one half was placed on the top of a precipice, exposed to view; the other half was placed at the foot of the rock, immediately below the nest, but concealed from sight, being covered over with leaves and grass. The upper half had not been exposed more than an hour, when the horizon was dotted with "*Astvogels*," which came circling over it, and, ere the evening, it was all devoured; the remaining half was left untouched, and continued, where it had been placed, until the whole surrounding atmosphere was loaded with the pestilential effluvia arising from it. When thus in a state of putrefaction, another portion of *fresh* meat was then exposed in the valley, close to where this lay; and, although this latter was instantly discovered, and devoured within twenty-four hours, the decomposed carrion still remained for weeks quite untouched.

2.—The "*Condor*," or Black Vulture, is the next most numerous variety. It is black, except the secondary quills of the wings, which are white; the tail is broad and fan-shaped. It is bare on the head, and neck, and wattled in red skinny filiments; the feathers are rugged, and its expanse of wing seems greater than any bird of this class. It devours carrion voraciously, and is disinclined to soar aloft in the air.

3.—The "*Ixalanga*" of the Kaffirs, is sometimes confounded with the above species, but is a different variety. It approaches nearest to the Sociable Vulture, *(Vultur auricularis.)* Its head and neck are also bare and of a red colour, and folds of red skin originating behind the ears and encircling the upper parts of them, hang down on either side. Its throat is covered with blackish hairs, ending in a ruff of curly feathers at the end of the neck. Its colour is of a blackish brown, rather lighter on the breast and under the wings. The expanse of the latter is frequently ten feet. It flies very high, and often rises in the air beyond the vision of man.

4.—The last species is the "*Percnopterus,*" or Egyptian Vulture. This is sometimes called the White Port Vulture, or Crow of Kaffirland. The feathers on its body are of a dirty white colour. The beak is yellow, and blunted at the point, which latter shades to black. Its claws are yellow. The tips of the wings are black. It is like an albatross, and the stretch of its wing is about three feet.

Of Eagles there are three varieties.

1.—The first called justly, the "King of the Mountains," is a majestic bird. On the wing, it has a lofty sailing flight, and, except for prey, seldom leaves the highlands. In colour, its body and breast are of a blueish black, and the head also, with white rings round the eyes. The Irides are yellow. It has a broad red band down the back. The tail is short and reddish in colour. The claws and beak are orange. By the Kaffirs it is called "Man Eater," from the tradition amongst them, that this is the first bird which attacks a man's body after death.

2.—The "Golden Eagle" *(Aquila chrysaeta,)* is, in Africa, similar to that known in other parts of the world. It is more slenderly made than the preceding species. Its tail and wings are long, and its body darker underneath than on the back, which, when it is on the wing, appears of a golden olive colour. It is a very wary bird, and fights fiercely for its nest and young.

3.—The last variety of Eagle, is the "*Preist,*" or Sea Eagle, a species of the *Haliætus lencocephalus.* Its body is of a blueish grey colour: the tail similar, and of a fan shape. The head is quite white. Its shriek is of the most discordant kind, and is incessantly kept up, when on the wing. This bird is very frequently found along the Eastern, Southern, and Western coasts of Africa.

The largest variety of Raptorials is, however, found amongst the Falcons, some of which are very beautiful. Those met with, numbered eight varieties.

1.—The most elegant of these, is called by

the natives, the "*Jackall-vogel:*" it is supposed from the similarity, in marks and colour, between the animal and the bird. In shape it somewhat resembles a buzzard, the wings being short for its tribe. The beak is of a blackish brown colour; the feet and claws yellow; the feathers of the tail are red; the back slate coloured; the breast, throat, and belly, of a reddish brown, and barred transversely with dark brown. Underneath the wings is also barred in a similar manner, only in brown and white.

2.—Another variety of this species is very common through Kaffirland, being smaller than the preceding, about fifteen inches in length, and twenty in the span of the wing; whereas the other is about twenty inches in length of body, and about two feet six inches across the wings.

An encounter of rather a curious character, once took place between the author and one of these birds. A friend in England having an ology for collecting birds' eggs, wrote out, requesting that he would send, from Africa, a few additions to his cabinet, particularizing those of the Raptorials. Some time after the receipt of this letter, a "*Jackall-vogel's*" nest came to view, built on the top of a large tree, which grew out of the face of a perpendicular and lofty "*krantz*," or precipice, having in it two fine eggs. With all the eagerness of school-boy days, the determination was at once formed of scaling the dizzy height, and of robbing the nest. Being rather ashamed, however, of the undertaking, and the tree standing over a path in a very conspicuous part of the valley near the town, the early hours of morn were selected for the perpetration of this ovarious burglary. Rising, therefore, while it was still dark, he repaired to the foot of the "*krantz*," and proceeded to climb up between the tree and the face of the rock; the first stages of the work were easily accomplished, and he soon rose some forty feet into the air; just as he was trying, however, to make over his footing from the rock to the stem of the tree, another bird of the same tribe, who was sitting on her nest, hitherto unseen in a crevice of the rock, perceiving the points of some ten fingers grappling close to her domain, flew out, and with one or two strokes of her formidable beak upon the said fingers, soon made him let go: his hold being thus loosened, he lost his footing, and came down headlong.

Beneath the rock lay the bed of the river, filled with large stones, and which were thinly covered with water. Had he fallen into this, little of him would have remained to tell this story. As it was, however, having let go with one hand before the other, the fall was thus swerved in a sidelong direction, and so brought him clear of the river, and into the centre of a dense "*Vyacht-um-bige*" thorn tree. This, breaking his fall, saved his life, but at the expense of his skin and clothes, which were lacerated and torn in a most serious manner. So bruised was he, that he felt little inclined to renew the attack; still not liking to be vanquished by a bird, he mounted once more, this time scaling the tree instead of the rock. Having reached the first fork of this, he found himself stopped by the slender length of the branches, on which the nest rested, and which would not bear the weight of the body. Demurring as to how to proceed, he was fiercely assailed by the second falcon, on whose eggs he meditated his attack. She had been complacently watching him, from her lofty eyry, and encouraged by the former successful onslaught of her neighbour, now tried the force of her talons on his face and courage. For several minutes, he resolutely maintained his position, to the eminent danger of his eyes, which she attacked violently, but at length he had again to beat a retreat; and it was not until he returned a *third* time to the charge, in the afternoon, accompanied by a friend, a rope, and a basket, that he succeeded, through the aid of these, in obtaining his prize, and depositing the eggs in his friend's receiving cabinet.

3.—Besides these "*Jackall-vogels*," a "Grey Falcon" is also common in the upper parts of Southern Africa. Of this there are *three* varieties. The first is a large grey bird, of a very thoroughbred form. The neck and legs are of a dark brownish colour, and it has a semicircle of black feathers on the back of the neck; in size, it is about equal to the smaller kind of "*Jackall-vogel.*"

4.—The next of the species is a smaller bird, also grey on the back and wings, but of a yellowish colour on the breast, and is there marked with transverse bars of reddish brown. Its beak, legs, and claws are yellow.

5.—Another is similar to this, but its beak, legs, and claws are pink, or flesh-coloured. It is also of a lighter shade of grey, and, in every way, a more delicate looking bird.

6.—The sixth kind of Falcon is of a beautiful form. Its tail feathers are very long, thin, and forked at the ends. The wings are sharply pointed, and barred across with brown stripes; the quills being of a bright white tint, which causes them to glitter in the sun. It is about fourteen inches in length, and on the wing its flight is very rapid.

Beside these, there are (7) the "*Falco Serpentarius*" of Cuvier, or Secretary-bird, also a Falcon; and (8) the Locust-bird, (possibly one of the Tringæ,) has been classed as a Falcon. It is like a dark brown plover, with white breast.

Of Buzzards, there are four varieties.

1.—The commonest is the "Brown Carrion Buzzard," with a full fanned tail. A white ring is marked at the end of each tail feather, caused by a white belt of colour on the extremities of the feathers. It is a shy bird, and generally is seen near the slaughter-houses and offal holes along the skirts of the camps on the frontier.

2.—Another kind somewhat resembles the smaller "*Jackall-vogel*," being of a reddish brown colour, but with a red head. The tail and wings are full and handsome, and the whole size of the bird is about fifteen inches.

3.—There is also a large Buzzard, of a grey colour on the back and wings. The head is black, while the breast and under part of the wing is white. This is, however, a very rare and wary species, and is styled the "Mountain Cock," from its peculiar attachment to the mountain districts, and the highest rocks.

4.—The last of this class is the "Turkey Buzzard," or, as it is generally styled in Kaffirland, the "*Boemvogel*." This is a large, heavy, black

buzzard, which strays about through the bush.
It is a useful scavenger, and a Colonial fine is
inflicted on any who shoot them. The body,
wings, and tail are of a glossy black; the primary quills in the wings and tail being white.
The head and neck are bare, red, and wattled
like a turkey. They usually stray about in
pairs, seldom more than six being seen together. They make a kind of monotonous drum-
ming sound.

Next on the list appear the Kites and Hawks.
Of the former of these there are but two.

1.—The first is a handsome and graceful
bird, with a fan tail, with which it pilots itself
through the air, using it like a fish's tail. It
is brown in colour; barred on the body, back,
and wings, with black. On the breast, belly,
and under the wing, it is white. The head and
throat are black; beak, legs, and talons yellow;
the length of the body is about thirteen inches;
the span of wing seventeen inches. Through
the summer months they are often seen, and
are very destructive to young chickens.

2.—To this may be added what is called by
the colonists the " Tiger-hawk." It is properly
the " African Kestrel," and is of frequent appearance through the districts and frontier of
the colonies. It is similar to that of Europe;
a game looking bird, and fleet upon the wing.

1.—Of Hawks, that called the "Spring Hawk" is the most graceful. It is so called, because it is usually first seen on the wing at the beginning of spring, being looked upon as a harbinger of summer. It is a large symmetrically formed bird, black barred with brown on the back; cinamon brown on the breast, thighs, and underwings; the head is black, the wings and tail are long and forked like those of the martin. Its size is about ten inches in length of body, and eighteen across the wings; the forks of the tail projecting about six inches beyond the centre feathers: the beak, legs, and talons, are of a bright yellow.

2.—The "White Hawk" of Kaffirland, is also a handsome bird. In length, it is about twelve inches, and seventeen in the span of wing; the tail is large and fanned; the beak much curved, and in colour, together with the talons, is of a bright orange. The whole plumage is of a snowy white, which, when the bird is soaring in the air, glistens brightly in the rays of the sun.

3.—The "Merlin Hawk" is also common. This is a small one of about seven inches in length, with a tail six inches more. The tail is fanned, transversely barred with clouded brown stripes, and tipped with a fringe of white. The primaries are brown; the general colour of the head, neck, and back, is a greyish slate. Under the wing is barred with brown; on the belly and round the vent it is white; the thighs and breast light cinnamon; the head and beak are finely formed; the latter black; the legs, feet, and claws yellow; the latter of these are curved long, and very sharp. It is a thorough bred Merlin, and of a very beautiful kind.

4.—There is also the "White Merlin." This is a very rare variety. In size and form, it much resembles the above, but in colour it is different. Its back and wings are of a grey slate tint, but the breast is white. It is more feathered on the thighs and legs, than the other. These last, with its beak and talons, are of a pale yellow.

5.—The "Rufus Merlin" may close our list of Hawks. This is a very beautiful little Raptorial, with sharply pointed beak and talons, pointed wings and tail, and wary, rapid, flight. In size it about equals the last, while, in colour, it is a Rufus cinnamon tint, dark on the back of the body and wings, and lighter on the breast and under parts. The legs are well feathered, with black tips to the wings. The beak, talons, and legs, are yellow. It appears to prey principally on the finches, which it is usually seen pursuing over the "*vlaats*."

1.—Of Owls, we noticed *three* varieties.

The " Large Horned Owl " of the mountains
about eighteen inches in height: the legs feathered to the feet, the eyes large; the beak
singularly small, black, and compressed, almost
hidden in the feathers of the face. The back
and wings are of a mottled brown; the breast
white, mottled also with a light brown; the
horns, composed of four feathers, are about
three inches long.

2.—There is another, much more common
than the above, and answers to our " Brown
Owl. In size, it is about half that of the
former. In colour it is also mottled brown,
but of a lighter tint, and without horns.

3.—The most elegant is what is called the
" White or Keiskamma Owl," because principally inhabiting the bush, which grows along
the banks of that river, and the rocks overhanging its sources. It is very small, about the size
of a large thrush. On the back, it is of a greyish
brown, faintly mottled, and its breast and beneath its wings, are covered with a soft white
down. It is a rare bird, and seldom to be seen.

We may close this list, with *three* Crows, a
Chough, and a large Raven.

1.—The first of these is the "Common Carrion
Crow" of Africa, and looks more like a raven,
though not one. It is about eighteen inches in
length, and has a cut and thrust bill, which is

jet black, and very strong. The plumage of the body is quite black, excepting a patch of white feathers on the nape of the neck. Its feet and legs are black. It is very daring and impudent in its habits, but a useful member of the African " Board of Health."

2.—The "Kaffir Crow" is similar to this one, but quite black, and of a smaller size. One of these was taken young by some soldiers, when they were stationed at Fort Waterloo, in Kaffirland, during the war of 1846. He became so tame, that at length he would not leave the room in which the man slept who fed him, except when he went on duty or parade, and then the bird was always to be seen, attending on the company in which his benefactor marched. One luckless day, a cur dog seized upon him, and ere he could be rescued, broke his leg. His master attended on him during his sickness, bound up the leg in splints, and cured him; still he was henceforth always lame, and hopped about instead of walking.

At length the route came. Meantime, Mr. Crow had become a cunning and an educated thief; and it was accordingly decided to leave him behind. He was therefore set at large by his master, and the company marched for head quarters. Pleased with his good fare and company, however, the bird had no mind thus to

be cast off at pleasure, and, consequently, he
followed the soldiers on the wing, along their
march, flying from stage to stage, and always
alighting on his master's knapsack. He thus
arrived at the head quarter station, and has
long remained, and is still a pensioner there,
although his faithless master has again left him
for others to attend to, and has long since sailed
for his native shore.

3.—The other kind, is the " White-breasted
Crow."   This is less in size than either of these
others.   When on the wing, it has a more
rapid flight; its voice is most discordant; its
caw more resembling the barking of a wild dog
than the notes of a bird.   It is usually about
ten inches long.

The "Chough" of Kaffraria is similar to that
of Cornwall.   It is about half the size of the
common crow. Its beak is long, curved, and of
a bright scarlet colour.   Its plumage is of a
glossy black, and its legs and feet of a dingy
red.   It frequents the rocks on the sea coast,
building its nest in their fissures, and feeds
along the edge of the waves on the sand.

The "Raven" in its size, plumage, habits,
and general appearance is, in Africa, exactly
similar to that seen in the other quarters of
the world; and is too old a favourite amongst
naturalists to need more to be said here of it.

With it we close this brief sketch of the Raptorial ornithology of these districts, and pass on to say a few words of some their feathered neighbours.

The next, Game Birds claim to be the most prized; and of these some are well worthy of note.

The first on this list certainly stands the "*Paauw*." This is the "*Bustard Capensis*." Of it there are three varieties. The Common or "Grey *Paauw*," the "Gum *Paauw*," and the "Bush," or "Tuffed" one. They are large heavy birds, usually weighing from thirty to fifty pounds.

1.—The bodies of the first of these are usually about three feet nine inches long. Their span of wing is seven or eight feet. The head is about four inches and the beak three. The wings and tail primaries are black, with large white spots upon them. The tail is barred across. The neck and breast are white. The head black, with a white spot in the centre, and a ring of white round the neck. The throat and back of the neck, grey grouse and cinnamon colour. The secondaries of wings, anteriors, tail coverts, and back, mottled grouse and Rufus brown. The neck of this species is longer and thinner than in the others, and has less of the cinnerous tints about it.

2.—The " Gum *Paauw* " is usually smaller, and is found frequenting the "*mimosa*" bushes on the plains and "*vlaats*."

3.—The last, or " Bush *Paauw*," is the monster bustard of Kaffirland. It is brighter and richer in the tints of its plumage, and has a large top-knot, or tuft of feathers on its head, The legs are usually about ten inches on the lower joints, and eight on the thigh. The feet, of course, like all of the tribe, having but three toes. The largest of these birds ever seen, weighed, when shot, fifty-six pounds.

4.—Another of the Cursorials is the " *Korhaan*," of this there are four varieties, differing only in the colour of their plumage. The commonest are black and white ; others are grey ; there is also a bluish one, and one a dark grey, which is also a small bustard, and is said by some to be the same as the "*Florican*" of India. Its height is about sixteen inches. It stands erect, with the neck (about five inches long) perpendicular, which is very thin and slender, and the head is small for the size of the bird ; the beak is short, and like that of the " *Paauw* " slightly curved. Its general colour is, as described in each description, although, in all, on the back, tail, and the back of the neck, it is of a cinnerous brown. The throat, breast, and belly, being the part of its plumage which most varies, are grey, blue, dark slate colour, and white. Around the eyes there are circles of white feathers, and completely encircling the head, a band of black feathers. At the back of the head and inclining backwards, it erects these black feathers when alarmed, which gives it the appearance of having a short weeping crest. On the breast and under the wings, is a soft down; while the peculiarity of the bird is the colour of this, which is of a most delicate pink shot with purple, which causes, in different lights, a most beautiful variety of tints in the plumage. It frequents the banks of rivers, flies heavily on the wing, and seldom rises high into the air. Its flesh, like that of the "*Paauw*," is amongst the greatest delicacies of the table, and whilst alive it certainly is a most graceful ornament to the natural history of Africa.

5.—The "*Dickop*" is also a highly-prized game bird. This is the "*Ædicnæmus Capensis*," or Stone Plover. It is a handsome bird, about eighteen inches in length, and two feet span of wing. In colour it is a mottled grouse brown; on the breast and throat it is white; its beak and legs black, and in shape similar to a plover; the eyes yellow, and the head and neck large for the size of the bird.

Amongst the "*Rasores*," there are numerous

objects of the sportman's gun. Three kinds of Partridge, the Red, and Grey-winged, and the Mottled or Common kind; also a smaller kind called the Namaqua Partridge. Two quails, the Common Brown, and the Button Quail; the latter is a very small mottled bird, and with a white breast of a game-like appearance. The Pheasant, as it is called, is more like a Grouse, but is in fact the "*Leipoa Ocellata;*" the same bird which is found in Australia, and is there called by the natives "*Ngowoo.*"

Of Guinea Fowls there are two varieties. The Common Mottled one, and the Tufted or Crested "*Gallinæ*; the latter is a very handsome and graceful bird.

To these may be added the "*Umkungele*" of the Kaffirs, or Wild Turkey: a large black bird somewhat similar in size, shape, plumage, and habits, to the domesticated one, but wary and difficult to shoot. It always builds its nest in the face of precipices.

Beside a long list of the "*Gallatores*," such as the Plovers, Curlew, Herons, Sandpipers, Stilt-plovers, Cranes, Haddadah, and Egrets, there are also several worthy of note amongst the "*Gallinules*," as much prized by connoisseurs in game. Of these none come before the "African Painted Snipe" for beauty. The length of this little bird is about seven or eight inches, the length of the beak two, and the legs three. The back, wings, head, and breast, are a mottled metallic greenish brown. The belly is white; the throat light cinnamon; round the chest there is a ring of white. The tail and its coverts are dark grey barred transversely with black; a yellow streak runs longtitudinally along the head. The primaries of the wings are dark grey with rows of large cinnamon circular spots running along them, and edged with black. The tail is short, and the wings rounded at the points, and with white epaulettes. The bird is large and more like a small plover; the legs and beak are deep yellow.

The "African Grebe" is a handsome bird, about the size of the European species. The neck is long and the head small, of a mottled black and brown plumage. The cock is of a much brighter tint than the hen.

The "Kaffrarian Baldcoot" is smaller, about the size of a widgeon. The neck is thin and slender, the head quite bald, with two wattles of red on the top, the beak, head, and body black, and formed like a duck; the feet being those of the coot, with four scolloped toes.

The "*Anser Capensis*," or Kaffrarian Goose, is also worthy of note. It is the size of a small common goose, but with a shorter neck. Its total length is about two feet, and two feet six span of wing; the beak is about the size of that of a large mallard, and the breast feathers similar in plumage to that bird. The back is dark brown; the secondaries of the wings of a cinnamon colour, the primary quills being a dark green; over the wings are epaulettes of white; the head is brown; the throat grey. Around the neck is a ring, and in the centre of the breast is a large spot, of cinnamon brown.

With this may be named the " African Darter." It is about two feet nine inches long; the tail is fanned, and the beak very long, narrow, and sharp; it is also serriated with small teeth, inclining backwards. The body is black, and along the back lie several long narrow feathers, striped longitudinally black and white; the neck is very long, narrow, and curved, and in colour, it is on the male bird, cinnamon brown, on the female, grey; the throat is white, the back of the head and neck are of a mottled brown; the feet are large and webbed. This is, of course, a marine bird, usually found at the mouths of the tidal rivers along the coast. Beside these, there are, of this class, the widgeon, teal, waterhen, and *five* varieties of wild ducks: the most remarkable of which, is the " *Vildemaakeon*," or spurwinged goose. This is a handsome black duck shot with a golden tint, with a white breast. It is like a large Muscovite duck, and inhabits dry salt "*vleys*." It is armed at the pinions with sharp spurs, similar to those possessed by the Secretary-bird.

Amongst the smaller tribes we must not here linger, so numerous and varied are they. The trees, bushes, reeds, grass, and, indeed, the whole landscape is alive with their flitting gaudy forms, delighting the eyes of the naturalist, and exciting his admiration and curiosity at every turn.

Shrikes without number, Flycatchers, Bee-eaters, Butcher-birds, Finches, Buntings, Cuckoos, Metches, Dedricks, Lories, Toucans, Parrots, Woodpeckers, Larks, Doves, and Honey Eaters, flock in countless numbers around, all demanding a reason why they should be excluded from the list, when others are described. We must therefore leave them to flit about through their forest glades, unheeded or unheard of save by those who live amongst them, and have the better opportunity of cultivating their acquaintance.

Ere leaving this ornithological notice, however, one remark we shall venture upon the " *Cinnyris* " or Honey Eaters—those little brilliant gaudy things, which have long been supposed only fit, while alive, to suck honey from the flowers in Africa, and to be set in glass shades, when dead, in Europe. We allude to them more particularly in connexion with their ability of singing. As a general remark, it certainly *is true*, that, in Africa, " the flowers are without scent, and the birds without song." Nevertheless, there are to this rule, (like all others,) very manifest exceptions: and this in particular, as relates, in the latter case, to the Honey-bird. Professor Swainson, in his able book on African birds, seems to imply a doubt of Mr. Barrow's assertion, in his book of African travels, that this bird was a songster. We are now happy in being able to confirm Mr. Barrow's assertion, that tenuirostral birds are *sometimes* gifted with a musical voice. For, whilst in Kaffirland, we had frequent opportunities of attentively watching these little birds, as they played in the trees in our garden: and we have sat for hours, listening to their sweet plaintive warbling, as they perched in the bushes close by. Those that we heard singing were varieties of the Scarlet-throated Sugar-bird of Kaffraria: *(Cinnyris Chalybea)* of Cuvier, which appears to be also the " *Sucrier à Plastron Rouge* " of Le Vaillant.

Leaving, however, with reluctance the Ornithology of the Cape, (for lack of space,) we next turn to glance at the Reptiles and Insects found among them. The species, and varieties, and multiplicity of these is untold. Above and beneath ground, their name is legion; whilst their sizes are as various as their forms.

Amongst the Reptiles, the Snakes, Adders, and Vipers are conspicuous; and, in very many instances, their bites and stings fatal and deadly. Of these we saw the *seventeen* following varieties.

1.—The largest and most formidable was the " *Python*," or Boa Constrictor of Natal. These enormous snakes are frequently found in the districts of the New Colony, and along the upper frontier of the South, or Old one, measuring from sixteen to twenty-five feet in length. They are large heavy reptiles, with bodies about six inches in diameter. They usually gorge themselves at a meal, and then lie for several days torpid and inanimate. While in this state, they are easily captured. In colour they are a light greenish brown, spotted with black. One measuring nineteen feet six inches in length, was brought from Africa, on board the same vessel with the author. Two days after leaving the Bay of Natal, it devoured a large fowl; and eleven days after that, two more. It then lay in a torpor for several days, and, when awakening from this, it cast its skin. By this time the vessel had crossed the line, and was nearing the colder latitudes, when in 12° north, it died, but more possibly from neglect and ill-treatment than from actual cold.

2.—The next largest to this is the " *Cobra-di-Capella*," or Hooded Snake, called by the Colonists the " *Ringeaault*."* The size of this species, is usually from five to seven feet in length, and five inches in diameter. Its colour is green, striped and spotted with brown. It has long flaps, or filiments, of skin, on either side of the head; which, when incensed, it spreads out in the form of a hood. It is very poisonous; its bite generally produces death within twenty minutes after the infliction of the wound, no remedies seeming to avail in bringing relief. It is, of course, much dreaded by man and beast.

3.—Somewhat partaking of the character of " Cobra," is the " Garter-snake," called by the Dutch the " *Kous-bande*," (literally the Stocking-band) this is the " *Naja Hæmachates*" of Dr. Smith, and is slightly hooded round the head. It is usually about two feet long, having a broad flat body and head, and a ridge along the back. Its colour is black, but spotted with white and straw-colour. Its bite is deadly, and its poison soon infuses itself through the blood.

---

* An account of a very narrow escape of the Author, from one of these snakes, is given pp. 80, 81, in his former work, "Kaffraria."

4.—The next in size to the "Cobra" is the "*Swaartz-slaange*" of the Dutch, or Black Snake. This is generally from four to five feet in length, and is a large heavy creature. It hangs about precipices, and is shy of notice, but, if attacked, fierce and poisonous. It generally appears about evening, and seems to feed principally on rats and rock-rabbits.*

5.—About the same size is the "*Boem-slaange*," or Tree Snake. It, as its name explains, frequents the roots and stems of trees; usually living in large holes, in the decayed parts of these. It is found in great numbers in the forests, and through the bush; and although much dreaded, appears less venomous than others. It feeds principally on birds and small subterranean animals, is of a brownish green colour, and, lying on a tree, would hardly be distinguished from the bark. It also often looks, when coiled up, like a huge fungus.

* A very curious discovery was made, in connection with this Black Snake. In a long large hole, situated in a "*krantz*," behind the roots of a large decayed tree, in Kaffirland, three nests of the Swaartz-slaange were once discovered, distant from each other about a yard. In each nest there was a deposit of eggs, numbering, respectively, eight, ten, and twelve. They were about the size of those of larks, quite white, and in form eliptical. The two first sets were freshly laid, the interior nest soft and somewhat soiled. Upon taking the eggs out, they were found to contain life, and on putting them on a stone, and crushing them beneath the foot, in each was found a perfect little snake, about six inches long; all alive, active, and vicious. The old one thus appeared to have deposited three distinct litters, containing in all thirty young ones, within the same year.

6.—Of those inhabiting the trees, none are more deadly, dangerous, and numerous than the "Whip Snake." This is a small delicate brown reptile, about two feet six inches long, and exactly the size and colour of a thick hunting-whip lash. It climbs along the stems and lower branches of the overhanging forest trees; and, when it has attained the extremities of the twigs, it coils its tail two or three times round them, and then dropping its body, and holding by its tail, it swings in the air, amidst the numerous pendant fibres and creepers, so that it is almost impossible to distinquish it. Whatever it comes in contact with, it bites, and the poison being very virulent, causes instant stupefaction, when the snake drops on its prey and sucks its blood. Thus partaking more of the nature of the asp than the snake, which, however, it resembles in appearance.

7.—Of Grass Snakes there are three; a large brown one spotted with black, and usually measuring about three feet in length; a black one of the same size and form, and of very frequent appearance; and a bright green one. This latter snake is so exactly the shade of the surrounding herbage, that it is quite impossible to see it. They seldom wait, however, to be molested by man, for, being very wary, the first intimation of their vicinity is generally given, either by their hissing, or their rustling retreat through the grass.

A wonderful instance of presence of mind in connection with one of these snakes, was once shown by an officer of the Rifle Brigade, (known to the Author) whilst out shooting in Kaffirland,   He and his companion had been regaling themselves at "*tiffen*," seated on a grassy knoll; and when about to resume their sport, and in the act of rising, this young man placed his right hand on the ground beside him.   He instantly became aware that, in doing so, he had placed it on a large grass snake: he felt the reptile trying to drag its neck and head from beneath his grasp, and, at the same time, it wound its body and tail closely round his arm.   His companion, seeing this, became so stupified from fright that he could render no assistance, and sat in mute horror, which was, however, soon turned alternately to wonder, admiration, and thankfulness. His friend feeling the position he was in, instantly pressed his hand firmer on the snake, (instead of suddenly withdrawing it, as ninety-nine out of a hundred persons under the same circumstances would have done,) and having ascertained that he had luckily placed it on the back of the snake's neck and head, he thus prevented it from drawing itself through his grasp. With his left hand he then felt his pockets, and with it drew from one of them, his large hunting knife; and seizing the blade of it with his teeth, he thus opened it, and then turning round with perfect *nonchalance* and *sans froid*, he, by one sure stroke, severed the snake's head from its body, and thus saved his own life and that of his companion.

10.—Allied to the species of Grass Snakes, is a small brown reptile called a Snake, but is properly a "*Seps*." It is about eighteen inches long, is rather prettily marked with lines of black, and has two small flippers, one on either side of the neck. It is very common in all the districts of Africa.

11, 12, 13.—To these may be added the *three* Water Snakes; green, brown, and black. The first and second of these are each about three feet long, and inhabit the rivers, lying in the rushes and sedge along their banks. The Black Water Snake is very large, frequently reaching five feet in length. These latter kinds are supposed to be harmless, and are timid and wary, always swimming away at the approach of men. They prey principally on frogs, lizards, and small iguanas.

14, 15.—The last of the genus are the Adders and Viper. Of these the "Puff Adder," is the most common, and the most deadly. The largest of these seen was three feet three inches long. The head two inches broad by two long, the tail round and thick; the circumference of the body was five inches. On the belly it was a pale straw colour, on the back light brown and straw-coloured. It was marked in stripes, somewhat resembling small gothic arches, laid one over the other, and fifteen in number. The mouth was large and triangular, and in it were found *twelve* fangs, six on either side, the outside pair were, from the roots to the point, three quarters of an inch long, very much curved, hollow throughout, and with bags of poison at the root. Through these cavities it ejects, or spirts the poison; and if, in its encounter with enemies, its fangs were broken, it had five other pairs, all remaining dormant, yet ready on emergency to be erected. This is the most deadly Adder in Africa, and possesses the peculiarity of springing backwards at its prey; thus throwing him off his guard, by first appearing to run away, then springing back, and throwing a somerset in the air, it seizes it as it comes to the ground. Of these there are two varieties, the Black and the Brown.

A dog, bitten by one of these Adders, died in forty minutes; whilst a man, bitten in the knee at nine in the morning, although the leg was amputated at four p. m. that day, was dead by midnight.*

Administering brandy in large doses, (in fact until intoxication is produced) seems the most efficacious antidote to the poisonous bite of these reptiles. Ammonia, if at hand, is beneficial; but the other seemed more generally successful when tried, on both man and beast.

16.—To this may be added the "*Scarpsticker*" of the Dutch, or Night-Adder;" a small dingy-brown Adder, spotted with black, about eighteen inches long.†

17.—There is also the "House-Adder," a small brown one, about a foot in length, which lodges in old walls, under floors, and found, not

* There is a tradition amongst the Kaffirs, that the young of the Puff Adder eat their way out of the womb of the old female, when the time of incubation is completed; thus "bringing through its life, death to its parent."

† A young traveller in the Colony, some short time ago, had a very narrow escape from one of these Night-Adders. He was riding on a journey, and in the heat of mid-day, he dismounted under a tree in the bush, off-saddled his horse, knee-haltered him, and turned him loose. He then put his saddle on the ground, and placing his head between its flaps, fell asleep. He slept till near evening, and then rising in haste, called in his horse, and saddled him. Ere mounting, however, he remembered that his near stirrup was too short, and in turning up the flap to draw down the buckle, he found a long Night-Adder, coiled in under it: having been attracted by the warmth, it had crept in whilst he was asleep. Had he, unwittingly, mounted, without discovering this, he would, of course, have been bitten by the Adder, the moment his leg had pressed him. As it was, by a single blow from his whip, he disabled his enemy, and soon succeeded in dispatching him.

unfrequently, under your pillow, and in your boots, bed, drawers, and such like localities.

18.—Added to these, there is a small and very venomous Viper, about ten inches long, often found in and about houses.

Several varieties of these seventeen species have been met with, but no more of a distinct class; and, indeed, when the experimental acquaintance of these is considered, together with the many unpleasant encounters persons in Africa have to be subjected to, it will readily be believed that these are considered quite an adequacy.

Added to which, the supplementary army of Scorpions, Tarantulas, Spiders, Hornets, Lizards, and others of smaller tribes, which also appear around, are, of themselves, quite ample to engage the attention and curiosity of the most insatiable naturalist. Amongst these latter too, deadly feuds and warfare are not only waged against their common enemy, mankind, but also among themselves.

We remember once watching, with great curiosity, three battles of this kind. The first of these, was between a large red Scorpion and a huge Tarantula. They engaged in mortal combat. The former using its poisonous sting, and the latter its fangs and breath; it lasted several minutes, both whirling round and round as they strove; at length the strokes of the Scorpion's tail became convulsed and less frequent, until, it gradually sank under the effect of its antagonist's fatal breath, and died first. The victor, although left alone in the field, seemed to have suffered considerably in the affray, and crawled away, as if to die in obscurity.

Another of these conflicts was between a Lizard and a Scorpion. In this the latter, also, was vanquished. The Lizard, having received one or two severe stings from the Scorpion, (which was a very large one) seemed to become infuriated, and rushing upon its enemy, ingeniously seized it in its mouth, between the head and tail, but so that the tail, being curled back, could not reach its head or body. It then commenced spinning round and round with great rapidity, and finally succeeded in severing the tail from the body, and thus killed it.

The last engagement was between a large black Hornet and a Tarantula. This lasted for several minutes, and, to my great amazement, the former was signally victorious, and succeeded in so stinging the Tarantula, that he died from the wounds. The Hornet was so little hurt, as to be able to fly away exultingly.

We close this chapter with a short notice of the Toads and Frogs of Africa—a tribe nearly as numerous, and as noisy, as the Kaffirs. Few who have heard their incessant croaking, will easily forget it through life. Of the former of these, we have seen three kinds, and, of the latter, two. They all vary in size, colour, and beauty of marking, but none seem to deserve special notice, save the " Monster Toad of Kaffraria," called by the Dutch the " *Donder-paade.*" This is a large ugly-looking monster, about eleven inches or a foot in length, and eight inches broad. In colour it is a brownish green, yellow on the under parts of the feet, throat, legs, and belly. On the back it is spotted with black, and on the sides is striped with the same colour. Its eyes are large and red, and the Kaffir tradition says that it spits fire. All animals are afraid of it, and horses shy from it with an inherent and manifest terror, quite equal to that which they evince at the sight of a snake or adder. It inhabits marshy places, and makes a loud discordant croaking noise.

A very curious account of sudden death, caused by this creature, was given in the Cape-town papers some few years ago, and which appeared to confirm the popular belief in its poisonous powers.

It was the case of three brothers, Dutch boers, who lived together in a large farm house, in the western district of Clanwilliam, in the old Cape Colony. One day, whilst two of them were out, a '*smouse*,' or pedlar, came to the farm, having amongst other articles, a quantity of Cape wine for sale. After some little bargaining, the Dutchman bought a cask of wine, and getting it tapped, he drew off a cupful, and drank it. Shortly after the pedlar had departed, the young man complained of thirst, and telling the servant to inform his brothers, should they return, where he was, and to prepare the dinner by the time he returned, he went out to a neighbour's spring, to obtain a drink of water. He had hardly gone, ere his elder brother came in, and enquired for him. Hearing where he was, and seeing the wine, he told the servant to bring him a cupful of it, and she having done so, he drank it and went out, saying he would go to the well, and seek his brother. Neither returned, and, some two hours afterwards, the third brother came home from hunting, and hearing what had happened, he went out in search of his brothers, and found them both together, lying at the spring, quite dead. He immediately sent for the Veldt-cornet of the district, and caused search to be made for the pedlar. He was easily found, and came to the farm, protesting his innocence of the murder of the Dutchmen, of which their brother accused him. In the altercation which took place between them, the farmer accused the pedlar of having poisoned the wine, which he had sold. This the latter indignantly denied, and to prove (as he said,) that he had not done so, he called for a large cupful of it. This he received, drank it, and, a few minutes afterwards, was a corpse.

The wine was then spilt out, and after the cask had been emptied, something was heard rattling about in the inside, the head was immediately stove in, when an immense " *Donder-paade*," or Monster Toad, was found in it.

This case caused great excitement at the time, and certainly seemed to confirm the belief, that this creature possesses some powerful poisonous properties, which, unlike the venom of the serpent tribes, is not imbibed by infusion through the blood, but by absorption in the stomach.

Of the more minute insects, we must here say nothing, but close this chapter with these brief remarks, referring the more curious in Natural history, to works treating more exclusively on that branch, of which many are to be procured.

Of the South African *pisces*, in an Appendix is given a condensed compendium of those, found in and about the Southern bays and shores of the African Continent, compiled, with great care and much intelligence, by Dr. Pappe, of Cape Town.

CHAPTER XIII.

THE idea, that the interior of the African continent is one vast uninhabited tract of sandy desert, is now, it is to be presumed, quite exploded. The latter researches of all intelligent travellers opening out the rich luxuriance of the soil, and densely populated districts of those parts of our globe, which ignorance had so long left wrapped in the misty clouds of supposed gloom, aridity, and inutility.

The districts and tribes stretching out on the North-western boundary of the Cape Colonies, are now pretty well known and defined. The Kaffirs, it is found, reach far across the continent. They and the people of Umzelekazi, who now dwell in the North-eastern interior, contiguous to Inhambane, (having been in 1837, expelled by the Dutch Boers from

the Kurrichenes mountains,) combinedly carry
their habits, language, and tribes, over vast
tracts of the interior districts. The Kaffir
Fingo tribes of the Amafenqu, the Amabace,
and the Matabele, are scattered everywhere
from Kaffraria, up to the confines of the Blue
mountains, near the Caledon river on the West,
and the Quathlamba, Drakensberg, and Lebombo ranges on the Eastward. The Basutos are
also Kaffirs, dwelling along the North-western
borders of the New Colony of Natal, and the
Dutch, and Trans Vaal Free States.

The Mantatees are a distinct race, residing
between these and the Amawazi, which latter
large and powerful tribes, inhabit the districts
to the Northward of the Lebombo mountains,
and the Pongola river. These Mantatees are the
only tribe of natives in Southern Africa, said
to be cannibals. It seems from what can be collected concerning them, that during the wars
of T'Shaka (or Chaka) and Dingaan, this tribe
being powerful and warlike, opposed the encroachments of these savage tyrants longer than
any others, and at length, so exasperated them
by their obstinate resistance, that they sent
the full force of their armies at several times
against them. This so distressed and harrassed
them, that, from dire necessity, they were compelled to become cannibals: having once, thus

tasted human blood, they could not relinquish it, and they have, consequently, ever since remained attached to the exercise of this barbarous usage.

Beyond these, are found the districts and people of the Baralongs, the Barmagalasitas, the Baphiris, the Bamanguatos, and the Bakone. All of these appear to be tribes sprung from an admixture of Kaffir and Negro blood, but partaking more freely of the latter.

The Bechuanas again, are a large Kaffir tribe, who stretch their habitations over an immense extent of country, towards the Northwestern part of the old Sovereignty, and reach, in fact, to the Damara tribes, who dwell along the Western coast. The habits of these people are quiet and industrious, and, that pious, zealous, and enterprising Misssionary and pioneer of civilization, Mr. Moffatt, has laboured amongst them for many years, most successfully. Through his endeavours, they have been extensively taught European handicrafts, and build their houses in towns and settlements, in English fashion. They also make their own clothes and hats, and manufacture several articles for culinary and domestic use very cleverly and well. The spread of the light of Christianity is also slowly following in the wake of that of civilization.

From amongst the Bapheris, the Bamanguatos, and the Bakones, it has been largely asserted that numbers of slaves are brought and taken in canoes, along the interior rivers, to the Portuguese settlements to Delagoa Bay on the Eastward, from whence they are shipped for North and South America. The districts, however, inhabited by these various tribes, are so unhealthy for Europeans, and are so thickly infested with the " *Tsetse* " fly, so destructive to cattle of all kinds, that few travellers have visited them, or at least returned to tell of their exploits. Towards the interior, and stretching along the coast to the Westward, the latest geographical researches have been made; in the former, through the discovery of the great salt lake, by Messrs. Oswell, King, and Livingstone; and in the latter, by Dr. Livingstone's recent discoveries towards Angola.

One of the greatest, and most important facts established by these, both in relation to science and the spread of Christianity, is, that these travellers were everywhere able to make their way by means of the Kaffir dialects and language; and to pass from the Eastern to the Western coast of Southern Africa, without meeting any serious, or, at least, insurmountable impediment: whilst finding, scattered over the greatest portions of the country, across which they travelled, numerous and intelligent tribes of natives.

So far from ascertaining that the districts of this country were arid, desert, or *"karoo,"* these explorators represent them as most abundantly watered, long and branching rivers flowing for miles together; of sufficient width and water to admit of being navigated by large canoes. The most extensive of these, towards the South latitudes, but North of the Pongola, is the Limpopo; the sources, course, and localities of which have been, of late, more satisfactorily laid down. It appears, from papers lately read before the Royal Geographical Society, to take its rise in the Witte Waters Raand, near the Magaliesberg Mountains, about 100 miles North of the Vaal river; and thence, flowing in a North by North-easterly course, to pass to the Eastward, most possibly falling as a tributary into a larger river, which again, towards the Northward, flows either into the new salt lake, N'Gami, or Lake Maravi.

Travelling from Kurumen in a N. N. W., direction, Dr. Livingstone, after the first stage of his last arduous journey, reached the town 23° 50' East Longitude, and discovered a course of Sekeletu, in 18° 17' 20" South Latitude, of the Sanshurch, or Chobe river, running East and West at 17° 28' South Latitude. Not far from this, was found the junction of this stream with the river Leeambye, and then, following the course of it through the district of Makolola and the Balotze valley, he accurately traced it to its junction with the river Leeba, which latter, through all its branches, he followed to its sources, in and near the Lake Dilolo, in 11° 30' South latitude.

From this point, the enterprising traveller took a Westerly direction, to the town of Njambi, 10° South latitude. From it he bore to the North East, as far as the river Checkapa, in 10° 38' South; and here, taking to the west, he finally reached St. Paul de Loando, the Portuguese capital and seaport, on the western coast of the province of Angola, situated in about 8° 50', South latitude. In 9° 51' 28" South, he crossed the Quango river, and there found it pursuing a straight course North and South. This large river is supposed to run into the great Congo, which again empties itself into the South Atlantic ocean, at Cape Padrone. The vicinity of the Chobe river was found extensively flooded; whilst the difficulty of travelling through the inundated land, was increased by the quantities of papyrus and reeds, found bound together by twining convolvolus.

At the town of Sekeletu, Dr. Livingstone

remained some time, and describes the natives as kind and docile ; but the most important fact brought to light by him whilst there, was the existence of a Portuguese slave-merchant's stockade, at Katongo, a Batoka village on the Eastern bank of the Leeambye river. That these traders in human flesh should have penetrated so far to the South, is a sign that they do not find a sufficient supply for their market on the upper districts of the Western coast.

From this point, he and his party proceeded up the river, towards the Barotse, in thirty-eight canoes, 33 feet long and 20 inches wide. "With six paddlers we passed," to use his own words, "through 44 miles of latitude, by one day's pull of $10\frac{1}{2}$ hours: if we add the longitude to this, it must have been upwards of 50 miles actual distance. The river is indeed a magnificent one: it is often more than a mile broad, and adorned with numerous islands of from three to five miles in length: these and the banks too, are covered with forest, and most of the trees on the brink of the water send down roots from their branches like the banian. The islands at a little distance seem rounded masses of sylvan vegetation, of various hues, reclining on the bosom of a glorious stream. The beauty of the scene is greatly increased by the date palm, and lofty palmyra, towering above the rest, and casting their feathery foliage against the sky. The banks are rocky and undulating; many villages of the Kanzeti, a poor, but industrious people, are situated on both of them. They are expert hunters of the hippopotami and other animals, and cultivate grain extensively. At the bend of Katima Molelo, the bottom of the river bed begins to be rocky, and continues so the whole way, to about latitude 16° South, forming a succession of rapids and cataracts, which are dangerous when the river is low. The rocks are of hard sandstone and porphyritic basalt. The main fall amongst these cataracts is over a straight ledge of rock, about 60 or 70 yards long, and 40 feet deep. The Tetze fly, in places, inhabits the banks."

Throughout the surrounding districts, the villages and towns are built on mounds, whilst the valleys are covered with rich pasturage, and at certain periods of the year, large herds of cattle. The principal town, or capital, of the Barotse country is Nariclo: it contains about 1000 inhabitants. The ridges of the high lands are covered with trees, and abound in fruitful gardens, in which were found the sugar-cane, sweet potato, two kinds of manioc, two kinds of yam, bananas, millet, maize, and Kaffir corn. The river contains an abundance of fish, so that the valley was always spoken of by the natives as a land of plenty. The climate no where could be said to be salubrious, fever being every where prevalent, and this, even amongst the natives, is often very fatal.

Of this fever Dr. Livingstone had eight attacks, the last very severe. He says, speaking of this in one of his letters, "I never laid by. I tried native remedies, in order to discover if they possessed any valuable means of cure; but after being stewed in vapour baths, smoked like a red herring, over fires of green twigs in hot potsherds, and physicked *secundum black artem*, I believe that our own medicines are more efficacious and safer. I have not relinquished the search, and as I make it a rule to keep on good terms with my professional brethren, I am not without hope, that some of their means of re-establishing the secretions (and to this, indeed, all their efforts are directed) may be well adapted for this complaint."

The accurate geographical position of this river, its junction with the Leeba, as well as the course, tributaries, and their sources of this latter, have all been furnished, by this enterprizing traveller, to the Royal Geographical Society, and are now determined and laid down in their new and valuable maps of this continent. The only point to cause regret, is the unfavourable reports he has had to furnish of the climate of these various districts. Still, notwithstanding this, as he says, "I have met Arabs, from Zanzibar, subjects of the Imaun of Muscat, who had been quite across the Continent; they wrote Arabic fluently in my pocket book, and boldly avowed that Mahomet was greatest of all the prophets," we cannot but confess, it leads to thoughts and reflections of some seriousness, when, in connection with the assertion, he exclaims, "Shame upon us Missionaries, if we are to be outdone by slave-traders!"

Of the *fauna* of these districts, he gives but a brief account; but describes them as peopled with countless herds of game. He writes: "Eilands and buffalos! their tameness was shocking to me: 81 buffalos defiled slowly before our fire one evening, and lions were impudent enough to roar at us. On the South of the Chobé, where Bushmen abound, they are seldom heard, these brave fellows teaching them better manners. My boatman informed me that he had seen an animal, with long wide-spreading horns, like an ox, called "*Liombika-lela*," perhaps the modern Bison. Also another animal, which does not live in the water, but snorts like a hippopotamus, it is like that animal in size, and has a horn, and may be, possibly the " Asiatic Rhinoceros."   And we passed some holes of a third animal, which burrows from the river, inland; has short horns, and feeds only at night.   I did not notice the burrows at the time of passing, but give the report as I received it.   Sable Antelopes abound, and so does the " *Nakong;*" and there is also a pretty little Antelope on the Seskeké, called " *Teeanyane.*" which seemed new to me."

The birds are in great numbers on the rivers, and the Sand-martins never leave it.   The novelties in trees, shrubs, and flowers were, of course, most numerous.

So interesting and valuable are the remarks of this indefatigable pioneer to civilization in South Africa, that we here insert the main substance of two of the last letters received from him, and which have been kindly placed at our disposal.   They will appear in full, together with the tables of his astronomical observations in the journals of the Royal Geographical Society, which has awarded to Dr. Livingstone, the gold medal for 1855, as a mark of their approval of his discoveries.

The first of these letters, describes his journey from the confluence of the Leeba, and Leeambye rivers, to St. Paul de Loanda, and bears date at Pungo Andongo, Angola, December 24th, 1854.   He says :—

"In my last letter, dated 20th September, 1853, I reported my return to the town of Sekeletu, on the Chobé, after having visited the country of the Barotse, and the river Leeambye or Zambesi, as far North as its confluence with the Leeba; and I mentioned my intention of proceeding to Loanda, in order, if possible, to open a path, whereby commercial intercourse might be maintained with the Western coast, as a means of ameliorating the condition of the people of the interior. The present communication is intended to convey a sketch of the journey from the point at which my last terminated, viz., the confluence of the Leeambye and Leeba, latitude 14° 11' 3" South, longitude 23° 40' 30" East, to Loanda, the capital of the Portuguese possessions in Western Africa.

"Sekeletu, who by the abdication of his sister, now possesses the chieftainship, and the principal men of his tribe, entered cordially into the project of opening a new road for commercial purposes.

"The commerce of the country over which Sekeletu now reigns, and that of numerous tribes situated more to the East, has been, until lately, completely neglected by Europeans. A large waterfall called Mosioatunya, is conjectured to have prevented the Portuguese from ascending the Zambesi; and the desert presented an insurmountable obstacle to commercial enterprize in the South: accordingly, when we first visited the country, we saw many instances in which valuable ivory had been allowed to rot, like the other bones, just where the animal had fallen. Indeed tusks went by the name of "mere bones," ("*marapohela*"—bones only); and though the inhabitants soon acquired an idea of their superior value, they have not, up to the present time, received prices sufficient to stimulate them to proper efforts to procure large supplies. Elephants abound in the land, and there are many daring hunters: but a few pieces of cloth present only a very small indication that tusks are of more value than the flesh. The elephants have always been killed more for food than for profitable barter; and other articles of trade, such as bees' wax, which abounds in some parts of the country, are thrown aside as useless.

"The common methods of killing elephants may be mentioned. The hunters having observed the path by which certain elephants, or a herd go to water, select the highest overhanging trees, as best adapted for their purpose; they are armed with spears, having very long handles, made of very light wood, and blades about two feet long, furnished with a barb on the shaft. As the animals generally drink during the night, the men perch themselves on branches hanging nearly over the path, and when the elephant comes unsuspectingly along, they plunge their spears into his body; the wounded animal rushes madly away, and as the spear is held in by the barb, the motion of the body causes the long handle to swing in different directions; contact with trees produces the same effect; and as the motions of the blade are uniform with those of the handle, the numerous internal gashes soon bring this strong animal to the ground. Another method is by means of a log of wood, having a poisoned spear-head inserted. It is suspended on a branch above the elephant's path, by means of a cord, which again is secured to a small wooden catch on the ground. When the catch is touched by the foot of the elephant, in passing along, the beam falls on his back, and the barbed spear-head remains. In this case the trust of the hunter lies in the poison. Still another method is that of deep wedge-shaped pitfalls, carefully covered over and plastered, so as to have the same appearance as the rest of the path. Many females and young animals are destroyed by this last means; but it is evident that with better arms, and the prospect of a speedy and profitable sale of the ivory, much more produce would appear. The present means are often rendered futile, by one elephant helping another out of a pitfall, or by the sagacious beast snuffing danger in the wind, and abruptly leaving the country. Even when successful, it can only be with one animal, for the others at once forsake the district if one of their number falls a victim.

" A variety of considerations having induced me to try Loanda first, Sekeletu showed his cordiality, by furnishing men, oxen, and canoes; and, being desirous of ascertaining the value of ivory among the white men in that direction, he committed four tusks to our care for the purpose, which we subsequently disposed of, at Cassange, to his advantage. Taking leave of the chief and principal men on the banks of the Chobé, my company consisting of none but men of Zambesi, and these chiefly Barotse, we descended that tortuous river to its junction, with the Leeambye, which we ascended, visiting Sesheké, and the different villages on its banks, at each of which, orders had previously issued, " that we must not be allowed to become hungry."

" On reaching the country of the Barotse, we learned that a foray had been made by one of the under chiefs, and that several villages had been destroyed, in the very direction that we intended to take. Having demanded the return of the prisoners, as the only means of ensuring our safety, I succeeded in getting eighteen into my charge, and these were restored to their relatives, as we approached their different habitations, in our progress up the river.   As we had previously seen, the Leeambye makes a sharp bend away to the Eastward, from the confluence of the Leeba, and flows from East to West. But the Leeba comes from the North, so that we supposed by ascending it, we should approach the source of the Coanza, and, by descending the latter, might at last reach Loanda.

"We discovered afterwards, that the Portuguese map, which represents the Coanza as rising in the East, is erroneous. With the above impression, however, we ascended the Leeba for 40 or 50 miles, when a cataract, preventing further progress in canoes, we remained waiting for a few days, for a party that had been detached at the confluence, before commencing the journey on oxback. The party was sent from the junction, with five captives belonging to Masiko, a Barotse chief, who lives East of that point, and proceeded in the same direction during five days. Two of the prisoners being little girls, shorter marches than usual were made; and the actual distance may, therefore, be not more than 80 miles. Though travelling Eastward thus far, the party did not again come near the Leeambye. From this, the fact that we could get no more information about it in the North, it may fairly be inferred, that this noble river the Leeambye, holds an Easterly and Westerly course for a considerable distance, beyond where we left it.

"The party having returned together with an embassy of Masiko's principal men, bearing a present, and friendly message, we left the river, and proceeded N. N. W. through a portion of the county called Londa, the paramount chief of which is well known to the Portuguese by the title of Matiamvo. The inhabitants called Balonda, belong to the true woolly headed negro race, and differ remarkably from the Bechuanas and other tribes in the South, in their treatment of females, and in the practice of idolatry. They swear by their mothers, and never desert them, they allow the women a place and voice in their public assemblies, and frequently elevate them to the chieftainship. Near every village we observed an idol, consisting either of an image formed of grass and clay, intending to represent a lion, or alligator, or a block of wood, on the top of which the human face was rudely carved. In cases of sickness, or of non-success in hunting, offerings are made, and drums beat, before these idols, during whole nights. The Bechuanas (Kaffirs,) on the contrary, swear by their fathers, glory in the little bit of beard which distinguishes them from the sex which they despise, and though they have some idea of a future state, it exerts but little influence on their conduct. Their supreme God is a cow, and they never pray.

"The first Londa Chief of importance, whom we visited, is called Shinté, or Kabompa. His town stands in latitude 13° South. (13° 0' 21".) We were received in, what they considered, grand style. The old chief sat under a species of "*Ficus Indicæ*," on a raised seat, having some hundreds of women behind him, all decked out in their best, and that best a profusion of red baize. Some drums and primitive instruments, made of wood, were powerfully beaten; and different bands of men, each numbering about fifty or eighty persons, well armed with large bows and iron-headed arrows, short broadswords and guns, rushed yelling towards us, from different quarters. As they all screwed up their faces, so as to look very fierce and savage, I supposed they were trying whether they could not make us take to our heels. But they knelt down and made their obeisance to Shinté, which in all this country consists in rubbing dust on the upper and front part of the arms, and across the chest. When several hundreds had arrived, speeches were delivered. in which my history, so far as they could extract it from my companions, was given. "The Bible containing a message of peace;" "The return of two captives to Shinté;" The opening of a new path for trade," &c.; were all described. "Perhaps he is fibbing, perhaps not;" "They rather thought he was;" "But as they were good-hearted, and not at all like Balobale, or people of Sekeletu, and had never done any evil to any one, Shinté had better treat him well, and send him on his way." The women occasionally burst forth with a plaintive ditty, but I could not distinguish whether it was in praise of the speakers or of themselves: and when the sun became hot, the scene closed.

"Shinté came during the night, and hung around my neck a particular kind of shell, which is highly valued, as a proof of the greatest friendship; and he was greatly delighted with some scriptural pictures which I showed him from a magic lantern.

"The spirit of trade is strong in all Africans, and the Balonda chiefs we visited, all highly approved of our journey. Each expressed an earnest hope that the projected path might lead through his town. Shinté facilitated our progress to the next important chief, named Katema; and we again reached the Leeba, in lat.

12° 8' South, and 22° 55' East long. It had assumed the same Easterly and Westerly course as the Leeambye. After crossing it, we were obliged to go due North, in consequence of the plains of Lobalé, on our West, being flooded and impassable. It happened to be the rainy season, and never did twenty-four hours pass without frequent drenching showers. All the streams were swollen, so as to appear considerable rivers; but as they were generally furnished with rustic bridges, we may infer their flow to be perennial. Several extensive plains were crossed, with the water standing more than a foot deep; and broad valleys also, along which the water flowed fast towards the Leeba, deep enough to wet our blankets, which we used as pads on the oxen, instead of saddles. Both this, and the water in the rivers, was so clear, that, in using the bridges over the latter, though they were submerged breast deep, we could easily see the sticks on which to place our feet. This clearness of the water, which we observed in the Zonga, Chobé, and Leeambye, at the times of inundation, is the result of the rains falling on a mat of grass, so thick, as to prevent abrasion of the soil. As the tropical rains cause the plains of Lobalé to present a similar phenomenon, it may not be unreasonable to conclude, that the water of inundation to the Barotse valley, and lower parts of the Zambesi, is supplied by copious rains in the North, and, as the natives reported, comes chiefly from the Lobalé.

"We suffered less detention than might have been expected, from these rivers; for though we had to swim some of them, all (except two boys) knew the art; and we never stopped to dry our clothes, unless it were in the afternoons. We got drenched, either by rains or rivers, two or three times every day; but the sun was hot, and we suffered no inconvenience. If, however, we arrived at our sleeping-place damp, or got our blankets wet, intermittent fever was sure to follow."

*   *   *   *

"The country of the Balonda, through which we passed, was both beautiful and fertile; dense forests alternate constantly with open valleys covered with grass, resembling fine English meadows. The general surface, though flat, seems covered with waves disposed lengthways, from N. N. E., to S. S. W. The crest of each of these earthen billows is covered with forest, four or five miles broad; while the trough, about a mile wide, has generally a stream or bog in the centre of it, with the habitations and gardens of the inhabitants on the sides. The forests consist of lofty ever-

green trees, standing close together, and inter-
laced with great numbers of gigantic climbers.
The trees covered with lichens, and the ground
with mosses and ferns, indicate a much more
humid climate than is to be found in the South.
The only roads through these dense thickets
are small winding footpaths; and as an attempt
to stop an ox suddenly only makes him rush
on, we were frequently caught by the overhanging climbers, and came to the ground head
foremost.

"The streams, with which the country is well
supplied, differ remarkably in the directions in
which they flow. Many were flowing Southwards; but a distance of about twenty miles
brought us to streams running North-east, and
in much deeper valleys. I suspected that we
were travelling on an elevated table land, because the current of the Zambesi and other rivers was rapid, and we had large Cape heaths
and rhododendrons, which grow on elevated
positions, together with a wonderful lack of
animal life. This proved to be the fact, for
when we were about 40 miles E. S. E. of the
Quango, we came upon a sudden descent, perhaps about 2000 feet, which to me seemed
about the same height as Table Mountain at
the Cape. Ninety or a hundred miles West
from this descent, appeared as it were a range

of mountains; but it is only the edge of similar table land, identical with that on the margin of which we stood. This presents the same mountainous appearance to a person coming from the West: the intervening valley is called Cassange, and through it flows the Quango and other rivers.

"Only when we reached the declivity which forms the valley of the Cassange, could I perceive why all the rivers that flowed N. N. E., or N. W., ran in much deeper valleys, than those which followed an opposite direction. The slopes down to the feeders of the Casai and Quango, are more than five hundred yards long, and pretty steep, while the beds of the branches of the Leeba are never more than ten yards below the level of the surrounding country. The whole valley of the Cassange seems to have been a work of denudation, for on all sides the declivity presents the same geological peculiarities; viz., a covering of brown hœmatite, mixed with quartz pebbles, lying upon bright red friable clay slate. This, differing only in hardness and paleness of colour, continues to the bottom; but, towards the centre of the valley, it takes the form of argillaceous schist. A detached mountain, seven or eight miles S. S. W. of Cassange, called Kasala, and having perpendicular sides all round, possesses the same structure. I regretted much having no instruments to measure the elevations of these parts; but, after ascending again to Tala Mungongo, we appeared to descend again all the way to Ambaca, where we met primitive and secondary rocks—the latter containing metals.

"This country, as compared with that to the South, is well peopled. We came to villages every few miles, and often passed as many as ten in a day. Some were extremely neat, others were so buried in a wilderness of weeds, that, though sitting on the ox in the middle of the village, we could see only the tops of the houses. There is no lack of food; manioc, or the tapioca plant, is the staff of life, and requires but little labour for its cultivation. The seasons seemed to allow of planting or reaping all the year round. The Balonda were all extremely kind; and, indeed, had they been otherwise, we should have starved; for there is no game, and all the goods which I had brought from the Cape were expended before we started, excepting a few beads.

"When we came near to the Portuguese possessions, the tribes altered very much for the worse; and the Chiboqui so annoyed us by heavy fines, levied on the most frivolous pretences, that we changed our course from North West, to North. This did not relieve us long, for when we came nearer Cassange, we found our route obstructed by the M'Bangala, who demanded payment of "a man, an ox, or a gun," for leave to pass at all: a refusal on our part was sometimes followed by a whole tribe surrounding us, brandishing their swords, arrows, and guns, and tumultuously vociferating their demands. The more we yielded, the more unreasonable the mob became, till, at last, in order not to aid in robbing ourselves, we ceased speaking, after telling them that they must strike the first blow. My men, who were inured to fighting by Sebituane, quietly surrounded the chief and councillors; these felt their danger, and usually became more amicable. They never disputed the proposition that the ground they cultivated alone belonged to them, and all the rest of the country to God. This being the idea in the native mind, they readily admitted that they had no right to demand payment for trading on the soil of our common Father. But they pleaded custom; slavetraders always gave them a slave: my companions being all free subjects of Sekeletu, had as good a right to give me, as I had to give one of them; and the affair usually ended by our agreeing to give, to each other, food in token of friendship. I had to part with an ox; and their part of the contract was sometimes fulfilled, by sending us two or three pounds of the meat of our own animal, with many expressions of regret at having nothing else to give. It was impossible to avoid laughing at the coolness of the generous creatures. I had paid away my razors, shirts, and everything I could dispense with; but though I showed these extortioners the instruments and all we had, as being perfectly useless to them, the oxen, men, and guns, still remained. "You may as well give what we ask for, as we shall get the whole to-morrow, after we have killed you: or, "You must go back from whence you came, and say we sent you;" were some of the witticisms which, with hunger, were making us all sulky and savage. If Sekeletu had allowed my companions to bring their shields, I could not have restrained them; but we never came into actual collision, and as far as we are concerned, the way is open for our return. On tho last occasion on which we parted with an ox, objections were raised against one which had lost his tail, because they imagined a charm had been inserted into the stump, which might injure them; and the remaining four, still in our possession, very soon exhibited the same peculiarity of their caudal extremities. Attempts have frequently been made by the Balonda and other distant tribes, to open up commercial intercourse with the Portuguese, and these have always been rendered abortive by these borderers."

*　　*　　*　　*

"In the beginning of April, I reached the banks of the Quango, which was swollen, and its muddy waters flowing rapidly, I had at length made up my mind to part with my blanket and coat to the ferryman, for a passage. But a young Portuguese serjeant, Cypriano de Abren, made his appearance, and enabled us to enter the Portuguese territory, without further annoyance. Senhor Neves de Cassange performed a brother's part to me in the time of need, and, indeed, the Portuguese everywhere exhibited the greatest kindness all the way to Loando.

"I approached Loando labouring under severe illness, and extremely anxious as to what I should do for the support of my companions, who, without exception, are the best I ever travelled with, and who bravely followed me, though told by the blacks of every village West of Cassange, that, "the white man was taking them down to the coast for sale, and they would all be taken on board ship, fattened and eaten."

"I arrived in the city nearly knocked up, and suffering from fever and dysentry. Edmund Gabriel, Esq., Her Majesty's Commissioner for the suppression of the slave trade, most generously received me and my twenty-seven companions into his house. I shall never forget the delicious pleasure of lying down on his bed, after sleeping six months on the ground, nor the unwearied attention and kindness through a long sickness, which Mr. Gabriel invariably showed. May God reward him! My companions were struck with awe at the sight of a city, and more especially when taken on board Her Majesty's ships of war. The kindness of the officers of the cruisers removed the last vestige of fear from their minds, for, finding them to be all my countrymen, they saw the fallacy of the declarations made to them on the road. They were afterwards engaged in discharging coals from a ship for wages, and will marvel, to the end of their lives, at the prodigious quantity of "stones that burn," one ship could contain. They previously imagined their own little canoes, on the Zambesi, the best vessels, and themselves the most expert sailors in the world.

"His Excellency, the Bishop of Angola, then the acting governor of the province, received my companions with great kindness, and assured them of his protection and friendship, as well as the desire to promote commercial intercourse with the country of Sekeletu. He also sent a present of a horse, and handsome dress for that Chief, and shewed very great attention to myself in my sickness. The merchants, too, of Loando, took the opportunity of our return to send presents to Sekeletu; and as they give much more for the produce of his country than can be, or is done, by merchants from the Cape Colony, it is to be hoped that intercourse, either with Cassange or Loando, will promote the civilization of the interior.

"I return, because I feel that the work to which I set myself, is only half accomplished. The way out to the Eastern coast may be less difficult than I have found that to the West. If I succeed, we shall, at least, have a choice.

"My present intention is to proceed to Matiaamvo's town, previous to turning Southward. Taking it for granted that I shall come into his good graces, our progress through his country will be comparatively easy, and the route, upon the whole, not much longer than the zigzag way we were forced to adopt in coming here. The only thing which may hinder the execution of this plan, will be the wishes of my companions to return, as speedily as possible, by the path we already know. It is the first time they have gone into other lands, except for plunder; and they have followed my wishes so implicitly hitherto, it would not be right in me to thwart theirs.

"After making any arrangements with Sekeletu that may be deemed necessary, I propose to descend the Leeambye, to Quilimane. It may be advisable, in order to avoid the waterfall of Mosoiatunye, to cross overland from Sesheké to the river Maninché, or Loenge, (Bashukulompo river,) buy, or beg, a canoe, and descend in it to the Leeambye. The confluence of the Chobé is only two days distant from the waterfall, but the river is very rocky and dangerous, before reaching that point.

"In order that, should I succeed in reaching Mozambique, or Quilimane, I may not suffer the same dejection of spirits on my approach, I presume to request, that any of our officers who may be on that coast, be directed to make enquiries, respecting my arrival, towards the end of 1855. I am known to some of the subjects of the Imaum of Muscat, by the name *Naka.*" (Doctor.)

"In conclusion, I cannot omit mentioning the very great courtesy of the Portuguese authorities; and as their habitual politeness was in strict accordance with the wishes of the government of Portugal, it is of the greatest value."

*   *   *   *

One of the last letters that has been received in England, is dated from Cassange, the 13th February, 1855, and is descriptive of the province of Angola.   Speaking of it he says :—

"It possesses great fertility and beauty, and its capabilities, both agriculturally and commercially, are of a very high order : indeed, I do not fear contradiction, in asserting it to be the richest in resources in Western Africa.

"As I have now had the advantage of passing through the province twice, and have honestly endeavoured to obtain correct knowledge of the country, I venture to give you my impressions, as not calculated to mislead any, except those whose general views of the world are much more gloomy than mine.

"As we proceed from the coast inland, the country, except in the vicinity of rivers, presents a rather arid appearance.   There are not many trees, but abundance of hard coarse grass. But the low meadow lands, of several miles width, lying adjacent to the rivers, are sufficiently fertile, and yield annually fine crops of sugar-cane, different vegetables, and manioc, (the staff of life through all this part of Africa,) also oranges, bananas, and mangoes of excellent quality.

"Proceeding Eastwards, we enter on a different sort of country, about longitude 14° East.

It is mountainous, well watered with perennial streams, and mollified by fogs, deposited from the western winds, which come regularly to different places, at different hours, every day. Near the Mùria we enter dense forests, whose gigantic trees covered with scarlet or other coloured blossoms, and giving support to numerous enormous climbers, with the curious notes of strange tropical birds, present the idea of excessive luxuriance, and recall the feelings of wildness, produced when standing in similar sylvan scenery, in the interior of Brazil. The palm which yields the oil of commerce, grows everywhere. Pine-apples, bananas, and different kinds of South American fruit trees, first introduced by the Missionaries, flourish in the woods, though apparently wild, and totally uncared for. Most excellent coffee, from a few seeds of the celebrated Mocha, propagates itself spontaneously in the forests, which line the mountain sides. Cotton of rather inferior quality finds itself so well suited with climate and soil, that it appears as if indigenous. Provisions are abundant and cheap. Ten pounds of the produce of the manioc plant, which under the classical appellation, "*Revalenta Arabica*," sells in England for twenty-two shillings, may, in the district referred to, be purchased for one penny. Labour too is abuudant and cheap ; two pence per day is considered good wages, by carpenters, smiths, potters, &c., as well as by common labourers. The greatest drawback the population has, in developing the resources of the country, is the want of carriage roads for the conveyance of produce to markets. The slave-trade led to the neglect of every permanent source of wealth. All the merchandize of the interior, was transported on the heads and shoulders of the slaves, who, equally with the goods, were intended for exportation. And even since the traffic has been effectually repressed by the intervention of our cruisers, human labour for transport has alone been available. This is a most expensive and dilatory system, as the merchants and persons of smaller means, on whose industry, access to a proper market would have a most beneficial effect, possess no stimulus for exertion in cultivation. Some use is made of the river Zenza, by means of canoes, and considerable trade is carried on between the districts on the Coanza and Loanda, by the same means; but the bars at the mouths of both rivers, present serious obstacles to speedy transit.

"The country still farther inland, becomes gradually more open. Ambaca presents an undulating surface, with ranges of mountains on each side of the distance. It possesses a great number of fine little streams, which might be turned to much advantage, for water power and irrigation. Both it and Pungo Andongo abound in cattle. The latter seems more elevated; for as we cross the Lotell, the boundary between the two districts, we enter upon the same vegetation and trees, which characterize Lunda. Wheat, grapes, and European vegetables, grow in nearly the same spots, with bananas, and other tropical fruits. Indeed, by selecting proper localities, cotton, sugar, coffee, and other products of hot climates, might be raised to any amount in this beautiful and fine country, together with many of the grains and fruits of colder lands.

"No attempts have hitherto been made to develop the internal resources. It is but lately that Coffee plantations were turned to, as a source of wealth. Some were discovered during my journey, and the actual extent of the tree is still unknown. I saw it at Tala Mungongo, nearly 300 miles from the coast. Different kinds of gum are found, such as gum *Elenii*, India rubber &c.; and among metals, very superior iron everywhere abounds; rich copper ore exists in the interior of Ambriz, and there are indications of coal."

"Cassange is, at present, the farthest inland station of the Portuguese. It may be called the commercial capital of the interior. Trade in ivory and wax is carried on with great vigour and success; and large quantities of English cotton goods, are sent into the country beyond, by means of native or half blood Portuguese. The merchants treat their customers with great liberality. At the time I write, Captain Neves is preparing presents, consisting of cloth, beads, carpets, furniture, &c., of upwards of £50 value, for Matiamvo, the most powerful potentate East of this. This chief lives about longitude, 24° East, and monopolizes the trade, which but for him, might pass to tribes called Kanijika, beyond him.

"The deep valley of Cassange, is wonderfully fertile, but success in trade prevents the merchants from paying any attention to agriculture. The soil so far as present experience goes, would place Mr. Mechi's pipes for liquid manure at a discount, for it requires nothing but labour: and the more it is worked, the more fruitful it becomes."

*　　*　　*　　*

The following geological observations may not be unacceptable, as descriptive of the formation of this country.

"The igneous rocks in the district of Cazengo, appear to have evidently run through gorges in the mountain ranges, and have tilted up schist, gneiss, &c.; while, in the latter, veins, or rather cracks, may be seen, filled with a dark blue rock, exactly like clay slate. In the districts of Cazengo and Golungo Alto, abundance of excellent iron ore occurs, some strongly magnetic, other parts not, but all very largely impregnated with the metal. To the North, near the river Daude, petroleum is reported; and so it is said to occur likewise towards the South, under the dark red sandstone which forms the crust of the country. The spot reported is on the banks of the Coanza, and near Cambambe. Veins of copper appear also on the banks of this river, in the same district, but I did not see them. The rocks of Pungo Andongo are composed of large masses of conglomerate, rising about 300 or 400 feet above the surrounding country. They stand in parallel lines, nearly North and South in direction, and rather more than a mile in length. The conglomerate stands on horizontal strata of dark red sandstone, and this in a very small proportion to the other materials, form the matrix. There are granite, gneiss, porphyry, schist, clay, and sandstone, trap, syenite, greenstone, quartzite, &c., all round and water-worn, and forming immense masses of shingle. There is also a soft limestone, containing shells, found lying on the tops of some of the rocks.

"The government of the country may be described as a military one, and closely resembles that which Sir Harry Smith endeavoured, in vain, to introduce amongst the Kaffirs. The imposts are exceedingly light, consisting of a tax of eightpence on each hearth, and sixpence on each head of cattle. Something is also levied on gardens near the coast, and on weavers and smiths. The population is large, between 500,000 and 600,000 souls, being under the sway of the Portuguese; and, of this large number, the majority are free-born. In those districts, to the statistics of which I had access, the slaves did not form five per cent. of the entire population, and a very large proportion was dependent on agriculture alone. There are very few white slaves, comparatively; and from the polite way in which persons of colour are addressed, and admitted to the table of the more affluent, it might be inferred, that there is as little prejudice against colour as in any country in the world. Nothing struck me as more remarkable, than the change produced on convicts, by their residence in this colony. No sooner do they arrive than they are enlisted into the 1st regiment of the line, and perform similar duties to our Foot Guards in London. The 11,000 inhabitants of Loando, go comfortably to bed every night, although they know that the citadels, and all the arms in Loando, are in the hands of convicts, many of whom have been transported for life. The officers are not supposed to have been guilty of any offence against the laws of their country, and probably they may have considerable influence with the men; but their testimony even is, that the men perform their duty well, and are excellent soldiers. Some ascribe the remarkable change to the utter hopelessness of escape, the certainty of detection, and punishment of any crime, and the fear of being sent to the deadly district of St. Josa de Encoge, (something like, but not so bad as our Norfolk Island); but, however accounted for, the change is unquesitonable.

"Another pleasing thing observable in the population, is the ability of so many to read and write. It is considered a disgrace in Ambaca, for a free man of either colour, not to be able to do this. This general diffusion of education, is the result of the teaching of the Jesuit Missionaries, who were expelled the country, by Marquis di Pombal. If the results of their teaching have been so permanent, without anything like a proper supply of books, we may be allowed to indulge the hope, that the labours of Protestants of all denominations, who endeavour to leave God's Word behind them, will be not less abiding.

"The commerce of Angola has been remarkably neglected by the English; for though the city of Loando contains a population of 11,000 souls, clothed chiefly in the produce of English looms, and though, in many parts of the interior, cheap Glasgow and Manchester goods constitute the circulating medium, there is not a single English house established at the capital. For this anomaly, various reasons are assigned, the most cogent of which appears to be, that those who first attempted to develop a trade, unfortunately accepted bills on Rio Janeiro, in part payment of their cargoes, at a time when the increased numbers and vigilance of our cruisers, caused the bankruptcy of many houses, both in Rio and Loando. Heavy losses were sustained, and Angola in consequence, got a bad name in the mercantile world. No attempt has ever since been made. Still with the same difficulties and burdens as the English encountered, the Americans carry on a flourishing trade with Loando.* A very large proportion of the goods imported in other ships, are English manufactures, taken in exchange for colonial produce, which has gone by the expensive and circuitous route of Lisbon, i. e., produce on which the expense of port dues, freight, commission, &c.,

* "The Americans, it is said, do not hesitate to co-operate with slavers, whereas the English traders cannot do this."

is paid from Loando to Lisbon, and thence again to London.   As the same expenses are incurred on English manufactures, a British merchant carrying goods direct, to and from England, and dealing in Loando in a liberal spirit, would probably establish a lucrative trade.

"In connection with this subject, I may be allowed to call your attention to the rivers Casai and Quango. These are reported by intelligent natives, who profess knowledge of the country, and are believed by Portuguese traders, to join somewhere North of Cassange, and form the Congo or Zaire of Captain Tuckey. The directions in which I saw those rivers flowing, appear to favour the idea.   The Casai, according to the report of Matiamvo's people, whom we met, flows E. N. E., even beyond the residence of their Chief, and as that is a mouth, or 300 miles from the ford, if it really makes a large bend round to the N. W. after that, we can form an idea of the great importance of the attempts of Commander Bedingfield and others, to establish commerce on the Congo.   It is scarcely possible to estimate the ultimate effect, which success in this most laudable effort would produce. These rivers drain such a vast extent of populous slave-producing territory, that they assume features of peculiar interest. The influence of the English squadron on the coast, is powerfully felt throughout the country. Of this I have had ample evidence, and no wonder it is so, for one feels proud of his countrymen, to see the zeal and energy, with which the officers of our cruisers apply themselves to the suppression of the trade in slaves."

*   *   *   *

To these interesting notices, nothing can be added respecting the far in-laying districts, of the South of this vast continent; but it is earnestly to be hoped, that this enterprizing man may be spared and protected throughout that laborious journey, on which he is now travelling, and that he may be permitted to return to his native land, with the accurate and interesting narrative of what he has seen.

His observations having passed through the Royal Observatory at Cape Town, have been received in London; and the results of his explorations as laid down therefrom, appear in the map attached to this volume.

*   *   *   *

Since the above has been in the press, accounts have been received of the further progress of Dr. Livingstone.

After leaving Angola, he endeavoured to press on towards the Eastern coast of the continent. He succeeded in penetrating some considerable distance into the interior, but whilst there, his supplies failed him.   He was consequently compelled to abandon his intention of further advances in that direction, and passing down towards the Southward, he came once more into the old Cape Colony.   He is now on his homeward bound voyage: and his arrival in England is anxiously anticipated with pleasure, by all who are interested in the researches of science and geographical knowledge.   May he long be spared to be the pioneer of civilization in Africa.

BEECHUANA KAFFIR HERDSMAN.

CONCLUSION.

In bringing to a close this volume, descriptive of Southern Africa, we have but a few words to add to those already written.

In a colonial and commercial point of view, it must be allowed, that this country is, and always has been, very much undervalued. Its resources have not been developed, its districts are but partially inhabited, and its soil is scarcely anywhere cultivated as it ought to be. Possessing a climate along its Southern shores, which is surpassed in its salubrity, by no part of the known world, it seems negligent, not to have availed ourselves more of it as a naval and military "*sanatarium*," for our invalid officers and men, from the more unhealthy climes on our foreign stations, as well as a more enlarged destination for emigrants. Mismanagement and misrule, (which now most happily are being speedily remedied,) may hitherto have conduced to embolden the frontier tribes of the Cape Colony in revolt, and render property there insecure: but this, it is very sanguinely to be believed, as hoped, will be so no more. Whilst the present crisis in the Mission fields of Christianity, is one of the brightest which has ever dawned upon these darkened shores. The banner of the cross, at length in the hands of English churchmen, as well as other Christians, is being unfurled, and is shaking out her crimson folds, to the Southern, Eastern, and Western winds of Africa; while scarcely a ship which sails across the Southern main, does not now bear to her ports, not only bales of merchandize and earthly wealth, but Missionaries and their families also, who go to swell the ranks of those already in the spreading fields. Education is beginning to scatter her seeds of knowledge far and wide.   Legislation, with her laws, is becoming more firmly implanted, and more extensively known.   Science is showing the glimmering lights of her lamp.   Commerce is increasing, and religion and civilization, it is believed, are being firmly implanted and propagated.   Thus is there a larger promise of peace and plenty to the land itself, and wealth and refracted strength held out for Britain, the mother-country.

The increasing stores, also, of geographical knowledge of this hitherto "*terra incognita*," cannot but tend, in time, to develop the riches of the continent, and stimulate commerce and public enterprize.

At the same time, it cannot but be felt, that the growing apathy, so extensively visible through England, in connection with colonial matters, is not one of the healthiest signs of our present national prosperity. The Empire of Britain, as the " Queen of the Ocean," lies, it must never be forgotten, in her maritime power; and, if that be once negligently suffered to decline, the stability of her sceptre will not be long so sure. It may be true, that our Colonial possessions are sufficiently extensive to warrant the prohibition of larger annexations to them, but it may be questioned, how far this plea is sufficient to justify the abandonment of any portion of them. As a foster mother to these many infant children, Britain truly is highly to be eulogized, not only for nurturing and defending her Colonies everywhere, but for giving to them, when old enough to wield it, an inherent power of legislation. It is well, not only to rule them, but to teach them how to rule themselves, and to give them the opportunity of so doing when expedient; but it ought also to be remembered, that to do this *too soon* in their history; or to abandon them as self-supporting communities, before they are strong enough to stand by themselves, is a false philanthrophy, or even amounts to an injustice. Hence is the dire necessity for our not neglecting our vast Colonial Empire, but upholding, fostering, feeding, strengthening it: that so it may be a mighty universe of colonial orbs and satellites, revolving round England as the centre planet.

Following the same rule throughout, may she long be seen the Divine instrument, for thus implanting and propagating sound laws and pure religion, amongst the rising and distant nations of the world: but we trust never to be seen adopting the humiliating (though perhaps, to some, apparently expedient) alternative, of the *abandonment* of her children, when amid difficulties.

A supineness and apathy about the consideration of matters connected with colonial interests, seems to indicate a tendency to neglect them; from which it is, that the adoption and support of such a policy as this mentioned arises. But such a feeling most happily, is not visible amongst many of our rulers; nor yet with those who aid in the spread of religious truth abroad. Nevertheless, it is very much to be feared, that it does exist amongst other classes of the community, and it is humbly hoped, that the foregoing pages (however imperfectly,) may be a means of extending the knowledge of, and increasing the interest in, these parts of our Colonial Empire.

This hope is mainly based on the effort which has been made to condense into a portable and readable form, those points of interest to the general reader, which may tend not only to amuse, but to be instructive : whilst to those who are personally interested in the matter, we hope pleasure and information, and not "*ennui*," may have been afforded, by the perusal of these compiled and cursory notices of Southern Africa.

ROYAL OBSERVATORY AT THE CAPE OF GOOD HOPE.

THE END.

APPENDIX I.

The South African Animal Kingdom, arranged systematically, in Classes, Orders, and Genera, according to its organization; as far as has been ascertained.

DIVISION I.

VERTEBRATA.

CLASS I.

MAMMALIA.

ORDER I.—BIMANA.

Africander	Earthmen	Kaffir
American	Englishman	Malay
Bechuana	Fingoe	Mantatee
Bushmen	Frenchman	Mosambique
Dane	Gona	Negro
Damara	Griqua	Portuguese
Dutchman	Hottentot	

QUADRUPEDS.

ORDER II.—QUADRUMANA.

Ape	Barbary Ape	Lemur
Baboon	Chimpanzee	Monkey

ORDER III.—CARNARIA.

(Feræ)

Sub-order I.—CHEIROPTERA.

Bat   Vampire Bat

Sub-order II.—INSECTIVORA.

Chrysochloris	Desman, or Musk	Mole
	Rat	Shrew

Sub-order III.—Carnivora.
(Plantigrada.)

Aard-vark	Hyæna	Margay
Canis	Hyæna-dog	Ocelot
Cat	Ichneumon	Otter
Civet	Jackall	Pointer
Dog	Jaguar, or Ounce	Proteles
Felis	Leopard	Ratel
Fennec	Lion	Viverra
Ferret	Lurcher	Wolf
Greyhound		

Order IV.—Mursupialia.
(none known)

Order V.—Rodentia.

Bathyergus	Helamys	Porcupine
Echimys	Jerboa	Rabbit
Gerbillus	Mus	Rat
Hare	Musk-rat	Vole

Order VI.—Edentata.

Anteater	Manis	Ornithorhynchus
Aard-vark	Megatherium	Orycteropus
Echidna	Mylodon	

Order VII.—Pachydermata.
(Belluæ.)

Adapis	Hippopotamus	Mastodon
Anoplotherium	Hog	Phacachærax
Dinotherium	Hyrax	Proboscidea
Elephant	Mammoth	

Order VIII.—Solidungula.

Eguus	Quagga	Zebra
Horse		

Order IX.—Ruminantia.

Addax	Giraffe	Ox
Antelope	Gnu	Sheep
Bison	Goat	Springbok
Buffalo	Koodoo	Steinbok
Gazelle, *(oribe)*	Oryx	Zebu

Order X.—Cetacea.

Dolphin	Manatus	Porpoise
Grampus	Narwhal	Whale

CLASS II.

AVES.
(Birds.)

ORDER I.—ACCIPITRES.

Buzzard	Hobby	Owl
Condor	Ichthyiaëtus	Polyborus
Eagle	Kestril	Raptores
Falconidœ	Kite	Sarcoramphus
Gos-hawk	Lanner	Serpent-eater
Gypæctus	Merlin	Sparrow-hawk
Harpy-eagle	Milvus	Turkey-buzzard
Hawk	Osprey	Vulture
Hen-harrier		

ORDER II.—PASSERES.
(Insessores.)
Sub-order I.—DENTIROSTRES.

Accentor	Myzantha	Sylvia
Anthochæra	Oriole	Tailor-bird
Chatterers	Ouzel	Tanager
Crow Shrike	Pardalotus	Tasmania-Shrike
Entomyza	Pipit	Thrush
Field Fare	Pipra	Tyrant-Elycatcher
Flycatcher	Regulus	Wagtail
Grackle	Scissor-tail	Waxwing
Glyciphila	Sedge-warbler	Wheat-Ear
Honeysucker	Shrike	Wood-Swallov
Meliphaga	Stone-chat	Wren
Muscicapidæ		

Sub-order II.—FISSIROSTRES.

Goat-sucker	Swallow, (seven)	Swift
Night-hawk		

Sub-order III.—COINROSTRES.

Alanda	Fringillidœ	Quiscalus
Amadavat	Geospiza, (Finch)	Raven
Bunting	Grosbeak	Regent bird
Buphaga	Jay	Rook
Cactorni	Lark	Sparrow
Canary bird	Linnet	Starling
Corvidæ	Ortolan,(C.Cockioli)	Titmouse
Cow-bunting	Parus	Whida-bird, (long-
Crow	Poëphila	tailed Finch)

Sub-order IV.—TENUIROSTRES.

Anabates	Cynnyris	Nectariniadæ
Certhia, (Creepers)	Dendrocolaptes	Nuthatch
Chough	Hoopoe	Rifle-bird

Sub-order V.—SYNDACTYLI.

Alcedo	Halcyon	Kingfisher
Bee-eater	Hornbill	Motmot
Dacelo		

ORDER III.—SCANSORES.
(Zygodactyli.)

Cuckoo	Musophaga, (or	Plyctolaphus
Honey-guide (or	Plantain eater)	Psittacidæ
Sparm)	Parrot	Touraco, (C. Lory
Lory	Cuculinæ	Woodpecker

ORDER IV.—GALLINÆ.
(Gallinacea.)

Cock	Leipoa	Quail
Columbidæ	Partridge	Ring-dove
Guinea fowl	Pheasant	Turkey
Hemipodius	Pigeon	Turtle dove

ORDER V.—GRALLATORES.
(Brevipennes.)
Cursores.

Ardcidæ	Plover	Himantopus
Bittern	Rail	Hoplopterus
Bustard	Rallaidœ	Ibis
Coot	Redshank	Jabirn
Crane	Sandpiper	Ostrich
Curlew	Scolopacidœ	Stilt
Demoiselle	Snipe	Stone-curlew
Œdicnemus	Flamingo	Stork
Otidœ	Gallinule	Totanus
Parra	Heron	Umbre

ORDER VI.—PALMIPEDES.
(Anseres.)

Albatross	Darter	Gannet
Anatidœ	Duck	Goose
Aptenodytes	Fin-foot	Grebe
Cormorant	Frigate bird	Gull

ORDER VI., *(Continued)*

Hawk	Penguin	Thalassidroma
Nettapus	Petrel	Teal
Pachyptila	Puffin	Tern
Pelicanidœ	Rhynchops	Widgeon
Pelican	Scoter	

CLASS III.

REPTILIA.

ORDER I.—CHELONIA.

Emydœ	Tortoise	Turtle

ORDER II.—SAURIA.*

Alligator	Ichthyosauris	Megalosaurus
Chameleon	Iguanidæ	Shink
Dendrosaura	Iguana	Plesiosaurus
Enaliosauri	Iguanodon	Telcosaurus
Gecko	Lizard	

ORDER III.—OPHIDIA.

Aconitias	Cæcilia	Serpents
Blind worm	Hydrophis	Snakes
Boa Constrictor	Python	Viper

ORDER IV.—BATRACHIA.

Frog	Natter-jack	Toad
Hyla	Phryniscus	Donder-paad
Lepidosiren	Pipa	

CLASS IV.

PISCES.

(Fish.)

ORDER I.—ACANTHOPTERYGII.

Acanthurus	Blenny	Centronotus
Agriopus	Bonito	Centropomus
Anampes	Blepharis	Coryphæna
Angler	Boar fish	Cottidæ
Anlostoma	Centriscus	Dactylopterus
Batrachoideæ	Centrolophus	Dolphin

(* The gigantic Saurian remains here included, were discovered and visited on the banks of the Q'Nabaga river, in Kaffirland, in the year 1853, by the Author.

ORDER I. *(Continued.)*

Dory	Otolithus	Scorpæna
Dragonet	Pilot fish	Surmullet
Gobroidæ	Pomfret	Sword-fish
Goby	Polynemus	Tetrapturus
Gurnard	Ribbon fish	Toxotes
Labrus	Sciænidæ	Trigla
Mackerel	Scomberidiæ	Tunny
Mugil	Sebastos	Wrasse
Mullet		

ORDER II.—MALACOPTERYGII.
(Abdominales.)

Achirus	Cyprinidæ	Ophidia
Apodes	Ell	Murœnidæ
Barbel	Flying fish	Pimelodus
Belone	Gadus	Pleuronectidæ
Carp	Garfish	Remora
Cobitus	Gymnotus	Siluridæ
	Hake	Sole

ORDER III.—LOPHOBRANCHII.

Hippocampus	Pegasus	Pipe-fish

ORDER IV.—PLECTOGNACHII.

Aluterus	Orthagoriscus	Ostracion
		Tetraodon

ORDER V.—CHONDROPTERYGII.

Chimæra	Lamprey	Ray
Dogfish		Sharks

DIVISION II.

ANNULOSA.

CLASS I.

INSECTS.

ORDER I.—COLEOPTERA.
(Beetles.)

Acanthocinus	Apion	Book-worm
Anobium	Ædemeridæ	Brachycerus
Aphodiada	Blethisa	Brachelytra

Bostrichus	Death-watch	Meloe
Brenthidæ	Diamond-beetle	Mylabris
Byrrhus	Dytiscus	Notoxidæ
Calandra	Elator	Oil-beetle
Callistus	Erotylus	Parandra
Calosoma	Glow-worm	Petalocera
Cantharis	Gyrinus	Pimeliidæ
Carabidæ	Halticidæ	Ptinus
Cassida	Helopidæ	Rhynchophora
Cerambycidæ	Heteromera	Rose-chafer
Cetoniadæ	Hister	Rutelidæ
Cicindela	Horiadæ	Salpingidæ
Cistela	Hydrophilus	Scaradæides
Claviger	Lady-bird	Scolytidæ
Clerus	Lamellicornes	Sphæridiadæ
Clytus	Lagriidæ	Staphylindæ
Coccinnella	Lampyridæ	Taxicornes
Cockchafer	Longicornes	Telephorus
Copridæ, (Rhinos-	Lucanidæ	Trachelides
ceros)	Lymexylon	Trimera
Curculio		

ORDER II.—ORTHOPTERA.

Acrydium	Earwig	Phasmidæ
Blattidæ	Grasshopper	Phyllium
Blatta	Locusts	Pneumora
Cricket	Mantis	Saltatoria
Deinacrida	Mole-cricket	

ORDER III.—THYSANOPTERA

ORDER IV.—NEUROPTERA.

Ant-lion	Panorpidæ	Raphidia
Dragon-fly	Perlidæ	Scorpion-fly
Ephemeridæ	Petalura	Sialidæ
Hemerobius	Phryganea	Snake fly
Libellulidæ	Planipennes	Termitidæ
Mantispa	Psocidæ	Trichoptera

ORDER V.—HYMENOPTERA.

Aculeata	Ant	Bee
Andrenidæ	Apidæ	Bembex

ORDER V. *(Continued.)*

Bracon	Evaniadæ	Mellifera
Carpenter-bee	Formicida	Mutillidæ
Cephus	Fossores	Proctotrupidæ
Chalcididæ	Gall-insect	Psithyrus
Chrysididæ	Golden wasp	Sandwasp
Cimbex	Hornet	Scoliadæ
Cinips	Humble-bee	Sirex
Crabro	Ichneumon	Sphegidæ
Diploptera	Larridæ	Terebrantia
Driver-ant	Mason-wasp	Teuthredinidæ
Eumenidæ	Megachile	Vespidæ

ORDER VI.—LEPIDOPTERA.

Acherontia	Heliconidæ	Pontia
Alucitidæ	Hepialida	Polyommatus
Anthroceridæ	Hesperidæ	Pyralidæ
Apatura	Heterocera	Pyralis
Argynnis	Hipparchia	Rhopolocera
Ægeriidæ	Leucophasia	Satyrus
Bombycidæ	Limenitis	Sesia
Bupalus	Lithosiidæ	Silkworm moth
Butterfly	Lycænidæ	Sphingidæ
Callimorpha	Melitea	Stauropus
Cerura	Moths	Thecla
Colias	Nemeobius	Thymele
Cossus	Noctuidæ	Tineidæ
Cynthia	Nymphalidæ	Tortricidæ
Geómetridæ	Pamphila	Uramidæ
Ghost-moth	Papilio	Vanessa
Gonepteryx	Pierus	

ORDER VII.—HEMIPTERE.

Aphis	Cimbex	Lantern-fly
Aphrophora	Coccus	Membracis
Boat-fly	Coreidæ	Negro-fly
Bug	Frog-hopper	Psylla
Cercopidæ	Homoptera	Tettigonia
Chermis	Hydrometidæ	Velia
Cicada	Kermes	

ORDER VIII.—APHANIPTERA.

Chegoe	Flea	T'Setse

ORDER IX.—STREPSIPTERA.

ORDER X.—DIPTERA.

Asilus
Athericera
Æstrus
Bibio
Bombylidæ
Bots
Breeze-fly
Chironomidæ
Culex
Diopsis
Fly
Gad-fly
Gnat
Humble-bee fly
Leptidæ
Mosquito
Notacantha
Sheep-tick
Simulium
Stratiomidæ
Syrphidæ
Tabanus
Tanystoma
Tipula
Wheat-fly

ORDER XI.—ANOPLURA.

Louse

ORDER XII.—THYSANURA.

Lepisma

Podura

CLASS II.

MYRIAPODA.

ORDER I.—CHILOGNATHA.

Julus

Glomeris

ORDER II.—CHILOPODA.

Centipede

Scolopendra

CLASS III.

ARACHNIDA.

(Pulmonaria.)

Acaridæ
Chelifer
Diadem-spider
Hydrachna
Mite
Phalangidæ
Scorpion
Spider
Tarantula
Tick
Trap-door Spider

CLASS IV.

CRUSTACEA.

(Malacostraca.)

ORDER I.—DECAPODA.

(Brachyura.)

Anomura
Astacus
Æthra
Birgus
Calappa
Cancer

ORDER I. *(Continued.)*

Crab	Lobster	Pilumnus
Crawfish	Macroura	Pinnotheres
Eriphia	Maxia	Porcellana
Gecarcinus	Ocypoda	Prawn
Hermit-crab	Pagurus	Scyllarus
Hippolyte	Palæmonidæ	Shrimp
Lambrus	Parthenope	

ORDER II.—STOMAPODA.

Squilla

ORDER III.—AMPHIPODA.

Grammarus

ORDER IV.—LÆMODIPODA.

Cyamus

ORDER V.—ISOPODA.

Æga	Limnoria	Porcellio
Bopyrus	Oniscidæ	

ORDER VI.—ENTOMOSTRACA.

Apus	Cladocera	Cytheria
Argulus	Cyclops	Daphnia
Branchiopoda	Cypris	Lernœadæ

CLASS V.

CIRRHIPIDIA.

Acasta	Balanus	Lepas
Acorn-shell		

CLASS VI

ANNELIDÆ.

ORDER I.—DORSIBRANCHIATA.

Abranchiata	Sabella	Tubicolæ
Amphitrite	Serpula	Vermilia
Arenicoli		

ORDER II.—TERRICOLY.

Earth-worm	Lumbricus	Naides

ORDER III.—SUCTORIA.

Leech

CLASS VII.

ROTATORIA.

Polygastrica   Polythalamia   Rotifera

CLASS VIII.

ENTOZOA.

Acanthocephala   Filaria
Ascaridæ   Tenia

DIVISION III.

CLASS IX.

MOLLUSCA.

(Shells.)

ORDER I.—CEPHALOPODA.

Ammonites   Nautilus   Spirula
Argonaut   Octopus   Tetrabranchiata
Cuttle-fish   Sepia

ORDER II.—GASTEROPODA.

(Zoophaga.)

Achatina	Doris	Periwinkle
Achatinella	Ear-shell	Phorus
Anastoma	Emarginula	Pleurotoma
Ancylus	Fasiolaria	Purpura
Aplysia	Glacus	Phytophaga
Atlanta	Haliotus	Phyllidea
Ampullaria	Helmit-shell	Physa
Ancilla	Helix	Rotella
Buccinum	Janthina	Sealaria
Bulimus	Limax	Siliquaria
Cancellaria	Limpet	Slug
Carinaria	Littorina	Snail
Cank-shell	Lottia	Stomatia
Cassis	Magillus	Triton
Crepidula	Nassa	Terebellum
Chiton	Natica	Tornatella
Clausilia	Nematura	Turbinella
Conus	Nerita	Turritella
Cypræa	Nudibranchiata	Turbo
Dolabella	Onchidium	Vermetus
Dolium	Paludina	

Order III.—Conchifera.

(Dimyaria.)

(Bivalves.)

Alasmadon	Isocardia	Pholas
Anodonta	Lima	Pinna
Arca	Lucina	Polyodonta
Aspergillum	Lutraria	Saxicava
Cardiaceæ	Mactra	Tellina
Cardium	Mussel	Teredo
Cytherea	Oyster	Ungulina
Donax	Pectens	Unio
Etheria	Pectunculus	Venericardia
Iridina	Perna	Venus

Order IV.—Brachiopoda.

Terebratula.

Order V.—Pteropoda.

Limacina

Order VI.—Tunicada.

Ascidia   Pyrosoma

CLASS X.

RADIATA.

Order I.—Echinodermata.

Asterias	Euryale	Sea-egg
Echinus	Pentacrinus	Spatangus

Order II.—Acalepha.

Jelly-fish	Portuguese man-of-war
Physalia	Medusa

Order III.—Polrbi.

Actiniæ	Gorgonia	Retepora
Flustra	Lucernaria	

CLASS XI.

INFUSORIÆ.

Euchelides   Monad

CLASS XII.

SPONGES.

Halicondria

APPENDIX II.

As a very valuable addition to the notices on the subject of natural history, we here subjoin, in the form of an Appendix, the substance of a most intelligent little pamphlet; which was published at Cape Town about three years ago, by Dr. Pappe, M. D., on the South African Ichthyology; a portion of science hardly yet touched upon, except by him.

It is much to be wished, that one so competent, and possessing so many opportunities for local investigation, would compile a larger work on this branch of natural history, and publish it in a form more likely to become generally known and useful.

In the introduction attached to the pamphlet, (the substance of which is here given) some remarks are made on the extensive use of fish as an article of food, at the Cape; and one remarkable fact is mentioned, that there are no less than *twelve* different kinds of fish caught at the Cape, which are also natives of the Mediterranean sea: whilst no Indian, and only one American species *("Scomber grex")* are found there.

DR. L. PAPPE'S SYNOPSIS

OF THE

EDIBLE FISHES AT THE CAPE OF GOOD HOPE.

TRIGLIDÆ.

1. TRIGLIA CAPENSIS CUV. AND VAL. (?) *(Roode Knorhaan; red Gurnard of the Colonists.)*—Head, back, upper part of body, and fins, rose red. Belly silvery, white, shaded by rosy patches. Scales very small; lateral line nearly parallel. Interior surface

of the pectoral fins dark yellowish-green, with large black marks towards their bases, speckled with a number of pure white irregular spots.   Iris red.   Length twelve inches.

Baron CUVIER, in giving a very short diagnosis of this species, specimens of which were sent him from the Cape by DELALANDE, remarks that "the dark spots at the inner surface of the pectoral fins were wanting;" but I have reason to believe, that his specimens had faded, and that through the effects of the spirits, in which they were preserved, the natural colours had been more or less obliterated. Experience, and the accounts of the fishermen here, convince me, that this and the following species, are the only ones of the genus, caught in our Bays. CUVIER's observation, that the fish bears a great resemblance to the *Trigla Kumu* of New Zealand, is perfectly correct.

Flesh firm, but palatable.   Caught in summer with the hook, but not very common in Table Bay.

2. TRIGLA PERONII. CUV. AND VAL. *(Graauwe or bruine Knorhaan; grey Gurnard.)*—Head large; forehead sloping; body declining in breadth towards the tail. Muzzle projecting; teeth small but numerous; upper mandible longest, divided into two lobes, and beset at its margins with five denticles.   Two spines, unequal in length, are placed above each eye, and a strong spine at each side of the occiput; opercular and scapular spines, pointed sharp.   Anterior side of the first ray of the first dorsal fin slightly serrated; the second and third rays of that fin longer than the remaining seven.   Ridges of dorsal grove, armed with a row of twenty-four blunt denticulations. Pectoral fins large, reaching beyond the vent; tail lunated. Lateral line smooth; scales small, oval.   Head, back, and sides, brownish-grey, mottled with white spots; belly pure white, mixed with purple.   Pectoral fins olive-green on the inner surface, edged with azure, and embellished by a large black mark, sprinkled with white and sky-blue dots.   Lower jaw and part of the pectoral and caudal fins pale-red, tinged with yellow.   Iris with white aurora-red.   Length from seven to fourteen inches.

This species appears to be nearly related to *T. Lyra*, of Europe, and although it does not correspond in every particular with CUVIER's description, yet I think that it is the same fish, which was anatomized by that Prince of Naturalists.

Not often caught in Table Bay; flesh equal to that of the preceding species.

SCORPÆNIDÆ.

3. SEBASTES CAPENSIS. CUV. AND VAL. *(Jacob Evertsen.)* Body oblong, robust.   Head large, bony, channelled above and between the eyes, and armed with spiny processes; gill covers and preoperculum strongly toothed at the margins.   Eyes very large, protruding from their sockets. Mouth wide, gaping; lips

fleshy; teeth crowded, paved, small, sharp, and curved in both jaws. Soft rays of dorsal fin longest. Liver unequally three-lobed, gall-bladder of an oval form, and the pylorus provided with numerous cœcal appendages. Air-bladder large. Tile-red, with shades of orange, white and yellowish-green; marked on the sides with a few flesh-coloured spots. Belly white, tinged with orange. Palate and peritoneum greyish-white. Length from twelve to fifteen inches.—Called *Jacob Evertsen*, after a Dutch Captain, remarkable for a red face and large projecting eyes.

This fish though common to Table Bay almost at all seasons, is highly prized for its flesh, by most colonists.

4. SEBASTES MACULATUS. CUV. AND VAL. *(Sancord.)* Simi-lar to the former, but shorter, of a more slender form, and with eyes, neither projecting, nor mouth much gaping. Liver rather large, three-lobed; gall-bladder narrow and club-shaped; pylo-rus without regular cœcal appendices, but surrounded by a glandular greasy mass. Natatory bladder wanting; palate and peritoneum black. Snout obtuse; teeth criniform, arranged in a band around the inner edge of both jaws. Upper part of body tile-red, mingled with orange and shaded with brown. Scales with greenish-brown edges. Belly white, clouded with orange, and tinged with yellow. Length eight to twelve inches. Dorsal fin dim tile-red, sprinkled with yellowish-green irregular marks, and with darker chesnut-brown spots at the base of the mem-branous portion of its first spiny rays. Hue of pectoral, anal, ventral, and caudal fins, orange with carmin-red; the eight lower rays of the pectoral fins detached at top from their con-necting membrame. Iris yellow.

A very delicious fish, but not very common. Caught chiefly in winter. Dr. A. SMITH, in his illustrated work on South-African Zoology, has confounded this species with the former. Though in their general outlines closely related, both fishes are however easily discerned, not only by outward appearance, but yet more by their anatomical differences, the one having a swim-bladder, and the other not; and from the colour of the palate and peritoneum, which are white in the first species, but black in the second.

SCIÆNINÆ.

5. SCIÆNA HOLOLEPIDOTA. CUV. AND VAL. *(Kabeljauw.)* Body elongated, stout. Head large, rounded, bony; mouth moderately large; both mandibles armed in front with a row of strong, short, pointed, cylindrical, hooked teeth; none on the palate. Dorsal fin divided by a deep notch; its soft rays longer than the spiny. Caudal fin truncate. Head purplish-blue, with aurora-red, mottled with yellow and green shades. Back and

sides above the lateral line greenish-blue, marbled with faint orange and purple; fins often rose red; lower part of the body pale flesh-red, mixed with green, purple, and white.

A large fish, from two to three feet long. Common on the coast, and at the mouth of rivers; caught with the hook and drag net. Is one of the staple fishes on the market, dried and salted like *Cod*, and exported to the *Mauritius*, and elsewhere. Its flesh when young, is good, but firm and dry in adult individuals.

6. OTOLITHUS ÆQUIDENS. CUV. AND VAL. *(Geelbeck.)* Body oblong; head conical: mouth middle-sized; lower jaw pointed, longest. Teeth in both mandibles nearly alike, numerous, sharp, crooked; the anterior ones of the upper jaw, largest. First dorsal fin low, spiny; caudal semilunated. Back and sides above the lateral line, dull bluish-purple, intermixed with green and orange; upper surface of head flashed with aurora-red; lower parts silvery white, tinted with purple grey. Inside of mouth gamboge-yellow.* Iris orange.

Clumsy, attaining a length of three feet and more. Flesh dry, but fit for salting. Common along the whole coast, where it is caught abundantly with the hook or net. It forms an article of food for the poor and *lazy*, and it is also prepared for exportation.

7. UMBRINA CAPENSIS. MIHI. N. SP. *(Baardmannetje.)* Snout obtuse, thick, truncate; lower jaw shortest with a barbel; dorsal fins distinct. Head reddish-brown tinged with gold. Back and sides ash-coloured on a silvery base. Lower jaw and belly white, sprinkled with minute dark dots. Scales large. Iris silvery.

Measures from two to two and a half feet, and is reputed for its delicious flesh. Chiefly caught in False Bay, during summer.

8. CHEILODACTYLUS FASCIATUS. CUV. AND VAL. *(Steenvisch.)*—Body oblong, spindle-shaped; head small; lips fleshy, retractile; the upper one longest. Eyes middle-sized, placed near the crown; mouth small; teeth velvety. The five last rays of the pectoral fins extended beyond their membrane, cartilagenous; second ray largest, being three inches long; the other three, shorter and shorter. Caudal fin forked, scales large, almost quadrangular; seven longitudinal stripes, covered with smaller scales, along the whole extent of the dorsal fin. Head olive-green, intermixed with orange; upper part of sides brimstone-yellow, tinged with green, purple, and orange. Body crossed by five or six irregular, vertical, purplish-brown bands. Belly yellowish-white, mottled with olive-green. Mouth and

---

* Hence the vernacular name Geelbeck (yellow mouth.)

pectoral fins deep orange; the lengthened rays of the latter rose-red, upper ones and tail variegated with purplish lines. All other fins yellowish-green, with purplish-brown stripes or blots. Iris yellow. Length thirteen, breadth four and a half inches.

A good table fish, caught with the hook. Not very abundant in Table Bay.

9. CHEILODACTYLUS BRACHYDACTYLUS. CUV. AND VAL. *(Steenklipvisch ; Pompelmoesje.)*—Body oval; head small; lips fleshy, the upper one a little projecting; mouth obtuse; teeth criniform. The last six rays of the pectorals, cartilaginous, slightly detached from their connecting membrane, the second and third of them longest. These are rose-red, while the remainder, as well as the ventral fins are of an orange hue. Opercular and pre-opercular scales very small; those of the body rather large. Head, back, and flanks, greenish-brown; lower parts and belly, silvery-white. Operculum and pre-operculum rose-red, tinged with silver and golden bronze. Middle-line sprinkled with six or seven dirty-white irregular dots. Fins brownish-green. Iris silvery, encircled by a yellow ring; pupil dark blue. Total length seven inches, breadth two and a half inches.

Lives amongst the rocks at Green-point, and feeds on small Crustaceæ. Its flesh is tender and wholesome.

SPARIDÆ.

10. SARGUS HOTTENTOTTUS. A. SMITH. *(Hangberger.)*— Body broad, nearly ovate; head small, projecting in front; incisors firm, trenchant, similar to the human.—Colour blackish-brown, tinted with purple; back and sides crossed by five broad black vertical bands; belly silvery-white. Length about eighteen inches.

Common to Table Bay from June to August, and much in request particularly at the time when it is with roe. It is also cured and pickled for economical purposes.—From the circumstance of its being chiefly taken in deep water, near a place called *Hangberg*, (overhanging rock,) it has received its present colonial name. It feeds on shell-fish, and is caught with the hook.

11. SARGUS CAPENSIS. A. SMITH. *(Hottentot Fish.)* Body much resembling that of the former, but more attenuated at base, and destitute of any bands or vertical stripes. Head purplish; back dull bluish-green with a metallic gloss; sides beneath the longitudinal line, silvery, with a reddish tint. Iris white.

Caught at all seasons with the hook, and is not only a superior table fish, but forms when salted and dried, an article of exportation. Mostly confined to Table Bay, and the West Coast, where it is found abundantly.   Length from twelve to fourteen inches.

12. CHRYSOPHRYS GLOBICEPS. CUV. AND VAL. *(Stompneus.)* —Forehead arched, rounded, almost gibbous, muzzle obtuse, small; teeth thick, firm, tubercular, standing in four rows on the sides of both jaws. Body broad. Crown above the eyes olive-green with aurora-red. Back bluish-grey; belly white, silvery; a black spot at the insertion of the pectorals. Iris red; pupil dark. The younger individuals have six or seven brown longitudinal stripes, and six transversal dark bands, which disappear in the adults.

A favourite fish, and often caught in great abundance during summer, with the drag-net. It also makes an excellent pickle-fish.

13. CHRYSOPHRYS LATICEPS. CUV. AND VAL. *(Roode Steenbrasem.)*—Head very large, gibbous; crown elevated, broad, convex, tapering towards the snout; eyes almost vertical; mouth of a moderate size; muzzle pointed, but blunt; lips fleshy. Upper mandible armed in front with four large, strong, conical teeth, and the lower one with six corresponding with those of the upper; middle teeth smaller than the lateral. Rows of sharp pointed teeth inside the mouth, followed by bands of round, granular molars. Soft rays of dorsal fin higher than the spiny; caudal nearly truncate. Scales large. Liver divided into two unequal lobes of an ochreous hue, and with the gall-bladder proportionally small; gullet dilated into a big, strong, muscular stomach, of an oblong shape; pylorus supplied with four short cœcums of different length. Swim-bladder large, simple, and firm. Intestines a little longer than the whole fish. Head faint purple with aurora-red; back dull greyish-green; sides and belly slightly flesh-red, on silvery ground. Groove between the maxillary and intermaxillary bones, saffron-yellow. Fins reddish.

This bulky fish often exceeds four and a half feet in length, and fourteen inches in breadth. It is very voracious and feeds generally on crabs, and cuttle-fish. (Sepia and Loligo.) As food, it is much prized, and is also cured for exportation. Not very common in Table Bay, but caught abundantly in False Bay, and on the shores of Hottentots' Holland.

14. CHRYSOPHRYS CRISTICEPS. CUV. AND VAL. (?) *(Roman.)* —Body of a beautiful orange colour, shaded by silver. Head and jaws of a deep orange hue. Between the eyes a falcated band of pure indigo blue, and a narrow stripe of the same colour, running along each side of the dorsal; a broad, silvery

line extends from the dorsal nearly to the anal fin. All fins crimson, with a shade of silver. Iris red. Young specimens do not exhibit the vivid hues, so remarkable in adults. Head and back reddish-brown; flanks and belly orange. An azure dot stands in the centre of the middle line.

One of the prettiest and most delicious fishes in our markets. Its flesh is generally acknowledged to be a superior dish. It is common in the waters east of Table Bay, and especially near the *Roman Rock*, where it is caught with the hook and drag-net in great numbers. A strayed individual, caught in Table Bay on the 14th of June, 1849, measured sixteen inches in length, and seven in breadth.

15. CHRYSOBLEPHUS GIBBICEPS, SWAINS. (*Baaische Roode Stompneus; Poescop.*)—Head very large, broader than the body. Front obtuse, truncate; the profile almost vertical. Eyes near the crown, which is elevated and gibbous. Lateral line terminating at the lower side of the tail. (Swainson.) Mouth middle-sized; teeth strong. Back and sides rose-red; lower parts silvery. Length from one and a half to two feet.

A large snow-white spot in front of the forehead, enhances the beauty of this singular fish, which ranks amongst the choicest in this Colony. It is rare in Table Bay, but frequently caught with the hook in False Bay, Mosselt Bay, Fishock, and in similar localities. It is also exported.

16. PAGRUS LANIARIUS. CUV. AND VAL. (*Dageraad.*) Front higher than in *Chrysophrys*. Strong conical teeth in the upper jaw, which are directed forward, and project from the mouth, the two outer teeth being longer and thicker than the rest, and those of the lower jaw much smaller. The whole fish is of a dark rose-colour, with a black spot at the insertion of the pectorals, and with another on the extremity of the dorsal fin. Lower jaw white; iris silvery; length twelve inches.

Highly prized for its delicious flesh. Not found in Table Bay, but frequently caught with the hook in the waters towards the East and South of Cape Town. This handsome fish owns its surname of *Laniarius* (butcher,) both to its colour, and to its sharp teeth, and voracity.

17. LITHOGNATHUS CAPENSIS. SWAINS. (*Blaauwe Kaapsche Steenbrasem.*)—Body elongated, fusiform; head lengthened, projecting; mouth small, terminal; the maxillaries thick, enlarged, very hard; tail slightly forked. (Swainson.) Back dark marine-blue; belly white, tinged with purple. Length two and a half feet and upwards.

An excellent table fish and very fit for pickling and salting. Caught with baited hooks during summer; especially in Hout Bay.

18 PAGELLUS AFER. MIHI. N. SP. (*Roode Kaapsche Stompneus.*)—Body ovate, broad, somewhat compressed. Lower jaw a little shorter than the upper one. Mouth obtuse; front teeth conical, stronger and larger than those within; both jaws paved internally with two rows of round molars. Lateral line well marked. Head and back aurora-red, mottled with blue and gold on a silvery ground. Sides of the body crossed by five or six sky-blue, broken, longitudinal stripes. Lower mandible and belly white. All fins faintly rose-red; apex of the tail orange. Iris purplish. Length 12—14 inches. Dorsal $\frac{11}{12}$. Anal $\frac{3}{8}$. Caudal 11. Pectoral 15. Ventral $\frac{1}{5}$.

One of the best fishes in the market. Its flesh is white and delicious. Superficially examined, it bears some resemblance to the Cape Silverfish, (*Dentex Argyrozona,*) from which it is easily distinguished, not only by its broader form, and less vivid hue, but also by the absence of the six rose-red longitudinal bands, and by the formation of its teeth. Caught with the hook during winter, and pretty common on the market.

19. DENTEX RUPESTRIS. CUV. AND VAL. (*Bastard Silverfish; Seventy-four.*)—Body large, bulky; teeth of the outer row large, cylindrical, curved, and pointed; the four front ones of its jaws strongest. Scales large; lateral line broken. Back and sides above the lateral line aurora-red, clouded by ultra-marine, blue, green, and faint purple, with an orange tint towards the tail. Lower parts of the body aurora-red, tinged with orange, and shaded with ultra-marine blue. (A. SMITH.) Length about two feet.

Rarely found in Table Bay, but considered one of the very finest fishes in the Colony. It is chiefly confined to the East of the Cape, where it is caught with the hook or net in great abundance. It is also cured for foreign markets.

20. DENTEX ARGYROZONA. CUV. AND VAL. (*Silverfish.*) Body oblong; eyes large; mouth of a moderate size; teeth like those of the preceding species.—Head, back, and sides above the lateral line aurora-red on a silvery base; hue below that line, faint flesh-red, striped with five to six narrow, longitudinal, pale, rose-red bands. Belly white, silvery; fins purplish-red; Iris scarlet. Length from sixteen to twenty inches.

This very voracious fish feeds principally on small fish and crabs. It is common on the Cape market throughout the year, and forms also an article of export.

21. CANTHARUS BLOCHII. CUV. AND VAL. (?) (*Windtoy.*) Body broad, oval. Head tapering towards the muzzle, and forming a curvature above the eyes. Jaws free, somewhat

protractile. Anterior teeth small, but sharp; inner rows velvety. Spines of dorsal fin strong, spiny; pectoral fins round at base, and pointed at the apex; scales middle-sized. Tail unequal, upper side longest. Length 12 inches; breadth nearly 5 inches.—D. $\frac{11}{13}$; A; $\frac{3}{12}$; P. 17; V. $\frac{1}{5}$; C. 17. Head and back olive-green; sides silvery, with faint rosy gloss; fins pale rose-red. Pectoral fins with a black spot at their insertion. Iris silvery.

A delicious table fish, more commonly caught in winter, and often put up in bundles along with Sargus Capensis, (Hottentot fish,) from which it is easily distinguished by a very superficial examination.

22. CANTHARUS EMARGINATUS. CUV. AND VAL. (*Dasje.*) Body lanceolate; front roundish, with a curvature hardly perceptible; muzzle pointed and partly concealed beneath the suborbital bone, which has a deep emargination in front of the eyes. Front teeth small, but crowded, pointed and sharp. Scales minute; lateral line moderately bent and well marked. D. $\frac{11}{12}$. A. $\frac{3}{10}$. V. 5. P. 15, C. 17. Head, back, and sides faint brown, on a silvery ground; a greenish-blue metallic lustre above and in front of the eyes. Body striped with some narrow, yellowish, longitudinal bands; pectoral fins, with a dark spot at their base; abdomen white, tinged with light brown. Length, twelve to fourteen inches.

Rare in Table Bay, but more frequently caught in the several Bays to the East of the Cape. Its flesh is highly esteemed as food.

23. BOOPS SALPA. CUV. & VAL. (?) (*Bamboesvisch; Stinkvisch.*)—Body subovate, attenuated at both ends; mouth small, obtuse, not protractile; external teeth broad, trenchant; scales minute. Head olive-green; with a flash of gold; body silvery with eight to ten longitudinal golden stripes. Iris yellow. A black speck at the base of the pectoral fin. Length, twelve inches, or more.

The fish feeds only on *Algæ*, and is caught principally in localities, where there is an abundance of sea-weed. Amongst the latter, the Ecklonia buccinalis (*Zeebamboes*) and our large Sargassa, (*S. longifolium* and *S. integrifolium*) are its usual haunts, and hence the vernacular name of *Bamboo-fish*. On account of its vegetable nourishment, it exhibits at times a particular smell, when embowelled, and is for that reason called *Stink-fish* by some of the fishermen. It is a rich and delicate fish, and though scarce in the Cape Town market, is common in Saldanha Bay, were it is dried and salted for home consumption.

SQUAMIPENNES.

24. PIMELEPTERUS FUSCUS. CUV. & VAL. (*Bastard Jacob Evertsen*).—Body oblong, bulky; head small; snout obtuse;

teeth strong, cutting, singularly ranged in one row ; eyes large, protruding.   Fins thick ; covered by scales, whence the scientific name (Fat-fin).   Two dorsal fins, united at base.   Length, two feet.

This fish is of a uniform dusky brown colour.   Its flesh is well flavoured and very nice.   Caught chiefly in Simon's Bay and along the East coast.   Feeds on shell-fish.

25. DIPTERODON CAPENSIS. CUV. & VAL.   (*Galjoenvisch* ; *Galleon-fish,*)—Body oval ; outer teeth strong, large, trenchant, resembling those of *Sargus*. Lips fleshy ; mouth proportionally small.   Two dorsal fins ; the second as well the anal, and part of the caudal, thick, covered by very minute scales.—Head, back, and fins, ash-coloured grey, or faint brown ; sides with six silvery vertical bands, reaching the middle of the belly, which is silvery-white, and tinged with purplish-red.   Length, from fifteen to twenty inches.

This fish, more plentiful in the Western Division of the Colony, is highly esteemed as food, and always fetches a good price.   It is however, disliked by some, on account of the many black veins, traversing its flesh, and is at times rather unwholesome, from being too rich, and requiring good digestive organs.   It is caught with the drag-net, during summer.

SCOMBERIDÆ.

26. SCOMBER CAPENSIS. CUV. AND VAL. (*Halfcord.*) Body oblong, adipose ; muzzle obtuse ; lower jaw somewhat projecting ; teeth numerous, small, velvety. First dorsal fin spiny, connected by a membrane ; second dorsal fin longer than the anal. Pectoral and ventral fins equally long ; caudal forked. The lateral line is bent at the upper part of the body, but becomes straight towards its end.   Head, back, and sides, dark marine-blue, with a broad greenish-yellow streak, running from eye to tail, which latter is crested. Abdomen white, silvery ; fins yellowish-green.   Iris white.

A large fish, measuring from two to three feet. It is rather uncommon in Table Bay, but taken with the hook occasionally.   Its flesh being very rich and deemed unwholesome, it is not in much request, and is therefore chiefly used as pickle-fish.

27. SCOMBER GREX. MITCHILL. (*Mackerel.*)—Body oblong, rounded, fat, smooth, covered with minute scales ; teeth small ; dorsal fins two ; caudal fin deeply forked ; tail bearing finlets ; its sides not carinated at base. Has a natatory bladder. Form and colour much like that of the common Mackerel. Body and sides light-green, with darker stripes of the same hue. Length, about eighteen inches and upwards.

This species, which is caught with the line, is little liked on account of its greasiness. It is common in Table Bay during winter, and is chiefly pickled.

28. THYRSITES ATUN. CUV. AND VAL. (*Snook; Snoek.*) Body cylindrical, elongated; jaws protracted; the lower one longest. Mouth wide; teeth large, conical, trenchant, sharp; the palate beset with smaller ones. First dorsal fin very long; tail without a lateral keel; skin rather naked. Back blackish-blue with metallic lustre; sides and belly silvery. Length, often exceeding three feet.

This voracious fish is caught with the hook, in immense numbers, almost all the year round, but more frequently during summer. It is very strong and ferocious, and is despatched after being pulled on board, by blows on the head, with a kind of knob-kerrie. Its flesh is highly prized by the majority of the Colonists, who also salt and dry it for home consumption, and as an article of trade.

29, LICHIA AMIA. CUV. & VAL. (*Leervisch.*)—Body compressed, oval, nearly rhomboid; broadest in the middle and attenuated at both ends. Mouth moderately large; jaws of equal length; front teeth in a number of rows, small, but sharply pointed and closely set. A line of large teeth on each side of the palate. Dorsal fins two; first one with eight detached prickles, the foremost of which is turned forward. Anal fin, shorter than the dorsal; tail without lateral keels. Head, back, and upper parts of the sides steel-blue; lower parts silvery shaded with faint brown. Fins yellowish; belly pure white. Length, from two to three feet.

Taken occasionally in Table Bay, but not in great repute, its flesh being deemed dry and rather insipid.

30. TEMNODON SALTATOR. CUV. (*Elftvisch.*)—Body oblong, slightly compressed; mouth large; lower jaw longest; both mandibles armed in front with detached trenchant, pointed sharp teeth, and within and behind with smaller ones. Dorsal fins two; first smaller and lower than the second; its rays jointed by a delicate membrame. Tail destitute of a lateral keel and spurious fins. Length about two feet.

This fish is uniformly lead-coloured, shaded with dark green on its back. From leaping now and then out of the water, it has obtained its name of Saltator, (Jumper.) It is held in great esteem as a table-fish, and the younger individuals are truly deemed a dainty. It is often caught in Table Bay, particularly in summer.

31. CARANX TRACHURUS LACEP. (*Maasbanker; Bastard Mackerel.*)—Body spindle-shaped, broad, compressed. Each jaw with a row of straight minute teeth. Lateral line armed

with scaly, carinated, prickly bands. Dorsal fins two; first low and small. Pectoral fins long, falcated; two detached spines before the anal fin. Scales minute. Upper part of the body of a bluish lead-coloured hue; lower parts silvery white. Iris gilt. Length, twelve to eighteen inches.

Caught in winter at both ends of the Colony. Its flesh is well flavoured and wholesome.

32. STROMATEUS CAPENSIS. MIHI. N. SP. (*Katunker.*) Body compressed, oblong-rhomboid; head obtuse, mouth small, not projectle; teeth velvety. One dorsal only, covered with epidermis; no ventral fin. Caudal nearly as long as the dorsal. Tail forked; scales small. Longitudinal line almost straight. Head olive-green, upper part of the body light-blue, with some faint yellow longitudinal stripes; belly silvery, with a red tint. Iris white. The specimen from which this description is drawn, measured thirteen inches long, and five and a half inches broad.

A good table fish, but not common. It is caught with the hook and net, chiefly East of Table Bay.

33. LEPIDOPUS ARGYREUS. CUV. AND VAL. (*Kalvisch; Scabbard-fish.*)—Body compressed, lengthened, narrow, riband-like; skin smooth. Head pointed, bearing a great resemblance to that of the *Snook.* Mouth gaping, large, armed with rows of strong trenchant teeth, and four larger ones in front. Under jaw projecting beyond the upper. Dorsal fin low and equal, nearly as long as the back; pectoral fins small, hooked; two round scales as rudiments of a ventral fin. Anal fin short, caudal small, forked. Lateral line straight. Colour of back faint steel-blue, on a silvery ground; the whole surface of the body clothed with a silvery dust. Length five feet; breadth from three to four inches.

This curious fish swims in undulating motions and with astounding velocity. It is but very rarely caught in the net. In the course of six years, not more than three individuals, to my knowledge, were taken in Table Bay. I found its flesh fine and delicious.

MUGILLIDÆ.

34. MUGIL CAPENSIS. CUV. AND VAL. (*Harder; Mullett.*) Body oblong, nearly cylindrical, robust. Head small, broad, flat; muzzle short, blunt; lower jaw with a depression, corresponding to a prominence in the upper one. Superior mandible provided with a row of fine, diminutive teeth. Scales rather large. Dorsal fins two; remote from each other; first with four spiny rays; pectoral fins pointed, caudal forked. Surface of

head and back dark steel-blue, mingled with oil-green; sides beneath the lateral line greyish-white, on silvery ground; cheeks, lower jaw, belly, and ventral fin, white. Fins greyish-green. Body crossed by nine narrow longitudinal lines. Interior of mouth pure white. Iris silvery. Length fourteen inches; breadth nearly four inches.

This species, as well as the following, enters the mouth of several rivers. Nursed in ponds, it grows extremely fat, and attains an uncommon size. A specimen so fed measured nineteen inches.

35. MUGIL MUTILINEATUS. A. SMITH. (?) (*Springer Leaping Mullet.*)—Greatly resembling the former, but easily distinguishable; its head being neither so broad nor flat, but rather a little convex on its top. Lower jaw more rounded, and body traversed by thirteen longitudinal narrow stripes. Colour of back and upper side greenish-brown; crown of head faint purple with oil-green. Gill covers tinted with gold; ventral fin purplish. Lower part of belly greyish-white, on a silvery base. Length twelve inches. It is in the habit of leaping constantly and with considerable velocity, when it finds itself entangled in a net; and hence its name.

Besides the two kinds of Mullet here described, there are three or four more species recorded as inhabitants of the bays and rivers of the Colony. All of them are caught with the net. They make good table-fish, but are more frequently salted or smoke-dried (Aokkoma). like the Herring, and, thus preserved, form a very considerable article of home consumption as well as of export.

BLENNIDÆ.

36. BLENNIUS VERSICOLOR. MIHI. N. SP. (*Klipvisch.*) Body elongated, smooth, slimy, spindle-shaped; head thick, obtuse forehead tapering towards the snout. Muzzle short, truncate; mouth small; lips fleshy; teeth in several rows; those of the first, strong, pointed, conic, hooked; inner ones small, paved. Dorsal fin nearly as long as the body, commencing right over the crown of the head; its first three rays longest, spiny, separated from the soft ones by a deep emargination. Ventral placed before the pectoral fins, and consists of only two rays. A small tentaculary, three-fid appendage above each eye-brow; and a tubercular excrescence near the anus, in both sexes. It is *ovoviviparous*. No fish perhaps displays a greater diversity of hues, than this, and to make out any *specific difference* amongst its many varieties, is next to impossible, I am thus inclined to unite them under *one* common denomination, expressive at once, of the changeable character of their colours. The following are the chief varieties observed by me in fresh specimens.

1. Prevailing colour blood-red, mottled with greyish-white irregular blots; abdomen purplish on a white ground; fins deep-red, tinged with greyish green. Iris purple. Length twelve inches. Caught principally amongst the rocks of Robben Island.

2. Head, back, and sides dark purple, marbled with reddish-brown, flesh-red, orange, and pale yellow marks. Belly white, shaded with purple. Pectoral rays striped with purplish-brown bands; dorsal, caudal and anal fins dull-brown, spotted with yellowish-green dots. Iris purple. Length ten to twelve inches. (*Blennius rubescens. Lichtenst?*) Extremely pretty; caught along with the former.

3. Upper part of body pale yellowish-brown; head olive-green; sides and belly gamboge-yellow, sprinkled with irregular greenish-white marks; pectoral and caudal fins without bands; dorsal and anal with faint-green spots. Iris yellow. Length eight to ten inches.

4. The whole of back, sides, and fins olive-green; belly of a deeper yellow tint, with some white blots along the lateral line. Iris yellow. Length six to eight inches.

The *Klip-fish* is greatly reputed for its flesh, which is nice, well-flavoured, and wholesome.

SILURINÆ.

37. BAGRUS CAPENSIS. A. SMITH. (*Bagger.*)—Body oblong, thick. smooth, slimy; head large, broad, nearly flat above; muzzle round, blunt; upper lip fleshy, with a barbel on both sides; teeth crowded, velvety; chin supplied with four barbels, which are shorter than those of the upper jaw. Dorsal fins two; second flat, fleshy, smaller than the first; pectoral fins moderate; anal large, caudal deeply forked. Upper part of head, back, and sides, dark greenish-brown; lower parts shaded irregularly with blue, yellow, and silver, and flashed with a bronzy lustre. Belly dull greyish-white, speckled with small brown dots, and clouded with purple. Base of tail red; fins faintly flesh-coloured. Iris yellow. Length twelve to sixteen inches.

Owing to its ugliness, this curious fish, which hides itself amongst stones in muddy water, the better to entrap its unsuspecting prey, is, from popular prejudice, less prized than it deserves. Its flesh is extremely delicate, and bears a greater resemblance to that of the Eel, than that of any other sea-fish caught in the Colony.

CLUPEIDÆ.

38. CLUPEA OCELLATA. MIHI. N. SP. (*Shad; Sardyn.*) Body compressed, elongated; head flattened at top; muzzle obtuse; upper jaw with a central notch, and a little projecting.

No teeth in either mandible; eyes and scales large. One dorsal only, tail deeply forked. Length six to seven inches. Head and back blue, changeable to green, and shaded with purple, yellow, and gold. Lower jaw and gill-covers silvery, with a reflecting golden lustre; sides above the lateral line crossed by a sky-blue longitudinal stripe. A line of eight to fifteen round, black, eye-light spots, extends from the upper edge of the operculum, along the whole body. Belly silvery. Iris gilt.

It would appear that this species stands intermediate between the common Shad, (Clupea alosa,) and the Twaite Shad, (Clupea finta,) possessing the toothless mouth of the former, but the size and colouring of the latter. Its natural length never exceeds six to seven inches. It is caught with the net, and used occasionally as a pickle-fish.

39. ENGRAULIS ENCRASICOLUS. FLEM. (*Ansjovis; Anchovy.*) Body slender; head and snout pointed: upper jaw projecting considerably. Mouth deeply and horizontally cleft far behind the eyes. Maxillaries and palate armed with small, but sharp numerous teeth. Scales large and deciduous; tail deeply forked. Top of head and back blue, with a tinge of green; flanks and belly silvery. Fins greenish-white. Length four to five inches.

Caught sometimes abundantly with the net, in summer, but little used in the Colony, the Cape salt being found unfit for its preservation as a condiment.

GADIDÆ.

40. GADUS MERLUCIUS. LIN. (*Stok-visch; Hake.*) Body elongated, slender; head broad, bony, depressed. Lower mandible protruding beyond the upper one; mouth very wide; teeth long, sharp, in a double row in each jaw; first row smaller and shorter than the inner one. Two dorsal fins; first three angular; caudal fin slightly lunate; ventral ovate, with five rays. No barble under the chin. Scales large. Upper part of the body dusky-brown, with a bluish, steel-coloured gloss; belly dirty-white. Iris yellow; inside of mouth black. Length from two to three feet.

It is remarkable that this fish, a notorious denizen of the European seas, was utterly unknown at the Cape of Good Hope, before the earthquake of 1809, (4th December.) At first it was scarce and sold at exorbitant prices, (4s. 6d.) Since that period it has yearly increased in numbers, and is now a standard fish in the market, being caught in great abundance.

English writers on Ichthyology comment very unfavourably on its merits, and call it a "coarse fish, scarcely fit for the dinner table." At the Cape its qualities are generally and fully appreciated; in fact, its flesh is highly delicate and but little inferior to that of the *Hadok*, (Gadus Æglefinus.) At times it makes its appearance in large shoals.

It is then abundantly caught, salted, and dried for exportation. The cured or dried *Cape Stok-fish* is an excellent dish, far superior to that insipid stuff, introduced from Holland or other countries.

XIPHIURIDÆ.

41. XIPHIURUS CAPENSIS. A. SMITH. (*Koningklipvisch ; King's Rock-fish.*)—Body almost cylindrical, moderately robust. Head large ; two rows of larger teeth in the upper, one of smaller ones in the lower jaw ; vomer armed with teeth of the same description. Two barbels pending from the under surface of the lower mandible. Pectoral fins of an oval form ; dorsal, caudal, and anal fins, united. Tail narrow, tapering, compressed, sword-shaped. Ventral fins none. Scales very small. (A. SMITH.) Has a large and very firm air-bladder. Flesh-coloured and clouded by a variety and intermixture of hues, difficult to describe. Lower surface, belly, and point of tail, tinted with pale purple.

This fish, in some respects, seems closely allied to the family of the *Gadidæ*, while on the other hand it somewhat resembles the *Murænidæ*. Although its habitat is deep water, and not (as its name implies,) amongst cliffs and rocks, yet it justly deserves the title of King's-fish, being without exception, the most desirable fish obtainable in our bays. It is rather scarce, is an expert swimmer, appears on the coast as a harbinger of rough, stormy weather, during winter, and commonly sells at very remunerating prices. DR. ANDREW SMITH, the intelligent South African traveller, gave the first description of this fish in his admirable *Illustrations of the Zoology of South Africa*. It was however known previously to *Barrow*, (1797,) who in his travels, (page 30,) mentions it in the following terms. "Another Blennius, called *King's Rock-fish*, is sometimes caught (in Table Bay,) to which, from its resemblance to the *Murænæ* of the ancients, naturalists have given the specific name of *Murænoides*."

I quote this passage for the purpose of contradicting Dr. SMITH, who says, "that during one of the several earthquakes, which occured many years ago, at the Cape, one or more sandbanks were formed near the entrance of Table Bay, and that not long after, *the first specimens* of this fish were obtained." It is evident that by some mistake or other, he attributed to the *Xiphiurus*, what applies to the *Stokvisch*.

PLEURONECTIDÆ.

42. SOLEA VULGARIS. CUV. (*Tong ; Sole.*)—Body oblong, flat, pointed towards the tail ; snout arcuated, projecting beyond the mouth, which is fringed below with small ciliated scales. Jaws unequal, armed on the under or white side only, with very minute, crowded teeth ; eyes small, spherical, placed near each other on the upper or coloured side. Dorsal and anal fins extending as far as the tail. Ventral fins near the head ; tail

slightly rounded; lateral line straight. Length ten to fifteen inches. Upper surface olivaceous-brown, obscurely spotted with patches of a deeper hue; scales small, roundish, ciliated, rough to the touch; the upper side apparently reticulated; fins tipped with purplish-brown stripes. Lower side dull white, mixed with faint purple. Iris yellow.

It is hardly required to say much of this, almost cosmopolitical fish, which is, for its delicacy, prized as well at the Cape as elsewhere. It is not common, however, in the colony, and it rarely surpasses the length of twelve inches, although there are instances known of individuals measuring a foot and a half.

RAIDÆ.

43. RHINOBATUS ANNULATUS. A. SMITH. (*Zandkruiper.*) —Body convex above, level below, tapering from head to tail. Head flat, nearly three-sided; eyes small; teeth crowded, paved, blunt; clusters of small thorns between the eyes, and minute spines along the dorsal line. Dorsal fins two, close to the caudal, which is oval, ventral fins small; skin rough, like shagreen. Length two feet and upwards. Upper side yellowish-grey, with a greenish shade, sprinkled all over with white eye-like spots; under surface faint flesh-red, bordered with white.

This fish which always dwells in localities, where the bottom of the sea is level and sandy, is rather scarce in Table Bay. Its flesh is tender and delicate.

44. RAIA MACULATA. MONTAG. (*Rog; Scate; Spotted Ray.*) Body rhomboid, horizontally flat on both sides; snout narrow, pointed, blunt; mouth, nostrils, and gills, on the under surface of the body. Teeth in many rows in both jaws; sharp, pointed, conical, and curved in *the male:* paved, broad, and flat, in *the female.* Tail long, thin, three-sided. furnished all along its edges with three lines of strong, hooked, but irregular spines, and with two small dorsal fins towards its end. Both surfaces more or less smooth, but snout and upper margin of the large pectoral fins, armed with clusters of hooked spines in *the male,* and with curved tubercular denticles in *the female.* *Male* provided with cylindrical cartilaginous appendages (claspers) to each ventral fin. *Female* larger than the *male.* Length two and a half feet and more. Colour above, pale yellowish-brown, sprinkled with numerous, irregular, faint, bluish-grey, spots. Under surface somewhat rough, greyish-white, tinged with purple.

A good table fish, and a fore-runner of bad weather. It is caught with the net.

To the number of edible fishes enumerated here, I feel bound to add one, which I never saw, but which I introduce on the incontestable authority of Dr. A. SMITH, who has given the following description of it, in the first volume of the *South African Quarterly Journal*, (1830) a publication full of interesting and useful information respecting the Cape Colony.

45. SERRANUS CUVIERII. A. SMITH. (*Rock Cod.*) Colour of back and sides brownish-yellow with blotches, streaks of irregular bands of dusky greenish-black; lower part of sides and belly reddish-yellow, with slight mixture of brown. Corsal fins deep dusky-brown, with the extremities of the spinous rays reddish; ventral fins towards apices brown, towards bases yellow; bases of pectoral fins bluish-white, finely spotted with orange; rest reddish-brown; tail even, or only very slightly rounded, with the hinder edge narrowly marginated with white. Eyes orange.

A full-grown specimen of this fish measures about two and a half feet; it inhabits the ocean along the East coast of Africa, particularly about Algoa Bay, where it is frequently caught, and highly esteemed as an article of food.

APPENDIX III.

To exhibit the wonderful profusion, and extensive variety of the vegetable kingdom in Southern Africa: we here append a Catalogue of trees, shrubs, plants, and bulbs, Indigenous and Exotic, seen growing in a garden near Cape Town.

CATALOGUE.

☞ All those marked with an asterisk are indigenous to Southern Africa.

* Acacia, horrida
    ,,   longifolia
    ,,   verticillata
    ,,   lophantha
    ,,   glauca
    ,,   procumbens
* Agapanthus, umbellatus
Agave, americana
* Aitonia
* Albuca, altissima
Aloe, soccotrina
* ,, arborescens
* ,, flavispina
* ,, paniculata
* ,, margaritifera
* ,, dichotoma
* ,, ferox
* ,, translucens
Althæa, different sorts
Amaryllis, formosissima
Amygdalus, persica
    ,,   necturina
    ,,   chimensis
* Anchusa, capensis
Anemone, different varieties
Angophora,
* Anthericum, floribundum
* ,, filifolium

Antirrhinum, majus
    ,,   bicolor
    ,,   coccineum
* Antholyza, æthiopica
    ,,   fulgens
Aquilegia, vulgaris
Araucaria, excelsa
* Arduina, grandiflora
* ,, bispinosa
* Aristea, spicata
Armeria, grandiflora
Artemisia, Absinthium
* Arum, Colocasia
* Asparagus, scandens
    ,,   officinalis
Aster, hortensis
    ,,   pedunculatus
* Babiana, tubiflora
* ,, villosa
* ,, rosea
* ,, rubro-cyanea
* ,, disticha
* ,, fragrans
* ,, grandiflora
* ,, plicata
* ,, flava
Bambusa, arundinacea
    ,,   dichotoma

* Belladonna, capensis
Bellis, perennis
* Bonatea, speciosa
* Brachystelma, tuberosum
Bromelia, Ananas
* Brunswigia, Josephinae
*   ,,   multiflora
*   ,,   falcata
*   ,,   pumila
*   ,,   curvifolia
Bryophyllum, calycinum
Buddleia, salvifolia
* Bulbine, alooides
* Buphone, toxicaria
* Buphone, ciliaris
* Burchellia, capensis
Cactus, several species
Calandrinia, speciosa
Calceolaria, mixed species
Calendula
* Calla, æthiopica
Callitris, cupressiformis
* Calodendron, capense
Camellia, two sorts
Campanula, (different sorts)
Canna, indica
    ,, lutea
Capsicum, annuum
Cassia, arborescens
    ,,   corymbosa
* Cassine, Maurocenia
*   ,,   capensis
Casuarina, two species
* Celastrus, pyracanthus
Celosia, cristata
Celsia, cretica
Centaurea, Cyanus
    ,,   americana
    ,,   moschata
Centranthus, macrosiphon
Cephalaria, attenuata
Ceratonia, Siliqua
Cheiranthus, Cheiri
* Chironia, frutescens
Chrysanthemum, indicum
* Cineraria, mixed species
* Cissus, capensis
Citrus, medica
    ,,   Aurantium
    ,,   nobilis
* Clematis, flammula

* Cobæa, scandens
Coix, Lacryma
Convolvulus, mixed varieties
Coreopsis, tinctoria
Coronilla, glauca
* Cotyledon, orbiculata
* Crassula, arborescens
Crepis, barbata
* Crinum, revolutum
*   ,,   aquaticum
* Crocoxylon, excelsum
Crotalaria, laburnifolia
Cuphea, platycentra
Cupressus, three species
* Curculigo, plicata
* Curtisia, faginea
* Cussonia, thyrsiflora
Cyclamen, hederaefolium
* Cyanella, orchidiformis
*   ,,   capensis
*   ,,   lutea
Cydonio, vulgaris
Cynara, Scolymus
* Cyrtanthus, odorus
*   ,,   obliquus
*   ,,   Smithiæ
Cytisus, tomentosus
Dahlia, variabilis
Datura, arborea
* Daubenya, coccinea
Delphinium, Ajacis
Dianthus, barbatus
    ,,   Caryophyllus
Digitalis, purpurea
    ,,   (variety) alba
* Diosma, alba
*   ,,   serratifolia
Dolichos, lignosus
* Disa, grandiflora
* Echium glaucophyllum
* Ekebergia, capensis
Epidendrum, fuscatum
Eriobotrya, japonica
* Eriocephalus
* Erythrina, caffra
Escholtzia, californica
Eucalyptus, pulverulenta
    ,,   diversifolia
* Eugenia, capensis
    ,,   jambos
* Euphorbia, several species

* Ferraria, undulata
Ficus, elastica
,, Carica
Fragaria vesca
Fuchsia, varieties
* Feisanus, compressus
* Galaxia, ovata
* Galaxia, graminea
Gardenia, Rothmannia
* ,, Thunbergia
* Gazania, rigens
* Geissorhiza, rochensis
* Geranium
Gilia, tricolor
* Gladiolus, gracilis
* ,, psittacinus
* ,, tristis
* ,, Watsonius
* ,, trimaculatus
* ,, ringens
* ,, carneus
* ,, hirsutus
* ,, roseus
* ,, Milleri
Gloriosa, superba
* Gomphocarpus, arborescens
Gomphrena, globosa alba
,, (variety) purpurea
* Gonioma, Kamassi
* Grewia, occidentalis
Guilandina Bonduc
Hakea, pugioniformis
* Hebea, galeata
* ,, orchidiflora
Hedysarum, coronarium
Hedera, Helix
Heliotropium, peruvianum
* Hessea, spiralis
Hibiscus
* Hæmanthus, albiflos
* ,, coccineus
* ,, tigrinus
* ,, puniceus
* ,, pubescens
* Homeria, lineata
* Hyacinthus, corymbosus
* Hypoxis, elegans
* ,, sobolifera
Iberis, two species
* Imatophyllum, Aitoni
Impatiens, Balsamina

* Indigofera, cytisoides
Inga, vera
Ipomæa, coccinea
* Iris, moraeoides
,, florentina
,, germanica
,, Susiana
* Ixia, viridiflora
* ,, rosea
* ,, (variety) alba
* ,, cœrulea
* ,, monadelpha
* ,, maculata
* ,, conica
Jasminum, odoratissimum
Kennedya, (several species)
* Kiggelaria, africana
* Lachenalia, tricolor
* ,, pustulata
* ,, orchioides
* ,, vialacea
* ,, pallida
* ,, flava
* ,, pendula
Lagerstroemia, indica
Latania, borbonica
Lathyrus, odoratus
,, tingitanus
Laurus, nobilis
Lavandula, Spica
Lilium, candidum
* Liparia, sphærica
Lonicera, sempervirens
Lotus, jacobæus
Lupinut, luteus
,, hirsutus
,, varius
Lychnis, chalcedonica
,, cœli-rosa
Malcolmia, maritima
,, purpurea
Malva, fragrans
* Massonia, latifolia
Mathiola, annua
Matricaria, Chamomilla
Maurandia, Barclayana
Medicago, arborescens
* Melanthium, junceum
Melia, azedarach
* Melianthus, major
* ,, minor

* Melianthus comosus
* Mesembryanthemum, several
    species
Mespilus, germanica
Metrosideros,
* Micranthus, plantagineus
*   ,,   triticeus
Mimulus, guttatus
Mirabilis, Jalappa
* Monsonia, filia
Morus, nigra
Musa, paradisiaca
   ,,   coccinea
* Myrsiphyllum, madeoloides
Myrtus, communis
Narcissus, poeticus
    ,,   Jonquilla
    ,,   pseudo-narcissus
* Nerine undulata
*   ,,   corusca
*   ,,   flexuosa
Nerium, Oleander
Nicotiana, glauca
    ,,   tabacum
    ,,   rustica
* Niebuhria, triphylla
Nigella, damascena
Ocymum, Basilicum
* Olea, capensis
   ,,   Europaea
*   ,,   verrucosa
Oénorhera, grandiflora
    ,,   tetraptera
* Ornithoglossum, glaucum
Origanum, Majorana
* Osteospermum, pisiferum
* Othonna, pectinata
* Ovieda, corymbosa
* Oxalis, rosacea
*   ,,   fiava
*   ,,   tenalla
*   ,,   hirta
*   Bowiei
Papaver, Rhœas
Parkinsonia, aculeata
Passiflora, cœrulea
    ,,   alata
    ,,   edulis
* Pelargonium, triste
*   ,,   cucullatum
*   ,,   lateripes

* Pelargonium melananthum
*   ,,   astragalifolium
*   ,,   tenuifolium
*   ,,   rapaceum
* Petunia, nyctaginiflora
Phlox, Drummondii
Phœnix, dactylifera
   ,,   reclinata
Phormium, tenax
Physalis, Alkekengi
*   ,,   peruviana
Phytolacca, decandra
Pinus, moritima
   ,,   Pinaster
* Pittosporum, virdiflorum
* Plumbago, africana
* Podalyria, styracifolia
*   ,,   sericea
Polianthes, tuberosa
* Polygala, cordifolia
*   ,,   speciosa
*   ,,   myrtifolia
Populus, alba
* Portulacaria, afra
Poterium, Sanguisorba
Primula, Auricula
* Prockia, rotundifolia
Prunus, Armeniaca
   ,,   Cerasus
* Psoralea, pinnata
Punica, Granatum
Pyrus, malus
   ,,   cydonia
Quercus, pedunculata
   ,,   Suber
Ranunculus, different varieties
Reseda, odorata
Rhus, (several species
Ricinus, communis
Robinia, pseudo-acacia
* Rochea, falcato
*   ,,   coccinea
Rosa, several species
Rosmarinus, officinalis
* Royena, villosa
Saccharum, officinarum
Salix babylonica
* Salvia, aurea
*   ,,   coarctata
*   ,,   coccinea
*   ,,   officinalis

Sanseviera, zeylanica
* Satyrium erectum
*　　,,　　cucullatum
*　　,,　　carneum
* Scabiosa, atropurpurea
* Schotia, speciosa
*　　,,　　tamarindifolia
Sciodaphyllum, palmatum
Scorpiurus, vermiculata
Sempervivum, aboreum
* Senecio, pseudo-elegans
*　　,,　　hastulatus
* Septas, capensis
* Solanum, giganteum
　　　,,　　aggregatum
* Sparaxis, pendula
*　　,,　　liliago
*　　,,　　tricolor
*　　,,　　grandiflora
* Sparmannia, africana
* Spartium, junceum
Spiræa chamædry folia
* Stapelia, gutiata
* Strelitzia, reginae
*　　,,　　augusta
*　　,,　　juncea
*　　,,　　farinosa
* Streptocarpus, biflora
* Strumaria, crispa
* Sutherlandia, frutescens
* Synnotia, variegata
* Synnotia, bicolor
Tagetes, patula
　　,,　　erecta
* Teedia, lucida
* Tephrosia, grandiflora
* Testudinaria, elephantipes

* Thecoma, capensis
Thymus, vulgaris
Tradescantia, discolor
* Trichonema, purpureum
*　　,,　　cruciatum
*　　,,　　roseum
*　　,,　　filifolium
*　　,,　　caulescens
* Tritonia, aurea
*　　,,　　miniata
*　　,,　　crispa
*　　,,　　rosea
Tropæolum, majus
* Tulbaghia, alliacea
Valeriana
* Vallotta, purpurea
*　　,,　　(variety) minor
* Veltheimia, virdifolia
Verbena, several varieties
Vinca, rosea
　　,,　　(variety) alba
Viola, odorata
　　,,　　tricolor
* Virgillia, capensis
Vitis, vinifera (several varieties)
* Wachendorfia thyrsiflora
* Watsonia, rosea
*　　,,　　marginata
*　　,,　　aletroides
*　　,,　　humilis
*　　,,　　coccinea
* Willemetia, africana
* Zamia, horrida
*　　,,　　longifolia
Zea, Mais
Zinnia, different varieties
* Zygophyllum, Morgsana

APPENDIX IV.

For the curious in Statistics, and for reference, we here give a list of the Governors of the Cape Colonies, from their first formation to the present time.

We also insert with it a return of the population of the country, classified according to tribes, and from the last ascertained census.

LIST OF THE GOVERNORS OF THE CAPE UNDER THE DUTCH.

	NAMES.	Date of Appointment.	
1	Joan Anthony Van Riebeck	April 8	1652
2	Zacharias Wagenaar	May 2	1662
3	Cornelius Van Gualberg	Oct. 24	1666
4	Jacob Borghorst	June 18	1668
5	Pieter Hackins	June 2	1670
6	Coenrvad Van Breitenbach	Dec. 1	1671
7	Albert Van Brengal	March 23	1672
8	Yslrand Goske	Oct. 2	1672
9	Johan Bat (Van Herentals)	Jan. 2	1676
10	Hendrick Crudat	June 29	1678
11	Simon Van der Stell	Oct. 14	1679
12	William Adrian Van der Stell	Feb. 11	1699
13	Johan Cornelius d'Ableing	June 3	1707
14	Louis Van Assemberg	Feb. 1	1708
15	Mauritz Posques de Chavornes	March 28	1714
16	Jan de la Fontaine (acting)	Sep. 8	1724
17	Pieter Girbert Nood	Feb. 25	1727
18	Jan de la Fontaine (acting)	April 24	1729
	Ditto (effective)	March 8	1730
19	Adrian Van Rerval	Nov. 14	1736
20	Daniel Van der Hengel	Sep. 20	1737
21	Hendrick Swellengrebel	April 14	1739
22	Ryk Tulbagh	March 30	1751
23	Joachim Van Plettenberg	Aug. 12	1771
24	Pieter Van Reed	Jan. 23	1773
25	Oudshoorn died on his passage out to the Colony, on board the ship Asia.		

	NAMES.	*Date of Appointment.*	
26	Cornelius Jacob Van der Graff	Feb. 14	1785
27	Johannes Isaak Rhenius	June 29	1791
28	Abraham J. Sluysken (Commissioner)	Sep. 2	1793

First occupation under British rule.

1	General Craig	Sep. 1	1795
2	Earl Macartney	May 23	1797
3	Sir Francis Dundas (Lt. Gov.)..	Nov. 22	1791
4	Sir George Yonge	Dec. 18	1798
	Sir Francis Dundas (Lt. Gov. second time)	April 20	1801

On the reversion of the Colony to the Dutch, Jan. Wilhelm Jaussens. (Batavian Governor.)

Second occupation under the British.

1	Sir David Baird	Jan. 10	1806
2	Hon. H. G. Grey (Lt. Gov.) ..	Jan. 17	1807
3	Du Pres, Earl of Caledon	May 22	1807
	Hon. H. G. Grey (Lt. Gov. second time)	July 5	1811
4	Sir John Francis Caradock	Sep. 6	1811
5	Hon. R. Meade (Lt. Gov.)	Dec. 13	1813
6	Lord Charles Henry Somerset ..	April 6	1814
7	Sir Rufane Shawe Donkin (acting during the absence of Lord C. Somerset)	Jan. 13	1820
	Lord C. H. Somerset (returned)	Dec. 1	1821
8	General Bourke (Lt. Gov.)	Feb. 8	1828
9	Sir Galbraith Lowry Cole	Aug. 6	1828
10	Sir Benjamin D'Urban		1833
11	Sir George Napier..	Nov. 4	1837
12	Sir Peregrine Maitland	Dec. 19	1843
13	Sir Henry Pottinger	Jan.	1847
14	Sir Harry Smith	Jan.	1849
	Colonel George Mackinnon, (Commandant and High Commissioner for Kaffirland.)		1847
15	Sir George Cathcart	Feb.	1852
	General Yorke (Commandant of Kaffirland)..................	Feb.	1852
	J. Darling Esq., (Lt. Gov.)	Feb.	1852
16	Sir George Grey (Governor) ..	Nov.	1854
	General Jackson (Lt. Gov.) ...	Jan.	1854

NAMES. *Date of Appointment.*

NEW COLONY OF NATAL.

Colonel Smith	1845
Colonel West, (Lt. Gov.)	1847
C. Pine, Esq., (Lt. Gov.)	1849

RETURN OF POPULATION.

OLD CAPE COLONY.

Dutch	77,000
British	29,000
Hottentots, Mosambiques, and Malay	120,000
Total	226,000

NEW NATAL COLONY.

Dutch	12,000
British	5,000
Zulu Kaffirs	115,000
Total	132,000

TERRITORY BEYOND THE ORANGE RIVER.

Dutch	15,000
British	1000
Griquas, Hottentots, and Kaffirs	85,000
Total	101,000

BRITISH KAFFRARIA.

British	8000
Amaxosa Kaffirs (Umhalla)	42,000
Total	50,000

POPULATION OF KAFFIR TRIBES BEYOND THE BOUNDARIES.

Amaxosa, (Kreli and Sandilla)	100,000
Tambookies, (Faku)	100,000
Basuetos, (Mosesh)	90,000
Total	290,000

TOTAL POPULATION OF KAFFIRS.

Zulu tribes of Natal	115,000
Tambookies, (Faku)	100,000
Basuetos, (Mosesh)	90,000
Amaxosas beyond the Kei	100,000
Ditto in British Kaffraria	42,000
Total	447,000

Population of Hottentot Tribes.

In territory beyond the Orange river	85,000
In Cape Colony	120,000
Total	205,000
Fingoes in Kaffraria	5000
(Supposed) numbers of Interior Tribes	550,000

RECAPITULATION.

Total of Kaffirs and Fingoes	452,000
,, Hottentots and Malays	205,000
,, Interior Tribes	250,000
Total coloured population	907,000
Total of Dutch in Cape and Natal, and beyond the Orange river	104,000
Total of British in South Africa	43,000
Total European Population	147,000

END OF APPENDIX.